OXFORD WORLD'S CLASSICS

REVELATIONS OF DIVINE LOVE

JULIAN OF NORWICH (1342–after 1416) is the earliest woman whose writing in English can be identified, but little is known about her life. Julian herself dates to May 1373 the revelations which were to be the inspiration of her writing, and she also mentions that she was thirty winters old when they occurred, but she does not reveal her name. Julian's book survives in two versions, and a scribal note to the shorter text identifies its author as a devout woman called Julian, who is a recluse at Norwich and still alive in 1413. From legacies in four surviving wills it is known that there was a recluse named Julian at St Julian's Church in Norwich between 1394 and 1416, although Julian probably became a recluse before this. She dates two breakthroughs that she made in understanding her revelations to 1388 and 1393. It was probably in 1413 that Margery Kempe of Lynn, the Norfolk visionary and holy woman, reports paying a visit to consult Julian about Kempe's own revelations, but the year of Julian's death remains unknown.

BARRY WINDEATT is Professor of English in the University of Cambridge and Vice-Master of Emmanuel College. He is the author of *Oxford Guides to Chaucer: Troilus and Criseyde* (Clarendon Press) and translator of Chaucer's *Troilus and Criseyde* for Oxford World's Classics.

T0108100

OXFORD WORLD'S CLASSICS

For over 100 years Oxford World's Classics have brought readers closer to the world's great literature. Now with over 700 titles—from the 4,000-year-old myths of Mesopotamia to the twentieth century's greatest novels—the series makes available lesser-known as well as celebrated writing.

The pocket-sized hardbacks of the early years contained introductions by Virginia Woolf, T. S. Eliot, Graham Greene, and other literary figures which enriched the experience of reading. Today the series is recognized for its fine scholarship and reliability in texts that span world literature, drama and poetry, religion, philosophy, and politics. Each edition includes perceptive commentary and essential background information to meet the changing needs of readers.

OXFORD WORLD'S CLASSICS

JULIAN OF NORWICH

Revelations of Divine Love

Translated with an Introduction and Notes by
BARRY WINDEATT

OXFORD
UNIVERSITY PRESS

OXFORD
UNIVERSITY PRESS

Great Clarendon Street, Oxford, OX2 6DP
United Kingdom

Oxford University Press is a department of the University of Oxford.
It furthers the University's objective of excellence in research, scholarship,
and education by publishing worldwide. Oxford is a registered trade mark of
Oxford University Press in the UK and in certain other countries

Published in the United States of America by Oxford University Press
198 Madison Avenue, New York, NY 10016, United States of America

British Library Cataloguing in Publication Data

Data available

Library of Congress Control Number: 2014949676

ISBN 978-0-19-964118-5

Printed and bound in Great Britain by Clays Ltd, Elcograf S.p.A.

For my mother

QUEENIE WINDEATT
(1922–2012)

'The mother's service is closest, most willing, and most sure; closest because it is most natural, most willing because it is most loving, and most sure because it is most true.'

Revelations of Divine Love, chapter 60

CONTENTS

INTRODUCTION

DYING in Norwich—in May 1373—a thirty-year-old woman is gazing at a crucifix held before her eyes. Suddenly, blood trickles down from under the crown of thorns, and the painted artefact of the crucifix dissolves, filmlike, into moving image. This vision initiates a series of fifteen revelations that day, concluded by a sixteenth the following night. Duly recovered, the woman compiles two versions of a book—one much longer than the other—devoted to exploring and interpreting what had been shown in her visions. Her revelations bring her both joyous serenity and some anguishing bafflement: she can hardly doubt them, yet in their exaltation they seem to promise more than orthodox Church teaching. The outcome—self-effacing, yet implicit with spiritual autobiography—is a unique fusion of revelation with a searching theological enquiry into what has been revealed. From this experience derives the work of Julian of Norwich, the earliest woman whose writing in English can be identified.

A profound and radical thinker, Julian understands the divine redeeming of mankind from sin as a manifestation of Christ as mother of all humanity, whom he will bring through salvation to new birth and new life. Julian comes to see that it was needful that there should be sin in this world, yet the joy of humanity's redemption far outweighs the harm in mankind's fall. For Julian, despite our sinfulness, the human will remains fundamentally good, our bodily nature is nothing to regret, and our repented sins will be to our glory in heaven. In his love for us, which has no beginning as well as no end, God has always willed the salvation of the noblest thing he ever made, which is humanity. We cannot know everything here, and we may suffer, yet 'all shall be well, and all shall be well, and all manner of things shall be well' (ch. 27; p. 74).

The life of an anchoress[1]

At some point in her life Julian became an anchoress in Norwich. An anchoress was a female recluse who lived permanently confined

---

[1] This account of an anchoress's way of life is largely based on the various rules and recommendations in the thirteenth-century English guide for anchoresses, the *Ancrene Wisse*, which was much copied in later centuries. There were, however, many individual variations.

in a small cell usually built against the wall of a church.[2] The intending anchoress would have undergone some probationary testing before receiving approval to be enclosed, and assurance would also be required about sufficient arrangements for her continuing material support. Upon enclosure she would have taken solemn vows of obedience and chastity. The life of an anchoress was regarded as the living death of one who was as if dead to the world. Parts of the rite of enclosure were excerpted from the office for the burial of the dead, and the anchoress entered her cell singing the antiphon from the burial service, 'Here shall be my rest forever.'[3] The anchoress was then prayed for as if over a corpse, dust was sprinkled as at a burial, and the door to the cell was shut and sealed up from the outside. Normally the anchoress would never leave her cell alive again, and in some rites the sealing of the door is followed by a mass for the dead. Some anchorites were indeed buried in their cells, and one fifteenth-century rite for enclosure of recluses specifies provision of a shallow grave already dug within the anchorhold for the recluse to contemplate and to deepen himself.[4] Rather than admiring her ladylike white hands, an anchoress should use those hands to 'scrape up the earth every day from the grave in which they will rot'.[5]

Henceforward, the anchoress will live in a cramped and comfortless confinement bare of any ornament except a crucifix, and wholly dependent on others for all her needs of sustenance and sanitation.[6] The aim in principle was an austere habitation symbolically sealed off from the world, but in practice this was provided in some quite different accommodation.[7] A maidservant might occupy an adjacent

---

[2] Anchoress is the female of anchorite, a term for a recluse applied to both men and women and deriving from the Greek *anachorein*, to retire, retreat.

[3] On medieval English ceremonies for enclosure, see Ann K. Warren, *Anchorites and their Patrons in Medieval England* (Berkeley, 1985), ch. 4.

[4] Roberta Gilchrist, *Contemplation and Action: The Other Monasticism* (London, 1995), 190–2, and E. A. Jones, 'Ceremonies of Enclosure: Rite, Rhetoric and Reality', in Liz Herbert McAvoy (ed.), *The Rhetoric of the Anchorhold* (Cardiff, 2008), 34–49.

[5] Bella Millett (ed.), *Ancrene Wisse: A Corrected Edition of the Text in Cambridge, Corpus Christi College, MS 402*, 2 vols., Early English Text Society, original series 325, 326 (Oxford, 2005, 2006), 2.46 (my translation).

[6] In his *De Institutione Inclusarum* Aelred of Rievaulx forbids any 'paintings or carvings . . . hangings decorated with birds or animals or flowers' in a recluse's cell; see *Treatise and Pastoral Prayer*, trans. Mary Paul McPherson (Kalamazoo, Mich., 1971), 71.

[7] On the wide variation in the proportion of recorded anchorholds, see Warren, *Anchorites and their Patrons*, 29–41. An anchorhold at Leatherhead, Surrey, was 8 feet

room with access to the anchorhold, but some maids went home at night; such maids were to receive no set wage, only their food and subsistence, so that theirs was also a kind of religious vocation. The anchoress's cell will have a window into the church—at Leatherhead only 21 inches square—which enables her to witness the celebration of mass. Communion is allowed fifteen times a year. Any family feeling is considered no longer appropriate in one dead to the world, and more than infrequent family visiting of an anchoress is discouraged. Her cell may have a small window to the outside, but this window will be covered with a curtain, and any touching of those callers who come to the window to consult her is to be shunned. No wonder that in one rite of enclosure the recluse is to think of himself as convicted of his sins and committed to solitary confinement as if to a prison.[8] No wonder that imagery of enclosure and indwelling is so integral to Julian's text. When Julian comments that 'This place is prison, and this life is penance' (ch. 77; p. 155), she may be referring not only to life in this world but to the life in her anchorhold.

The anchoress's day is occupied with the recitation of a round of prayers which begin with her waking moments and only cease with prayers said just before going to sleep. In such a day, which in winter would have begun at 3.30 a.m. and ended at 7.00 p.m., the saying of prayers can hardly have taken less than five hours and possibly more.[9] Otherwise the anchoress was expected to keep silent as much

square; one at Compton, Surrey, was 6 feet 8 inches by 4 feet 4 inches, with a separate space for sleeping, and another at Hardham, Sussex, was no bigger. Much larger was an anchorhold at Chichester Cathedral, which measured 29 by 24 feet. One in Shropshire contained at least three rooms; another still extant at Chester-le-Street, Co. Durham, had four rooms. There is record of anchorholds with gardens attached. Two recluses inhabiting adjacent cells was not unknown. During reconstruction of St Julian's Church, Norwich, in 1953 the foundations of the anchorhold presumably once occupied by Julian were discovered to indicate a space in the cell approximately 9½ by 11½ feet. See Father John-Julian (ed. and trans.), *The Complete Julian of Norwich* (Brewster, Mass., 2009), 38.

[8] Rotha Mary Clay, *The Hermits and Anchorites of England* (London, 1914), 193.

[9] A typical day of prayer might be as follows: 3.30 a.m. Preliminary prayers and devotions; 5.00 a.m. Matins, Lauds and Prime of our Lady, with other devotions; 8.00 a.m. Terce of our Lady, Litany of the Saints, The Seven Penitential Psalms, The Fifteen Gradual Psalms, Devotions before the cross and to our Lady; 11.30 a.m. Mass, Sext and None of our Lady, meal and rest period; 3.00 p.m. Private prayers and meditation, some vernacular reading; 4.00 p.m. Vespers of our Lady; 5.00 p.m. Compline of our Lady; 7.00 p.m. Bedtime prayers and devotions. Prescribed gestures and postures accompanied prayers: standing, kneeling, prostration, outstretched arms, signs of the cross, striking the breast, kissing the earth.

as possible. Between Easter and harvest-time in mid-September the anchoress can eat two meals a day, except on Fridays. During the other half of the year the anchoress is to fast as much as possible, except on Sundays. No meat or fat should be eaten, and no dairy produce on Fridays or in Advent. 'Eat vegetable stew willingly, and get into the habit of drinking little', advises the *Ancrene Wisse*, bracingly. An anchoress should always eat alone, as is appropriate to one dead to the world. It does not greatly matter what an anchoress wears in her unseen life, but anything worn next to the skin should be rough and coarse in texture, and the anchoress 'may perhaps wear drawers of haircloth tightly fastened, with the legs firmly cross-gartered down to the feet'. However, the wearing of haircloth, or self-flagellation with holly or brambles should only be undertaken with a confessor's permission; scourging the front of the body or mutilating it with cuts are specifically forbidden. Following St Paul (1 Corinthians 11: 6) the anchoress should keep her head covered, but not for adornment. The hair can be cut or shaved four times a year. As to personal hygiene, frequent washing is encouraged. No rings, brooches, fancy belts or gloves are allowed.

The anchoress makes herself a recluse from the world in order to be free for God, and in her cell she inhabits a liminal space between this world and the next, yet the life of an anchoress was not without paradoxes. By the later Middle Ages, as recluses became more of an urban than rural phenomenon, the anchoress found herself immured at the very heart of the community she had left behind. Her seclusion—dependent as this made her on the practical and material support of others—must often have been symbolic and conditional rather than absolute, not that this need diminish her inward solitude nor her spiritual ambition. There is ample evidence from wills of the loyal support and affection that anchoresses enjoyed in their local communities. In return, the anchoress supported the community through her prayers, gave spiritual counsel, and should provide an example of holiness, although engagement with the world left behind outside the anchorhold is regulated so firmly and in such detail as to suggest that much could go wrong. The *Ancrene Wisse* advises that an anchoress may have a cat but not a cow, which will only entangle her with worldly distractions even if it helps contribute to her support. Anything made by the anchoress can be sold to help meet her needs, and for anchoresses to support themselves by their labour was well regarded by some (although not by all), but an anchoress must not conduct a business. Her needlework should be the sewing and mending of church vestments or clothes for the poor. Nor should an anchoress turn herself into a schoolmistress in teaching children, because this would distract her from her vocation. An anchoress is not to send or receive letters, and cannot write without permission, although with her confessor's agreement she can dispense guidance to those who seek it from her.

It was on account of Julian's reputation as such a spiritual adviser that she was consulted by Margery Kempe, a highly unconventional Norfolk visionary and holy woman, who records how she confided some of her own 'wonderful revelations, which she described to the anchoress to find out if there were any deception in them, for the anchoress was expert in such things and could give good advice' (see p. 168).[10] This reflects an assumption by the later Middle Ages that the lives of recluses would move beyond the ascetic towards contemplative experience: Julian's contemporary Walter Hilton (d. 1396) addresses to an anchoress the first book of his great guide to contemplation, *The Scale of Perfection*, while the celebrated English mystic Richard Rolle (d. 1349) wrote his *Form of Living* for a female recluse. In the account of her conversation with Julian, Kempe gleans her portion of the spiritual harvest from Julian's life as an anchoress. It was the solitary life as a self-martyrdom from every worldly consolation in order that, stripped and set free from all earthly and sensory distraction, the anchoress may pursue her path through prayer and meditation towards spiritual enlightenment.

Julian of Norwich: life and book

The author now known as Julian of Norwich divulges few details about herself, preferring her readers to focus on the revelations and not on their recipient. With studied anonymity she suppresses in her longer text some of the few personal details present in the shorter, including all reference to the author's being a woman. However, she does record precisely her age at the time, the date and hours of her revelations, and of her later breakthroughs in interpreting

[10] *The Book of Margery Kempe*, ch. 18. For a translation of Kempe's account of her visit to Julian of Norwich, see Appendix 2, pp. 168–9.

them, lending the historicity of a documentary deposition to an anonymized account of what transcends time and defies description. The longer version of her revelations records that they occurred, depending on which manuscript, on 8 or 13 May 1373, when she was thirty and a half years old (ch. 2; p. 40). She was born, therefore, in late 1342 and was thus an almost exact contemporary of Chaucer. Her text also records how it was 'fifteen years and more later' (i.e. in 1388 or later) before she gained insight into the key overall significance of her revelations (ch. 86; p. 164), and not until 'three months short of twenty years' after the time of the revelations (i.e. February 1393) that she finally interpreted her parable-like vision of the Lord and Servant (ch. 51; p. 108). Any context for the revelations in place or social circumstance had already been excluded from the shorter text, so it is ironic that with a few added words a scribal rubric to the shorter version undoes all Julian's self-abnegation and enables her identification. It declares itself a vision shown 'to a devout woman and her name is Julian, and she is a recluse at Norwich and is still alive in the year of our Lord 1413' (Short Text, p. 3, hereafter ST[11]). Four wills variously provide evidence of an anchoress named Julian at Norwich and at St Julian's Church in Conesford, Norwich, between 1393/4 and at least 1416.[12] The four benefactors—priests, a Norwich layman, and a pious noblewoman—provide a glimpse of Julian's circle and repute, while the wills' bequests to her maids give some hint of Julian's daily companions and helpmeets in 'her highly industrial location, at St Julian's cell, near the busy quays

---

[11] Reference to the ST, which is not divided into chapters in the sole manuscript, is by page number only. See Note on the Text and Translation.

[12] The earliest evidence for Julian's enclosure as an anchoress occurs in the will of Roger Reed, rector of St Michael's, Coslany, Norwich, who on 20 March 1393/4 bequeathed two shillings to 'Julian anakorite' (Norwich Consistory Court, Reg. Harsyk, 194v; now much damaged). In his will of 19 May 1404, Thomas Emund, a chantry priest of Aylsham in Norfolk, bequeathed twelve pence to Julian, anchoress at the church of St Julian in Norwich, and eight pence to Sarah, living with her (Lambeth Palace: Register of Archbishop Thomas Arundel, I.f.540d). In his will of 24 November 1415, John Plumpton, a citizen of Norwich, bequeathed forty pence to the anchoress in the church of St Julian's, Conesford, in Norwich, together with twelve pence to her maid, and twelve pence to her former maid, Alice (E. F. Jacob (ed.), *The Register of Henry Chichele, Archbishop of Canterbury 1414–1443*, 4 vols. (Oxford, 1943–7), 3.413). In her will of 26 September 1416, Isabel Ufford, Countess of Suffolk, left twenty shillings 'a Julian recluz a Norwich' (*Register of Henry Chichele*, 2.94–7). Bequests are also recorded in 1423 and 1428 to an unnamed anchoress at St Julian's, Conesford, but these are probably to Julian's successor in her anchorhold.

of King Street, Conesford'.[13] Julian was probably an anchoress well before 1394, but the dates of her enclosure and of her death are unknown. It is often claimed that even her own name is uncertain, for the anchoress might have taken 'Julian' as her name in religion from the patronal saint of the church to which her anchorhold was attached. In fact, there is little historical evidence for such a practice, and Julian was a not uncommon girl's name at the time. Nor does her book give itself a name, and the titles of all printed editions of Julian's work are editorial choices.[14]

It was probably in 1413, while visiting Norwich, that Margery Kempe felt herself divinely bidden 'to go to an anchoress in the same city who was called Dame Julian'.[15] Although Kempe gives Julian the title of 'dame', which was customary for nuns, all the wills naming Julian as a beneficiary refer to her as an anchoress or recluse rather than as a nun, as also does the rubric of the shorter text. Whether Julian was a nun before her enclosure as an anchoress remains a matter for debate. The nearby Benedictine nunnery of Carrow held the advowson of St Julian's Church (i.e. the right to nominate its rector), but no evidence remains to connect Julian with this house, although Julian's longer text has survived through copies made centuries later by exiled English Benedictine nuns. Julian may have received some early schooling from the nuns of Carrow and later may have enjoyed their support in her years as an anchoress. Indeed, Julian may have been still in secular life at the time of her revelations, for her account mentions her mother and others around her (ST, pp. 12, 15, 31). Whether this would be likely if Julian were already enclosed as an anchoress remains a matter of dispute: it is unclear whether an anchorhold could accommodate these onlookers, and whether the rules of enclosure would be waived in the event of grave illness. It may be that after the revelations, influenced by them, Julian entered religious life as an anchoress. It has been argued that Julian may have been a widow at the time of her revelations,

---

[13] Carole Hill, *Women and Religion in Late Medieval Norwich* (Woodbridge, 2010), 14.

[14] For this translation the traditional title has been used, which derives from the first printed edition of 1670 by Serenus Cressy. Separate titles have not been given to the short and long texts, which are versions of one work.

[15] Norwich was one of the most important medieval English cities, with a notably vibrant religious culture, and with more hermits and recluses recorded than in any other English town; see Norman P. Tanner, *The Church in Late Medieval Norwich, 1370–1532* (Toronto, 1984), 58.

with speculation that she had been a mother herself, not that this is necessary to explain the special place of an understanding of Christ as our mother in her meditations.[16]

If a laywoman, Julian evidently had the circumstances and the leisure to allow for devotion. The manuscripts of her work variously describe her as ignorant (ST, p. 10), and as a simple uneducated creature (ch. 2; p. 40),[17] and although the claim in the longer text may be to ignorance of Latin rather than to illiteracy, it was no doubt prudent at times for Julian to claim both. It may be that she refers simply to her lack of literacy at the time of her revelations rather than the education she later attained. Her likely revisions of her work—detailed and meticulously phrased—make it seem improbable that Julian could not read and write in English, as do her references to the alphabet as an elementary level of learning (chs. 51, 80; pp. 113, 159). Even so, Julian may well have worked at revising her text in a copy which had been dictated to an amanuensis for convenience rather than because Julian was unable to write herself: writing was a laborious process in medieval circumstances. Julian's text is a witness to its author's intellect and her knowledge of spiritual writings, but its learnedness is suffused and implicit, without direct citation of sources or other pointers to books read. Even biblical reference—with many echoes of John and Paul—does not always follow the letter so much as the spirit of the original, but Julian appears to echo scripture because she has taken its truths to heart, not because she is concerned to parade biblical citations to authorize herself. Her awareness of texts' content may have derived in part from hearing them read and from conversation with spiritual advisers, and so is re-expressed later in her own words. Julian's text is a marvel of stylistic subtlety and grace: rhetorically patterned, theologically precise, and with the impress of a distinct personality. It combines an unmannered rhetorical sophistication—which bespeaks an accomplished literacy—with some of the energy and fluidity of a more oral style.

---

[16] Sister Benedicta Ward, 'Julian the Solitary', in Kenneth Leech and Sister Benedicta Ward (eds.), *Julian Reconsidered* (Oxford, 1988), 10–31.

[17] The manuscripts of the long text variously refer to Julian in Middle English as 'unlettered' or 'that cowde [knew] no letter'.

The revelations

Julian's revelations, which start when the supposedly dying woman sees the blood on a painted crucifix begin to trickle and spread, prompt her to a lifetime of subsequent contemplation. In meditating on Christ's life, and especially his Passion, medieval people were encouraged to enter imaginatively into the scenes of that life and relive them in their mind's eye, imagining themselves present in heart and mind, and often enlarging and elaborating upon aspects and circumstances of Christ's suffering and the sorrows of those who witnessed it. In her *Book* Margery Kempe exemplifies such affective devotion, stepping through the frame and into the picture as she imagines herself acting as the Virgin's companion and helper during the events of the Nativity and the Passion. Such devotion was regarded as appropriate for beginners in meditation and especially for women, and an extensive literary and visual culture, including many reported visions, developed under its influence. It was believed that Christ's Passion was a historical event which, uniquely, made itself available to be witnessed and inhabited mentally by those living in later historical periods who could not witness the historical Passion physically. In the *Horologium Sapientiae* of the Rhineland mystic Henry Suso—of which a partial translation became available in medieval England—Christ remarks of his Passion: 'Even here and now it is granted to you through my dispensation in some fashion to look upon this.'[18] As such, the accessibility of Christ's life by means of meditation—his real presence in the meditating mind—was held to be a special extension of Christ's giving of himself in the incarnation. In recording her initial wish to receive a more intense awareness of the Passion, and to feel herself there, sharing and reliving the experience of his first followers at the foot of the cross, Julian acknowledges this type of meditation even as she proceeds to transcend it.

Having previously prayed for an experience of witnessing Christ's Passion, what Julian does see and contemplate of the Passion is highly selective. Not only do her revelations not correspond chronologically with the Passion narrative, but most of its events are omitted,

---

[18] 'Et hoc quoque iam in praesenti tibi aliqualiter videre dispensative conceditur' (*Horologium Sapientiae*, ed. Pius Künzle (Freiburg, 1977), 394). Suso adds that frequent recollection of the Passion makes the ignorant most learned and turns amateurs and simpletons into teachers (p. 494).

contrary to the consecutive approach to the chronology of events
followed in many medieval Passion meditations. Julian sees nothing
of the Last Supper, the Agony in the Garden and Betrayal, or the
trial. Julian is shown nothing of the bearing of the cross or of the
process of Christ's being crucified, both traditional objects of devotional meditation. The sorrows of Mary on Calvary—beloved topic
of affective devotion—are acknowledged only obliquely and almost
abstractly (ch. 18; p. 64). Julian specifically records that she was not
shown the Jews who put Christ to death, and in Julian's attention to
Christ's wounds there is no identification of those who inflicted them.
The moment of Christ's dying is not shown—or rather, Julian sees
a miraculous change—nor does she mention Christ's cry of derelic-
tion by God (Matthew 27: 46). Julian variously alludes to Christ's
descent into hell before his resurrection but passes in silence over
the confrontation between Christ and the devil which accompanies
that. The resurrection is mentioned in the Lord and Servant chapter
(ch. 51; p. 114) but otherwise sparsely.

As visions, Julian's revelations are strikingly dissimilar: they are
unequal in length, type, or content. Not all are of the Passion, not all
are primarily visual, and they prompt different kinds of revision after
meditation, becoming less visually centred as the work progresses.
The first and eighth revelations present almost cinematic close-ups
of the bleeding of Christ's head and the congealing and drying of
his body. This pathological focus is not for its own sake, but offers
a cue for meditation on the spiritual implications of these quasi-
photographic details, observed with a painterly eye perhaps influenced by the rich artistic culture of medieval Norwich.[19] The second
revelation develops an extended meditation from just one intently
observed visual shot of Christ's face discolouring on the cross. With
contemplation, the fourth revelation of Christ's body bleeding, as if at
his flagellation, develops into another dimension, so as to see Christ's
blood streaming through the firmament, and to envisage Christ's
blood, rather than the figure of Christ, as descending into hell and
ascending into heaven for us. Mysterious transformations of normal
space and dimension are deployed in other revelations, like the tenth,
which opens out from its initial focus on the wound in Christ's side.

[19] See also P. Lasko and N. J. Morgan (eds.), *Medieval Art in East Anglia 1300–1530*
(Norwich, 1974), and B. Windeatt, 'Julian of Norwich and Medieval English Visual
Culture', in N. Jacobs and G. Morgan (eds.), 'Truthe is the beste' (Bern, 2014), 185–203.

The third revelation of God 'in a point', or the first revelation's vision of something as small as a hazelnut yet understood to be 'all that is made', also work by challenging normal ideas of space and form. The concluding sixteenth revelation of Christ enthroned in majesty in the human soul is the culmination of Julian's pervasive spatial discourse of enclosing and inclusion. This last revelation of Christ's enclosure within us mirrors back across the book Julian's first revelation of our enclosure within Christ. Fundamental to Julian's interpretation of her revelations, this final vision prompts recurrent cross-references to her contemplations, as does the twelfth revelation of Christ glorified. For Julian, this twelfth revelation defeats all attempts to picture it, but presents God proclaiming himself in a prose poem of self-description ('It is I. It is I. It is I who am highest . . .', ch. 26; p. 74).

Understandings vouchsafed in words rather than images form the core of a number of revelations, where further insights may be developed in visual terms. Julian understands that: the devil is vanquished (fifth revelation); Christ thanks her for her youthful suffering (sixth revelation); if it were possible for Christ to suffer more, he would willingly do so (ninth revelation); Christ's question—'Would you like to see her?' (ch. 25; pp. 72–3)—introduces the vision of Mary at the Passion (eleventh revelation); Julian will be taken suddenly from her suffering and come to heaven (fifteenth revelation). It is two non-visual revelations—the thirteenth (on sin) and the fourteenth (on prayer)—that prompt the most extended contemplative commentary, culminating in Julian's parable-like account of the Lord and Servant. The seventh revelation—without a visual focus, and consisting of rapidly alternating feelings of exaltation and desolation—is exceptional in remaining unsupplemented by subsequent meditation, whether because Julian moved beyond such fluctuating feelings or because she saw them as worked through in the production of her revised longer text.

Turning revelation into writing—the text that Julian attempts to translate from the medium of moving image, visualization, and intuition in her revelatory experience—confronted Julian with intractable problems in both form and content that remain part of the challenge in reading her work. The original revelations as recorded in the short text do not present an immediately connected thematic sequence: they can seem fragmentary and enigmatic; a series of segments, without much foreground or background, and in no particular order.

Absence of formal subdivision within the short text perhaps retains
Julian's earlier sense of her experience as a stream of revelatory consciousness, where boundaries between revelations are still merging
and emerging to her perception. Along with such boundaries would
come an understanding of relative priority and significance that eventually enables the later demarcation and numbering of revelations. As
an answer to Julian's earlier prayer to have more bodily sight of the
Passion, her revelations' montage-like series of images and impres-
sions, sensations and heard words, is so singular and deconstructive
of traditional expectations as to pose real challenges to interpretation.
Julian's intensely individual focus in her visions opens up new insights
even into such iconic images. Yet although Julian's contemplative life
was founded on the unrepeatable revelations of May 1373, her subsequent inner life of heightened forms of insight and understanding is
no less part of her revelatory experience as a whole.

Visions and revisions

The survival of two authentic versions of Julian's text provides
a remarkable opportunity to chart the spiritual and creative process by which an account of revelatory experience is revised and
reinterpreted over a lifetime of meditative aspiration. Julian's work
survives in a shorter form, the Short Text (ST), preserved in one
mid-fifteenth-century copy, and in a version four times longer, the
Long Text (hereafter LT), only preserved complete in three post-
Reformation manuscripts. The shorter text survives in a manuscript
also containing some abridged versions of other contemplative texts,
which raises the possibility that this shorter text might itself represent an abridgement of the longer (whether by another hand or
by Julian herself for some particular purpose). Overall, however,
the nature of the shorter text points to its representing an authentic
earlier state of Julian's work. Only the short text includes certain
circumstantial details recording the revelations as an event: the priest
who brings the crucifix has a boy with him and addresses Julian as
'daughter' (ST, p. 5); Julian's posture on her sickbed (ST, p. 5) and
the position of her head and hands (ST, p. 5) are specified; the crucifix 'stood at the foot of my bed' (ST, p. 30); Julian's mother is present
at the bedside (ST, p. 15). On balance, such details would seem more
likely to have been recorded in a testimony written nearer in time to

the experience than to have been inserted into one abridged later, whether by a scribal editor or Julian herself. Yet the shorter text is still deemed worth copying as late as 1413 (probably within a few years of Julian's death), and the rubric in the shorter text which gives this date has some authority in implying that this text was copied by someone who knew or knew of Julian, by then in her seventies.

The date and purpose of the shorter text can only be deduced from internal evidence, but it remains a powerful statement that can stand in its own right. Its relatively undeveloped commentary on the revelations and its circumstantial details may identify it as a form of memorandum set down not long after the revelatory experience of May 1373, and perhaps connected with the process of Julian's gaining approval to be enclosed as an anchoress. A passage near the opening of the shorter text affirming Julian's belief both in Church teachings and also in 'paintings of crucifixes' (ST, p. 3) has been interpreted as reflecting a concern not to be associated with heretical Lollard hostility towards images, and this would be more likely to date from the 1380s than the 1370s. In view of the substantial revision occurring between the shorter and longer texts, such a later dating of the shorter might then imply a composition date for the longer version rather later than 1393, when Julian indicates that she was vouchsafed her crucial understanding of her revelations (ch. 51; p. 108). Yet if an anxiety about Lollardy really underlay this passage in her short text, Julian might have been expected to retain it in her longer version rather than omit it, since such concerns over heresy became more pressing later in Julian's lifetime, and may explain in part the lack of evidence for much circulation of the longer text. By the early fifteenth century—in the context of growing concerns about unorthodox texts in English—there were ample grounds for a female visionary to hesitate before publishing so profound and audaciously original a work as Julian's longer text. By the same token, this passage about the painting of crucifixes may indicate no more than that this particular redaction of the shorter text does indeed date from 1413 as it declares and has had a cautious disclaimer added to its opening sentences, which may not have been present in earlier copies of the short text. In the light of just how much Julian can be proven to have rewritten her work, it would be naïve to assume that a version of the short text copied decades after the event it describes would have remained unrevised as first written.

Unlike some visionaries (including Margery Kempe), Julian does not record in so many words that she was divinely charged to write down her revelations, but she does understand that God wants them made known. This is the context of her declaration in the short text, confronting and rejecting the notion that, just because she is a woman, she should not make public what she has learned by revelation, while also distancing herself from any problematic claim to be a woman who teaches (ST, p. 10). That this passage no longer appears in the long text suggests that Julian moved so far beyond such defensiveness about her vocation as thinker and writer that she no longer felt the need to address it. Yet her last chapter in the long text declares that her book is not yet completed (ch. 86; p. 164), and it may well be that Julian kept her full text to herself as work-in-progress. There was only ever one book for Julian to write, because there was only one subject: her revelations of 1373, understood cumulatively over time in response to the various challenges that Julian encountered in them, not least in that the revelations seemingly went beyond orthodox teaching. In responding to such challenges, it is quite probable that Julian's text developed through a number of stages and layers.

Taken as a whole, the features of the short text read as if earlier in that lengthy process of developing understanding and interpretation which the long text acknowledges to have occurred. By comparison with the longer version, the revelations in the short text are quite sparely related, closer to speech, and possibly dictated; they are introduced with little preface or context, and unlocated in time. Some of Julian's more vivid visual insights do not figure in the short text, including some details of her Passion revelations. Indeed, there is not only more meditation but also more visualization in the longer text. Absent from the short text are the parable of the Lord and Servant (ch. 51) and the chapters on Christ our mother (chs. 58–63), with the chapters of profound meditation that precede and follow. Express indications in the short text that Julian's work is aimed at contemplatives no longer appear in the longer version. References to Julian in the first person in the short text tend to be revised away in the long text, while references in the short text to 'he' and 'they' are rewritten into a more inclusive first-person plural 'we' that characterizes the long text. The short text is more tentative than the long text in presenting its account of the revelations, and more defensive in asserting its conformity to orthodox Church teaching. A sense of sin, as too of the devil, seems always near in the short text, reflected in a less settled and serene style.

Most of the shorter text's content is carried over into the longer, as if Julian works on and from a copy of the short text; passages undergo some re-expression, but much phrasing remains scarcely altered. Little material is positively discarded, and compression or resequencing in the longer text of material from the shorter is the exception (as in chs. 40–4; pp. 90–7). The longer text treats the shorter one curatorially, as if the words of the short text conserve the core documentary testimony of the revelations. It is around the short text that the longer version frames the apparatus of what can resemble an edition of this original testimony, with numerous additions of extended meditative commentary on the revelations' content. Textual divisions in the sole manuscript of the short text are signalled by blue initials rather than by chapter numbering, dividing the text into twenty-five sections. Only eight of such divisions correspond with the beginning of a new revelation, and there is no evidence as to whether these divisions are scribal or authorial. With the longer text come both the numbering of the revelations and the division into numbered chapters. The numbering of revelations apparently goes back to Julian herself, because cross-reference between revelations by number is instrumental to the way that Julian interrelates her thoughts about her revelations in the long text and draws her work into a whole. The chapter divisions are less clearly authorial, and the chapter summaries, at least in their extant form, apparently do not derive from Julian herself, but since she has only thought to number the first, second, and sixteenth revelations within her text, it is through the apparatus of these chapter summaries (in MSS S1 and S2), or the chapter headings (in MS P), that the other revelations are numbered and demarcated. What survive here may be layers of early editorial assistance, because it is likely that an enclosed anchoress would need clerical support in producing such an ambitious text.

Julian's mode of developing her text between its shorter and longer versions involves adding many new passages, as well as weaving new matter into existing sentences, transforming content and style through cadenced prose patterning. The succinct report in the short text is carried forward into new contexts where it is framed by understandings of her initial statements that Julian has come with meditation to perceive. A vivid core of initial perception is set within

subsequent interpretative commentary, in a way that allows for qualification and realignment of problematic passages. The long text has
evolved through the intensive interpolation into a version of the short
text of interleaved commentary in added paragraphs, as well as inter-
lineated expansions that incorporate new sentences into existing passages and new clauses into sentences surviving from the short text.
Much of what is now viewed as Julian's characteristic style and language is the work of the long text, where Julian gains control of what
previously seemed uncontrollably problematic, and such mastery is
reflected stylistically. A brief observation jotted down like a memo in
the short text ('love was revealed to me most of all—that it is closest
to us all', ST, p. 34) will be transformed in the longer text in terms of
what the soul now understands of God's will in the original insight
('the soul received most understanding of love; yes, and he wishes
that we perceive love in all things and rejoice in it', ch. 73; p. 149).

What had started in the short text as the story of Julian's visions
becomes in the long version the history of how she comes to understand them. As an authorial re-edition of the earlier text—and something of an unconscious autobiography in recording a process of
meditative retrospection—the long text now includes within itself so
much reflection on the earlier narrative of Julian's revelatory experience as to shift the balance and revise the focus of the briefer account
and refashion its genre. In essence, the short text had presented a narrative self-account of an experience of revelation. In the long text,
however, the original narrative line gives way to the more exploratory
unity of a meditative commentary. Here are foregrounded all the ana-
lytical subtleties of a contemplative and theologically-informed mind
that discerns patterns, categorizes, and subdivides with a spiritual
sense of number.[20] Indeed, it is commentary that comes to define the
continuity of the longer version. In the course of meditating on her
first twelve revelations Julian has interleaved many additional paragraphs, but her thirteenth and fourteenth revelations prompt Julian
to such an extended excursus of commentary that a narrative history

[20] Julian analyses 'three objects in our seeking' (ch. 10; p. 55), 'three ways of contemplating' (ch. 21; p. 67), 'three kinds of expression in our Lord' (ch. 71; p. 146), 'three
kinds of knowledge' (ch. 72; p. 148); she sees 'two attributes in what our Lord was conveying' (ch. 41; p. 91), 'two ways of working within one love' (ch. 48; p. 102), 'two kinds
of sickness' (ch. 73; p. 148), 'four ways in which the body dried' (ch. 17; p. 63), 'four kinds
of fear' (ch. 74; p. 150), and much more.

of the revelations received on the first day can barely re-establish itself before commentary on the completed revelations as a whole takes over until the text's conclusion. The questions implicit in Julian's initial account have prompted such an extended response that the narrative framework has been pushed outwards from within by the pressure of meditation at the centre of the work. A sense of its own narrative continuity no longer controls the book, for the first text has been turned inside out. Instead, the narrative of the original day's visionary experience is held in fractured form within what is now the real continuum of Julian's meditations on her visions. Julian's original narrative of two days ends up almost splitting at the seams under the exploration of its own implications, but this is the paradoxical effect of the several time-schemes. There are the two remembered days of revelation along with responses at that time, now seen through the retrospect not only of Julian's intervening meditations over many years but also, as she variously implies, of some subsequent illumin-ations (ch. 65; p. 139).

In the long text the modern reader gains access to a work that— for all its formal textualization and its alertness to Julian's fellow Christians—retains something of the layered, interleaved structure of a private working draft. It has not been reconfigured into a logical linearity for the benefit of readers who have not shared its author's experience and is criss-crossed with references forward to revelations that have not yet been reported. The acknowledged delay in reaching key understandings fifteen and twenty years after the original revela-tions would have been sufficient reason for the non-circulation of an uncompleted text, and beyond this Julian may have had other unre-solved uncertainties that go unreported in the text as it survives. It is entirely possible that there were more stages and states of Julian's text intervening between the short and long texts which do not survive, whether or not they were ever circulated or remained her working copies. Part of the text's great integrity as a commentary-in-progress derives from Julian's candid admissions of uncertainty and lack of understanding, which are left to stand in her text alongside a record of the process by which she did attain understanding, or accepted what she could not yet know. It is as an uncompleted project shared with the reader that the long text subsumes any more direct but simpler claim to didactic intent in the short text, instead reflecting through its very form the history of an individual's meditative exploration towards greater understanding. The long text adds no schematic contemplative programmes for readers to apply for themselves and is not structured by metaphors of spiritual progress: no ascents or pilgrimages are outlined. In essence, Julian offers her own experience as a witness, and her only claim on her reader lies in her conviction that her testimony's value lies not in any endorsement of her singular experience in her secluded life but in its import for all her fellow Christians.

'The noblest thing he ever made is mankind'

Some of the uniqueness of Julian's response to her visionary experience—and the consequent challenge for modern readers of the resulting text—lies in the depth and originality with which Julian considers her revelations from theological perspectives, which become inseparable from how the revelations are perceived. At the heart of the longer text, Julian's meditations on her thirteenth and fourteenth revelations include some of her most familiar concerns: the challenge represented by sin, the role of prayer, our 'godly will' that never consented to sin, and Julian's understanding of how Christ is our mother. There is much that is exploratory and much that may seem reiterative in Julian's method in these chapters, where Julian's characteristically independent exposition of the structure of the soul helps inform an understanding of the implications of the incarnation which unifies Julian's concerns in her meditations and how she resolves them.

THE STRUCTURE OF THE SOUL: SUBSTANCE AND SENSORY BEING

Made in God's image, there is nothing more like God than the human soul (ch. 58; pp. 126–8). Unlike the human body, which is created out of earthly matter, God would take nothing for the making of the human soul (ch. 53; p. 119). The soul is created, but out of nothing that is created, by God who is himself uncreated, and with the consequence that there neither can nor shall be anything between God and man's soul (ch. 53; p. 119). Moreover, all human souls were made all at once, and kept united to God (ch. 58; p. 126). Our souls have a pre-existence in the Second Person of the Trinity before individual bodies are created in the course of time.

As the higher part of the soul, God created its substance or essence, and the highest part of the soul, its apex, is that portion of the soul's substance that remains grounded in God's substance, his uncreated being. Our soul dwells in God's substance, and we participate in God's substance. Our soul, made from nothing, has a natural affinity to the unmade substance of God's nature. Julian avoids claiming that God and the human soul can be one and the same, suggesting rather that the substance of our soul exists in God without being identical to him. Julian also makes a careful distinction between what she was shown and what she nevertheless understands. Although she may have seen no difference between God and our substance, she understands that our substance is in God: which is to say, that God is God, and our substance is a created thing in God (ch. 54; p. 120). Moreover, although the soul may always be like God in nature and in substance, restored by grace, it is often unlike God in condition through sin (ch. 43; p. 95).

The other part of the soul is what Julian terms in Middle English our 'sensuality', or sensory being.[21] Julian goes beyond the conventional, in ignoring not only the traditionally gendered view of a masculine higher and a female lower part of the soul, but also the customary stress on a divisive split between body and soul. Nor in practice does Julian much emphasize substance and sensory being as higher and lower than each other—even if she acknowledges this (ch. 55; p. 122)—for there is only one soul, and all language of space, division, and higher or lower, may mislead. For Julian the sensory being is an integral part of us, for substance is united with sensory being at the very moment that the soul is embodied in a human being. Indeed, God is the means that keeps the substance and the sensory being together so that they shall never separate (ch. 56; p. 123), and this is effected in Christ's incarnation (ch. 57; p. 125).

What Julian understands by the sensory being is evidently more capacious and positive than many medieval definitions. It signifies that part of the soul concerned with bodily knowing and the feeling of bodily things. It is our bodily being in the world of time, informed by our soul, a nexus between the bodily and the spiritual, between

---

[21] 'Substance' remains a technical theological term, as it was for Julian, and so has not been translated. The modern English 'sensuality' is too limited and negative in meaning to translate Julian's Middle English 'sensualite', which has generally been translated as 'sensory being'.

the body and history. It includes, but is very much more than, the physical senses or sensuousness, sexuality, or, indeed, sensuality in the more restricted modern sense. It refers to our whole sensory consciousness, but includes both our psychology and our physicality as an individual consciousness. For Julian, any distinction between substance and sensory being does not correspond to a dualism between soul and body, because both substance and sensory being refer to the soul, although there would be no sensory being without the body. In assuming human nature Christ took upon himself our sensory being without sin and did not fail in that sensory being ('And these two parts were in Christ, the higher and the lower, which is but one soul', ch. 55; p. 122), with profound implications for understanding the dignity and worth of the sensory being. Substance and sensory being differ in completeness ('In our substance we are complete', ch. 57; p. 124), whereas in fallen humankind it will be through aspects of the sensory being that we fall short and remain incomplete. Yet Julian tellingly leaves this largely to implication, not explicitly condemning sensory being as such, or linking it with particular sins. This reflects Julian's benign view of our body, created by God and assumed by Christ. Instead of devaluing human bodiliness and distrusting the sensory being, Julian dwells on sensory being as a precious part in ourselves where body and soul are capable of redemption. God's mercy and grace are needed, but for Julian the sensory being will be brought to completion and to inclusion in eternity.

The relation of substance and sensory being in the soul is something that Julian returns to defining through some of her recurrent language of mutual indwelling—'our substance is in God, and I also saw that God is in our sensory being' (ch. 55; p. 121)—for the union of our substance and sensory being is located in God. Julian presses beyond convention in seeing God informing the lower part of the soul, and God is present in the soul at the very point where its two parts, substance and sensory being, are conjoined. At this point is the city of God where he is enthroned forever (ch. 55; p. 121). Indeed, Julian stresses that both substance and sensory being are integral to the soul (ch. 56; p. 123). In a reference to her sixteenth revelation, Julian even equates sensory being itself with the city of God: 'The noble city in which our Lord Jesus sits is our sensory being, in which he is enclosed' (ch. 56; p. 123). In Julian's understanding, the sensory being is not something to be suppressed or rooted out,

since the complementarity of substance and sensory being is fundamental. God has knit himself to our nature, and so in Christ our two
natures are united (ch. 57; p. 125). Moreover, the conjunction in us of
substance and sensory being has implications for our own judgement
(ch. 45; p. 98). Seeing only the outward witness of the sensory in this
changeable, transitory existence, people blame themselves (ch. 46;
p. 99), whereas God, beholding the union of substance and sensory
being, is able to excuse human weakness.

CHRIST OUR MOTHER

In what Julian calls the first creation there is a union between the
substance of the individual soul and the Second Person of the Trinity
that is foreseen from without beginning. This first creation therefore exists before the union of substance with the sensory being and
the body when the soul descends to earth at an individual's birth.
Moreover, it was ordained without beginning by the Trinity (ch. 53;
p. 119) that Christ should take on human nature, which was ordained
for him first of all (ch. 57; p. 125). The incarnation is hence a second creation, when the Second Person in the Trinity has taken the
lower part of human nature to which the higher part was united in
the first creation (ch. 55; p. 122). It is these first and second creations
that provide the theological foundation for Julian's understanding of
the motherhood of God, because Julian represents as maternal the
role of the Second Person of the Trinity in the creation and then the
reunification of the human soul by Christ's redemptive work through
his incarnation. In our Father we have our safekeeping in respect of
our natural substance, which is ours by our creation from without
beginning, and in the Second Person of the Trinity with regard to
our sensory being we have our restoring and salvation. Just as the
first refers to creation, the second refers to a re-creation; the first corresponds to nature, the second to mercy, and hence Julian sees God
rejoicing that he is our Father, mother, spouse, brother, and Saviour
(ch. 52; p. 115)—perhaps especially meaningful to recluses who have
forsaken for God all family ties.

For Julian, Adam's fall has already been redressed: the two parts
of the soul have been remade by Christ's redemption (ch. 57;
p. 125). The point is that while all members of the Trinity are united
in substance with humanity, only the Second Person is united with
human sensory being. Because soul and body are in union, mankind

must be redeemed and restored by the Second Person of the Trinity's taking upon himself the lower part of human nature, whose higher part was united to him in its first creation. Both parts were in Christ, the higher and the lower, which are but one soul. The higher part was forever at peace with God in perfect joy and bliss. The lower part, which is sensory being, suffered for the salvation of mankind (ch. 55; p. 122). In restoring human sensory being to its original relation with the divine substance through his incarnation, Jesus is cast by Julian as mother, just as his original creation of the union between human substance and sensory being is represented as a maternal act: 'And so Jesus is our true mother by nature at our first creation, and he is our true mother in grace by taking on our created nature' (ch. 59; p. 129).[22]

In Julian's understanding of Christ's first and second maternity, our redemption was always foreseen from without beginning in terms of motherhood and, by implication, regardless of the fall of man: 'God almighty . . . knew us and loved us from before there was any time. Out of this knowledge . . . through the prescient eternal counsel of all the blessed Trinity, he wanted the Second Person to become our mother, our brother, and our Saviour' (ch. 59; p. 129). Julian comes to understand three ways of contemplating motherhood in God: the first is God's motherhood in our first creation, the second motherhood is in the taking of our nature through his incarnation, but the third is a spreading outwards or a diffusion of grace that restores us to our natural place (ch. 59). It is this motherhood of works, a working of motherhood in action, that Julian explores in the maternal similitudes of her understanding of Christ our mother, which are founded in Julian's profound preoccupation with the Trinity, within which, as the wisdom of God, Christ may be called mother.

From the Old Testament Julian could have absorbed references to God as an attentive, protective parent nurturing her children (as in Isaiah 42: 14, 49: 15, 66: 13), while in the New Testament Christ, in rebuking Jerusalem, likens himself to a mother hen: 'How often would I have gathered thy childen together, even as a hen gathereth her chickens under her wings, and ye would not!' (Matthew 23: 37; also

[22] On the unique nature of Julian's thinking about this 'second maternity', see Caroline Walker Bynum, *Holy Feast and Holy Fast: The Religious Significance of Food to Medieval Women* (Berkeley, 1987), 266–7.

Luke 13: 34). Moreover, Wisdom, identified with the Second Person of the Trinity, is personified as female in scripture (as in Wisdom 7: 11–12, 25–7), and some Pauline texts represent God as bringing us to birth (1 Peter 1: 3; James 1: 18). Medieval affective devotion had already developed traditions of interpreting Christ as a mother who, in a paradox, by his Passion and death gives life and so brings to birth his children, who are breast-fed and nurtured by Christ as their mother. In one of his prayers, which were so influential on later affective devotion, Saint Anselm (1033–1109) had developed the Gospel imagery of Christ as mother hen.[23] The twelfth-century Cistercians Bernard of Clairvaux, William of St Thierry, and Aelred of Rievaulx employed maternal analogies to convey Christ's compassionate and nurturing role towards the human soul, and such scholastics as St Albert the Great, St Thomas Aquinas, and St Bonaventure drew on maternal imagery in discussing God the Creator, the Wisdom of Christ, and the Holy Spirit. There was also the traditional conception of the Church as our mother (see ch. 46; p. 100)—and Christ is the Church. Julian herself makes this connection and goes on to describe Christ's motherly hands diligently caring for us like a kindly nurse (ch. 61; p. 133). Some of Julian's boldest passages develop a double understanding of the incarnation that includes not only Christ in the womb but humanity in the womb of Christ: how in order to become our mother in everything Christ came down into the womb, but also how he carries us within himself to term and after the most painful labour he gives birth to us into life and to bliss. Having described how 'in the Virgin's womb he took on our sensory soul' (ch. 57; p. 125),

---

[23] And you, Jesus, are you not also a mother?
    Are you not the mother who, like a hen,
    gathers her chickens under her wings?
Truly, Lord, you are a mother;
    for both they who are in labour
    and they who are brought forth
      are accepted by you.
You have died more than they, that they may labour to bear.
    It is by your death that they have been born,
    for if you had not been in labour,
      you could not have borne death;
And if you had not died, you would not have brought forth . . .
So you, Lord God, are the great mother . . .

    Sister Benedicta Ward (trans.), *The Prayers and Meditations of St Anselm* (Harmondsworth, 1973), 153–4.

Julian moves—via the idea that Mary is thus the mother of all who will be saved—to a strikingly dual notion of our both perpetually being given birth to by Christ and yet of our perpetual enclosure secure within him, which Julian cross-references to her first and sixteenth revelations (ch. 57; p. 126).

Julian's account of Christ our mother works by comparisons, making the point that Christ's motherhood of us goes surpassingly beyond what earthly mothers can do. For Julian it is less that Christ acts like a mother than that mothers at their most maternal share in Christ-like characteristics. The mother breast-feeds her child, but our mother Christ feeds us with himself through the sacrament, which is the food of life. The mother lays her child upon her breast, but Christ (as in Julian's tenth revelation) leads us within his breast and wounded side to reveal part of the Godhead and of heaven's bliss. All the mother's care in birthing and upbringing is, for Julian, performed by Christ in our mothers by whom it is done. Even if an earthly mother might let her child perish, our heavenly mother Jesus will never let us perish (echoing Isaiah 49: 15). Our mother Jesus wants us to behave in spirit like a child who instinctively trusts in the mother's love (ch. 61; pp. 132–3), and indeed, in spiritual terms we never grow beyond childhood in this life (ch. 63; p. 136). Comparison with an earthly mother's love provides a uniquely potent way for Julian to convey the inexhaustible care of Christ across time, who will never cease from his labours until all his children are delivered (ch. 63; p. 135). Comparing God's care and a mother's upbringing of her child, the English guide for anchoresses, the *Ancrene Wisse*, describes the mother's playing hide-and-seek until she appears again to hug the child frightened by her disappearance, but in Julian's account Jesus our mother never exercises even such a playful deception and never pretends to be absent from us (ch. 61; p. 132). Nor does Julian dwell much on the mother's chastising the child, as some spiritual writers do (ch. 60; p. 131). If Julian was aware of other treatments of the motherhood of God, she has made them so much her own that her originality makes influence hard to detect. For Julian, the motherhood of God, expressed in Christ, is no mere metaphor or simile, but the taking on of our physical humanity in the incarnation. Julian could hardly be clearer or bolder in affirming the equality and equivalence that 'As truly as God is our father, so truly is God our mother' (ch. 59; p. 128).

'TWO KINDS OF PERCEPTION'

Another of Julian's most distinctive themes—her understanding of a 'godly will' in the human soul—also develops in association with her thinking on the structure of the soul and the motherhood of God. Julian's conviction about a godly will in every soul reflects the soul's two-part structure: 'Just as there is an animal will in the lower part of our nature which cannot will anything good, so there is a godly will in the higher part of our nature, and this will is so good that it can never will evil, but always good' (ch. 37; p. 87). It is through Christ's motherhood of us in redemption that we have this godly will intact and safe in him (ch. 59; p. 129), a kind of spark of the divine life in us. Julian's confidence in the impeccability of the soul is based on her conviction of predestination in Christ. Julian believes that all her fellow Christians will be saved, in the sense that all souls are predestined for heaven, although free to reject that predestination. In that God abides in the souls of the elect and their souls abide in God, that part of the will residing in the substance or higher part of the soul is indefectible from good and 'never assented to sin nor ever shall' (ch. 37; p. 87). This does not mean incapable of sinning—because 'in this life we cannot keep ourselves from sin as completely in perfect purity as we shall in heaven' (ch. 52; p. 117)—but our will, like that of the fallen servant in the Lord and Servant parable, is preserved intact in the sight of God (ch. 51; p. 109), even if neither the servant nor we may perceive it, and it is this confidence that resonates throughout Julian's text.

In addition to the union of substance between God and humankind, Julian sees those who will be saved as joining in the union of Christ's soul with God, which is represented as the most subtly intricate of knots: 'Christ's beloved soul was preciously joined to him in the making; with a knot so subtle and so strong that it is united to God . . . Furthermore . . . all the souls which shall be saved in heaven without end are united and joined in this unity, and made holy in this holiness' (ch. 53; p. 119). The implication is that sin may never sever the ties that knit God and the elect. If these ties are so close—'And so it is that there neither can nor shall be anything at all between God and man's soul' (ch. 53; p. 119)—where is the room for sin? Indeed, Julian declares of the soul's union in substance with God: 'And as regards our substance, God made us so noble and so rich that

we always work his will and his glory. When I say "we", that means
those who will be saved; for I saw truly that we are what he loves
and we do what pleases him, lastingly and without ceasing' (ch. 57;
p. 124). Not only does each individual participate in the union of
divine substance with the human soul, but through his assumption
of our human nature Christ makes his mercy generally available to
mankind (ch. 58; p. 127). Moreover, Julian describes Christ's union
with our humanity at the incarnation as if to imply that thereby all
humankind is to be saved ('he took on our sensory soul, and in taking
it on, having enclosed us all in himself, he united the sensory soul to
our substance. In this union he was perfect man; for Christ, having
united in himself everyone who will be saved, is perfect man', ch. 57;
p. 125). The implication is that the door to salvation stands open to all
who will seek it (except perhaps to unrepentant reprobates), but this
is not the same as an assurance of universal salvation, which Julian
never declares.

At the core of Julian's dilemma over her revelations is that she has
two kinds of perception (ch. 46; p. 99), which she distinguishes. One
is the revelations' assurance of unending love, protection, and salvation. The other is the common and universal teaching of the Church.
The attempt to reconcile what Julian understands to be the implications of her own revelations with orthodox Church teachings is the
impetus that drives many of Julian's meditative changes between her
short and long texts. Christ promises Julian, 'I shall keep my word
in all things, and I shall make all things well' (ch. 32; p. 81), and as
both Julian's revelations and Church teaching derive from God they
cannot be truly in contradiction, if only she can understand how they
serve to complement each other. One such orthodox teaching is that
we should acknowledge ourselves sinners, deserving blame and anger
(ch. 46; p. 100). Yet this is challenged by the revelations, both openly
and implicitly, since they do not show God blaming us for sinning,
and this costs Julian much uncertainty and unease. As early as her
third revelation, where Julian sees that God is in all things and does
all things, she is moved to wonder in that case 'What is sin?' Not
being shown sin, Julian comes to the traditional conclusion that sin or
evil is an absence or privation rather than any positive entity (ch. 11;
p. 56). Much later, in the thirteenth revelation—in response to her
wondering why God had not prevented the beginning of sin, in which
case all would be well—Julian receives from Jesus the answer that sin

had to be: it was 'befitting'. Nevertheless, 'all shall be well' (ch. 27; p. 74), even if—as is made evident—this may be in the fullness of heaven rather than necessarily in this life. As Julian will discover, this involves faithfully accepting that much remains undisclosed to us. Through many succeeding chapters Julian is left to struggle with conforming orthodox teaching with the optimistic and benevolent implications of her revelations, which often lie in the significance of what they omit to mention ('the revelation was of goodness, in which there was little mention of evil', ch. 33; p. 82). It is her meditations on such occlusions in her revelations that prompt some of Julian's most striking meditations: she does not see sin because, having no kind of substance in itself, it can only be recognized by the pain it causes (ch. 27; p. 75), and rather than worry why sin came to be, she is encouraged to see Fall and incarnation together, and to understand that although Adam's sin is the greatest harm, the redemption is much more pleasing to God than Adam's sin is harmful (ch. 29; p. 77).

It is Julian's contemplative confidence that God's love is without beginning which underlies her realization that our human sense of time may confuse our understanding of God's purposes in the role of sin, as also of prayer. To her early question 'What is sin?' the answer is an understanding that since God does everything, all is for the best conclusion, and nothing happens accidentally, although it may appear otherwise to us (ch. 11; p. 55). Enfolded as we are within God's beginningless love, sin diminishes to a non-entity because evil is non-being. Eventually, Julian attains her understanding that sin is not something inherent in human nature but derives from human imperception 'and the cause is blindness', whereas if we saw God continually we would not experience 'the craving that is conducive to sin' (ch. 47; p. 101). It is no accident that in her parable of the Lord and Servant Julian places no emphasis on original sin. Julian never describes humanity in terms of such a concept of inherited and ineradicable contamination. On the contrary, for Julian sin is not natural to mankind but unnatural (ch. 63; p. 135). As such, sin is not to be feared more than fear forms a useful spur to amendment (ch. 63; p. 135). As Julian sees it, many of our sins are not wholly intended, and one should not bother too much about 'sin that you commit against your will' (ch. 82; p. 161), nor despair because of our frequent falling (ch. 39; p. 89), nor busy ourselves with self-accusation (ch. 79; p. 158). Julian even goes so far as to declare that it is actually God's purpose that humanity cannot keep from sinning in this life (ch. 52; pp. 116–17), with the implication that the conventional emphasis on punishment and penalty for sin should give way to recognizing a kind of merit in the suffering of sin. Indeed, Julian roundly declares that our heavenly reward will be all the greater because of our sins (ch. 38; p. 88)—assuming, of course, that those sins are properly repented and forgiven. This belongs with Julian's positive view of our twofold nature in both body and spirit, whereby we actually have the potential to attain to greater spiritual goods through our fleshly createdness than if we had been created as spiritual beings alone (ch. 56; p. 124). None of this is to deny sin, but to deny it an ultimate power: we should hate no hell but sin (ch. 76; p. 153), because hell would be the separation from God to which sin may lead. It is in this context that Julian comes to understand how she can never see in God any blame or anger for human sin—nor, even more startlingly, can she see any forgiveness (ch. 49; p. 103).

As for how our prayers relate to a God who loves from without beginning, Julian's fourteenth revelation gives insight into how our praying has to be understood free of the misconceptions brought by our time-conditioned consciousness and our instinctual sense of cause and effect within that. If, as the Lord explains, 'first, it is my will that you should have something, and then I make you desire it, and then I make you pray for it' (ch. 41; p. 92), how can our prayers not be answered? Our praying cannot alter God, nor win results from God: our prayer appears to us to be answered only when and if it corresponds with God's will (ch. 41; p. 92). As such, prayer should be an alignment of our will with God's (ch. 41; p. 92), and goodness and grace are not earned by prayer (ch. 41; p. 92). It is God who prays in us, and since God is the source of prayer, and prayer is a gift of God, we should trust that he will answer the prayers he has initiated in us (ch. 42; p. 94). Moreover, since God is in everything, he is also present in his apparent refusal to answer our prayers (ch. 42; p. 94). By the same token, all our sorrowing and longing for union with him is Christ's longing in us (ch. 80; p. 159). Yet within all God's pre-existent ordinance that her revelations illuminate, Julian perceives an undiminished freedom for humankind through love.

Nonetheless, Julian wrestles with the implication of failing to see any blame or anger in God on account of our sin, when that sinfulness is not in question. The only anger she sees is on man's part, which God forgives (ch. 48; p. 102). It is impossible for God to be angry—for 'where our Lord appears, peace reigns' (ch. 49; pp. 103–4)—and if God might be angry even for an instant we could have no being (ch. 49; p. 104). Instead, Julian sees that God 'regards sin as sorrow and suffering for those who love him, to whom he attributes no blame, out of love' (ch. 39; p. 89). Julian perceives that even though she will do nothing but sin, her sin will not prevent the operation of God's goodness (ch. 36; p. 85). Although Julian and everyone will sin, God keeps us safe (ch. 37; p. 87), and our falling does not prevent him from loving us (ch. 39; p. 89). Julian comes to see that while sin will be justly punished, contrition and repentance are truly transformative, and we can be 'suddenly freed from sin and from pain, and taken up into bliss, and made equal with exalted saints' (ch. 39; p. 89). Hence, far from being shameful to them, the sins of the elect will be turned to glory, and in heaven the scars of their sins will be insignia of honour (ch. 38; p. 88). Our sorrows and tribulations will have been sent on ahead of us to heaven, where we shall find them when we get there 'all turned into very lovely and unending glories' (ch. 49; p. 105).

It is this hopeful theme—'And by his permission, we fall . . . and . . . we are raised to manifold greater joys' (ch. 35; p. 84)—that from the thirteenth revelation onwards looks forward to the parable of the Lord and Servant in chapter 51. Yet despite all the optimism, there remains a sense of unresolved questions. Seemingly pressing problems about the existence of evil and suffering, or the fate of the damned, are explained to be beyond explanation now, whether through our own imperception or as God's proper secrets and mysteries. Despite all the reassurance on sin, the Lord and Servant parable follows in answer to a moment of renewed crisis, when Julian still cannot negotiate the apparent gulf between Church teaching that the blame for our sin continually weighs upon us, and her astonishment that she saw God attributing no more blame to us than if we were as pure and holy as angels in heaven (ch. 50; p. 105). Since God has not shown her that sin is done away with, she must 'see in God how he sees it' (ch. 50; p. 105).

The lord and servant

The parable, or illustrative story, that Julian reports and analyses in by far her longest chapter (ch. 51) is not related as part of the

sequence of revelations, nor is it like those revelations, but it prompts
an exceptional degree and kind of interpretation. Both at its opening
and throughout, this parable of the Lord and Servant is presented in
terms of the problematic process of how it comes to be understood.
It appears as a spiritual vision in bodily form, but also as a more spiritual vision without bodily form: initially an imaginary vision, and
then in a more spiritual, intellectual understanding. The narrative
of the parable is a brief sequence of wordless actions, as if played out
in dumbshow, which invites decoding as a picture where every detail
of positioning, gaze, and appearance may carry implication. Julian
sees a lord sitting composedly and a servant standing by respectfully,
ready to do the lord's will. The lord sends the servant to a certain
place to do his will—destination and errand being undisclosed to the
reader. Out of love the servant hastens to do the lord's errand but
falls into a 'slade' (a valley or hollow). Although seriously injured, the
servant's greatest misery is that, having fallen, he cannot now see his
lord—even though the lord is very near—and 'like someone who was
weak and foolish for the moment, he was intent on his own feelings'
(ch. 51; p. 106–7). Julian attends carefully to see if she can discern
either any fault in the servant or if the lord attributes any blame to
the servant. Julian can see neither, for the fall did not arise from disobedience, but from the servant's good will, and he remains as willing and as good inwardly as before his fall. Julian also perceives the
double aspect of the tender gaze with which the loving lord regards
his fallen servant: outwardly with pity and compassion, and inwardly
with rejoicing at the rest and honour into which the lord will bring his
fallen servant. The lord concludes that it is only reasonable that the
servant should be rewarded more than if he had not fallen, and his fall
be turned into surpassing glory.

   This is where the original revelation came to an end, and despite
feeling that God continues to lead her understanding forwards, Julian
remains in a quandary about how to interpret what she understands
to have been revealed as an answer to her uncertainties. It is only
after three months short of twenty years that Julian receives 'teaching inwardly' to focus intently on all the details and qualities of what
was shown her in the parable. The implication is that every point in
the inward picture of the parable is open to be decoded. Particular
challenges and questions are posed by the following aspects: the
servant's good will in obeying the lord's command; the severe pains

and suffering of the servant consequent upon the fall; the absence of blame for the servant by the lord; and the servant's being rewarded more than if he had not fallen. This will prove an audacious reimagining that transforms understanding of humanity's sinfulness as represented by the story of Adam.

The rest of the chapter retains—and reflects through its form—the recursive history by which Julian returns meditatively to the signal details of the parable. Each return to the pictured scene picks up on details in order to press further with spiritual understandings, as if layers of understanding are built up. Julian has not rewritten her chapter from some late vantage-point of achieved understanding and so as to accord only with that. Partial insights have not been revised away out of the picture but left to document a journey towards understanding. Julian's impulse is that of the commentator, returning repeatedly to meditate so intently on the parable that it almost comes to have the presence of a painting, despite remaining in many spiritual aspects unvisualizable.

Julian's initial analysis (ch. 51; p. 107) is like something from her shorter text, confining itself to an outline noting the figures' manner of standing and sitting, their position, the nature of their clothing—but also, significantly, noting the inward goodness in both the lord and the servant. Julian already understands at this point that the lord 'is God', while the servant represents Adam, except that 'in the sight of God all men are one man, and one man is all men' (ch. 51; p. 109): both each and all, individual and community. Even at this early stage in her analysis, however, comes a key insight into the significance of the Lord and Servant parable for Julian's understanding of humanity's 'godly will'. The fallen servant may be unable to behold God, and his capacity for understanding has been numbed, yet unbeknown to him 'his will was preserved intact in the sight of God; for I saw our Lord commend and approve his will' (ch. 51; p. 109). From this remarkable insight—that the will in the fallen servant is still commendable to God, even if the servant cannot see this—Julian moves immediately to an equally bold insight: that our sinfulness is its own punishment and part of the pain of our separation from a God who does not blame or punish, a pain that reflects our own confusion in unproductive self-blame and self-loathing.

It is Julian's technique to recur a number of times during the chapter to various features of the Lord and Servant parable as these deepen in significance for her through contemplation. One such feature is the lord's sitting on the earth, where his clothing and looks are first sketched in descriptively (ch. 51; p. 109), but Julian soon returns to these features seeking interpretation. The strangeness of a lord's sitting on the ground in a barren and deserted wilderness signifies how the lord seeks no alternative resting place for himself but sits on that earth with which fallen humanity is mingled, waiting until Christ has restored the city to its beauty and splendour. Much later, Julian recurs to the lord's sitting in order to understand how the sitting betokens the Godhead, in whom there may be no labour, and eventually the lord's sitting undergoes a transfiguration ('Now the lord does not sit upon the earth in a wilderness, but he sits in his noblest seat . . .', ch. 51; p. 114).

Another recurrent focus for Julian's analysis is the positioning of the servant as he stands with the seated lord, an aspect to which Julian returns and progressively reinterprets. Having originally recorded only that the servant 'stands by . . . in front of his lord' (ch. 51; p. 106), Julian later observes much more particularly ('he stood very near the lord, not right in front of him but a little to one side, on the left', ch. 51; p. 110), but offers no commentary (see also 51/109, 113–14). Later, in a passage acknowledging how the servant represents the Son's redemptive purpose, 'he therefore stood before his Father like a servant, willingly taking upon himself all the burden of us' (ch. 51; pp. 112–13). Further on, the servant's position is interpreted by way of representing the longing and desire of those who shall come to heaven: 'this yearning and longing was represented in the servant standing before the lord, or rather, to put it differently, in the Son's standing before the Father in Adam's tunic' (ch. 51; p. 113). Later still, and more specifically, 'That he stood in awe before the lord, and not right in front, signifies that his clothing was not suitable for him to stand right in front of the lord' (ch. 51; p. 114). Finally, all this is swept away in the transfiguration of the chapter's close, where the son first stands before the father richly apparelled and crowned, and then 'the Son does not stand before the Father on the left side like a labourer, but he sits at his Father's right hand', even if Julian also carefully notes that 'as I see it, there is no such sitting in the Trinity' (ch. 51; p. 115).

Her method here typifies how Julian develops her meditation by revisiting aspects of the parable and thereby enlarging understanding.

The same technique can be observed in Julian's meditative interpretation of the servant's clothing, mentioned but undescribed early in
the chapter (ch. 51; p. 109). Somewhat later this clothing is visual-
ized very particularly: a labourer's white, unlined tunic, which is old,
sweat-stained, tight-fitting, cut short just below the knee, and all in rags
and tatters (ch. 51; p. 110–11). However, no further interpretation is
offered here, other than surprise that this was unseemly attire to wear
before so noble a lord. Further on, Julian returns to the tunic's spiritual
significance: 'the white tunic is the flesh' (ch. 51; p. 113), perceiving
that its unlined nature signifies that there was nothing between the
Godhead and the manhood of Christ, while its age and staining witness
to Adam's toil (ch. 51; p. 113). Further on again, the fact that it is about
to disintegrate into rags and tatters is to be understood as the tearing
of Christ's flesh by whips, nails, and thorns (ch. 51; p. 114). By the
chapter's end, Adam's old tunic—tight, threadbare, and skimpy—has
been made fair, new, white, and radiant by the Saviour, and seems finer
than the clothing Julian sees on the Father (ch. 51; p. 114).

Such a double understanding of the servant continues when the
servant's labour is likened to that of a gardener. This alludes both
to Adam's condemnation in Genesis to till the earth, and to traditions of Christ as a gardener of the human heart, developing from
his post-Resurrection appearance in the semblance of a gardener to
Mary Magdalene (John 20: 15). The servant gardener is to work at
producing and serving a food that is pleasing to the lord. The overlap
between this task and the servant's errand earlier in the chapter is left
to implication and unpressed. Since we also hear that there is a treasure in the earth (ch. 51; p. 111), and this treasure 'was grounded in
the lord in marvellous depths of endless love' (ch. 51; p. 111), both
food and treasure are probably the soul of humanity, which Christ
will redeem and bring back into God. Although this is 'the greatest
labour and the hardest toil that there is' (ch. 51; p. 111), Julian retains
no sense from Genesis of Adam's labour as a curse, or of the earth
as accursedly hard to cultivate. Instead, nature figures as benignly
abundant (ch. 51; p. 111), although something is lacking from glory
until the servant has restored the treasure to the lord. By this point
in her contemplation Julian can move boldly to see comprehended
in the servant both the Second Person of the Trinity and Adam as all
mankind (ch. 51; p. 112). From this, Julian proceeds to the stunning
heart of her insight in which—transcending our time-bound sense

of sequence and consequence—Adam's fall and Christ's incarnation
are understood as one. The parable brings Julian to the perception
that God's son could not but fall with humanity, and so 'God's son
fell with Adam into the hollow of the Virgin's womb' (ch. 51; p. 112)
at the incarnation. Finally, the chapter's concluding section invokes
Christ's harrowing of hell and resurrection as transformations of his
'fall' into incarnation, rescuing those souls eternally knit to him in
substance. This conclusion also works through a powerful reversal of
the clothing themes of the chapter that have gone before, in which—
with a glance back to the second revelation—Christ's resurrection
and glory transform 'our foul mortal flesh which God's son took upon
himself' (ch. 51; p. 114).

Julian has pursued the parallels between Adam and the second
Adam, Christ, with increasing daring as the parable narrative is
rehearsed repeatedly to yield up its further significances. One challenge to her analysis is the apparent mismatch in how this parable of
a fallen servant maps on to the narrative of the Fall of Man and its
traditional interpretation. Julian's silence on the subject of Eve and
of woman's culpability (in misogynistic tradition) is one key sign of
Julian's independence in rethinking the Fall. Unlike Adam's fall in
Eden, Julian's parable of a fall involves no rebellious disobedience of
an earlier prohibition, with a subsequent punishment for such transgression. On the contrary, the servant falls while eagerly obeying the
lord's command to run an errand, and falls inadvertently and as if
accidentally. It is striking that Christ's 'descent' into incarnation is
thus implicitly paralleled with the servant's accidental slip and loss
of his footing, suggesting the inevitability in both. Moreover, the
parable's narrative implies that an eagerness to love and serve that is
more associable with Christ is met with a wounding and with a mode
of blindness more identifiable with Adam. Julian sees that she must
carefully address the relation between the servant's degree of knowledge and the eternal wisdom of the Second Person of the Trinity
in his eternal purpose to redeem humanity (ch. 51; p. 112). The
traditional identification of the Second Person with all-foreseeing
Wisdom might otherwise fit unusually with the servant's accidental
fall by inadvertence: as he waits to start on his errand the wisdom of
the servant saw inwardly what there was to do (ch. 51; p. 113). Indeed,
the inequality implicit in a servant's service of even so magnanimous
a lord is an audacious way of representing the interrelations between

two Persons of the Trinity. As the servant waits to do the lord's command 'inwardly there was revealed in him a depth of love, and this love which he had for the lord was just like the love which the lord had for him' (ch. 51; p. 111). A love equal with God's might seem an unlikely attribute of Adam's, yet apt to the Persons of the Trinity. This double aspect of the servant as at once Adam and Christ—Fall and incarnation as one—is further highlighted by Julian's simultaneous perception that while his worn-out clothing points to Adam's age-old toil, it is as if this servant has never been sent out on any errand before and is fresh to his endeavour (ch. 51; p. 111). For Julian, it is the double identity of Christ and Adam that dissolves contradictions.

By comprehending in the servant both Adam and Christ, Julian understands something of the simultaneity of creation and redemption in the sight of God. Fundamental to Julian's understanding is her preferred emphasis less on an enduring eternity to come than on the beginninglessness of God's purposes in pre-existent love (ch. 53; pp. 118–19). Julian can shift the conventional interpretation of incarnation—whereby Christ assumes our humanity—with her understanding that Christ was the first of humanity, before humankind was created. As Julian sees it, Christ was already spiritually human before his incarnation, so that humankind was created in imitation of the pre-existing humanity of the Son. Just as our humanity imitates that of Christ, so Christ's motherhood of us pre-exists and is the fount of human motherhood, while (it is implied) the resurrected and ascended Christ retains humanity in heaven ('he is with us in heaven, true man in his own person, drawing us upwards', ch. 52; p. 116).

In the end, Julian's parable is so transformative of understanding because it transcends any allegorical reading. Prompted to attend closely to all the parable's details, Julian duly records in places what she has decoded: 'The standing of the servant signifies labour ... His springing forward is a reference to the Godhead, and his running refers to Christ's humanity' (ch. 51; pp. 113–14). Yet such equivalences do not suffice to explain the example as a whole. The impetus of the Lord and Servant parable is to serve as a kind of model to think through, whereby Julian can realize the fullest redemptive implications of the incarnation. The traditional debate between justice and mercy is superseded, because God's justice is mercy, and his mercy is just. Despite our guilt, God does not judge humanity as our guilt deserves. Adam's motivation and degree of guilt simply merit no comment from Julian, compared with the manifestations of God's love and goodness, represented by the lord's unworldly generosity to his servant, rewarding him more than if he had never fallen. As Julian observes: 'I saw, as I shall explain, many different characteristics which in no way could be attributed to Adam alone' (ch. 51; p. 108), and the servant—in a way that prompts comparisons with Langland's electrifying figure of Piers Plowman—becomes a figure through whom Julian can explore a Christ-like potential in humankind. In the figure of the servant are commingled Christ's virtue and goodness, and Adam's weakness and blindness, for—in Julian's liberating revelatory insight—it is because Christ has taken upon himself all our blameworthiness that the Father may assign no more blame to us than to Christ (ch. 51; p. 112).

'Take each thing along with everything else'

Julian's account of how her sixteen revelations were completed over two days in May 1373 modestly implies that she is not to have a later career as a habitual visionary, but the differences between her two texts suggest that in practice this was far from the case. There are hints that, although her sixteen revelations constituted a finite and unrepeatable historical event, Julian did experience later illumination and insight. Reaching the close of her account of the first fifteen revelations, Julian notes that she has recorded them as God vouchsafed them to her mind 'renewed by moments of illumination and inspiration, I hope, of the same spirit that revealed them all' (ch. 65; p. 139). After the sixteenth revelation Jesus 'would not let the vision be lost, but he revealed it all again inwardly in my soul, with more completeness' (ch. 70; p. 145). Recording her uncertainties over her second revelation, Julian remarks: 'And then at various times our good Lord gave me more insight' (ch. 10; p. 53). Some of Julian's references to the timing of her understandings could usefully be more precise but do imply spiritual illuminations received subsequent to the sixteen revelations. Indeed, if we take as seriously as Julian does all the multiple instances where she records herself as seeing and understanding by means of meditation on her revelations, then her extant text represents the outcome of sustained and continuous contemplative illumination and insight over many years.

Julian defines three modes of revelation in her experience, and identifies three stages or levels in her understanding of her revelations. Near the end of her first revelation Julian enunciates a threefold distinction in her revelatory experience: 'All this was shown in three ways: that is to say, by bodily sight, and by words formed in my understanding, and by spiritual vision' (ch. 9; p. 52). This distinction is then repeated much later, after the close of her sixteenth revelation, but with further comment on the varying extent to which these three modes of insight may be communicated to a reader: 'Concerning bodily sight, I have said what I saw as truly as I can; and as for the words, I have reported those words just as our Lord revealed them to me; and as for spiritual vision, I have said something, but I can never disclose it in full' (ch. 73; p. 148). Julian thus claims that bodily sights have been reported as accurately as possible (perhaps with the implication that only incomplete accuracy is available), while the mind's perception of divine voices appears to present least difficulty for accurate reportage, but spiritual vision can never be more than partially conveyed. Even so, in the concluding phase of her text, after her sixteenth revelation, Julian will return repeatedly to a radiance of light and vision: 'at the end of woe, our eyes will suddenly be opened, and in clearness of light our sight will be complete' (ch. 83; p. 162).

After meditating for nearly twenty years, Julian also acknowledges, by means of another threefold distinction, the comfort derived from what she sees as three stages and types of understanding: the initial teaching understood at the time of the revelations; the inward learning that has been accumulated over the intervening time; and the understanding represented to her mind by all the revelations comprehended as a whole 'from the beginning to the end—that is to say, of this book' (ch. 51; p. 108). Julian candidly acknowledges that she can no longer disentangle these stages in her mind, nor is she apologetic. Her text is largely unselfconscious about there being any divided authority between initial revelation and subsequent meditative commentary. There is little sense that Julian views the revelations as primary and her meditations as secondary or ancillary, for her insights in meditation are presented as if the outcome of a process continuous, equal, and of a piece with the revelations. Instead, Julian's threefold structure witnesses to how later understanding actually builds authenticity over time. Subsequent insights can authenticate rather than supplant the revelations. So, along with later meditation added in the longer text, some strikingly more detailed visualization is added to what is reported of the revelations, perhaps because meditation has enabled Julian quite literally to see more in her initial experience. From Julian's perspective this is evidently no contradiction to her conviction that 'I have said what I saw as truly as I can', and a similar accrual of text characterizes Julian's later record of the divine utterances that she initially reported. After presenting the divine words, Julian recurrently introduces passages beginning 'as if he said' or 'then he means this', which present, in the form of direct speech and as if they were divine locutions, Julian's own interpretative paraphrase of what she has come to understand the divine utterances to mean.[24] At some points (as in ch. 31, p. 79: 'we are . . . his crown'), Julian seemingly repeats as revelation or divine locution what has been attributed earlier to her own meditative understanding. Meaning emerges from an interplay between experience, memory, and meditation.

As a book of revelations Julian's text must have its origins and focus in what was revealed to her, yet it has also been crucially shaped by the implications of what she was *not* shown and did not or could not see. Julian contemplated equally intently what was—or was not—included in her revelations, and the impetus of her meditative text springs from its distinctive combination of the amplitude of vision and the anxiety of uncertainty. Julian's request for a vision of hell and purgatory is not answered (ch. 33; p. 81), nor is her curiosity satisfied about the spiritual progress of a friend (ch. 35, p. 83). Just as Julian makes precise inferences from her unusually precisely focused Passion revelations, so too she draws distinctive conclusions from what she is pointedly not shown, and she is not shown sin (ch. 11; p. 56). The only sins that are specifically included in revelations to Julian are impatience or sloth and despair (ch. 73; p. 148). Julian is not shown how she shall fall herself, or the extent of her sins: she wants to know but is not shown (ch. 79; p. 157). Julian includes no general taxonomy of the seven deadly sins, does not explicitly advocate withdrawal from the world or suppression of the senses, and makes no specific recommendation of virginity or celibacy. Uninterested in guilt, Julian observes that she is not shown self-imposed penance and asceticism but is shown that we should instead humbly bear the penance that Christ may give us. In any case,

---

[24] For a list of such attributive paraphrases, see the note to p. 56.

'this life is penance' (ch. 77; p. 155). In keeping with her avoidance of negativity about the body, Julian is not shown that our outer bodily part should compel our inward part, but she does receive a striking insight: 'that the inward part leads the outward part, through grace, and that both shall be united in bliss without end through the power of Christ—this was revealed' (ch. 19; p. 66).

Troubled by sin, Julian had longed 'to see in God how he sees it' (ch. 50; p. 105). At the heart of the Lord and Servant parable that she receives by way of answer is a human inability to see: the servant fallen into a place where he cannot see how he is regarded by the lord with a sustaining love. Three times in her meditations Julian is advised to accept for the interim that the answer to her uncertainty is that God's perspective must be different, and she receives understanding about two parts, two mysteries, and two judgements. Of the two parts, the first concerns 'our Saviour and our salvation' and is entirely open to those who follow Church teaching. The other part is hidden from us and is 'all that is over and above our salvation'—which perhaps concerns the destiny of those outside the Church but remains 'our Lord's private counsels' which we please God by leaving to him (ch. 30; p. 77). Julian is also shown two kinds of mysteries: the first are those secrets God wants us to know will remain hidden until the time of his choosing, while the second include 'all the preaching and teaching of Holy Church' (ch. 34; p. 83). Thirdly, Julian considers two judgements: God judges us in accord with our substance, whereas men make judgements according to our changeable sensory being, with predictably mixed results. Yet with an assurance as serene as it was presumably hard-won, Julian aligns her revelations with the former judgement ('that lovely, gentle judgement that was shown throughout the whole lovely revelation, in which I saw him attribute to us no kind of blame', ch. 45; p. 98), while Church teachings are assigned to the second and lower judgement. Assured that 'the smallest thing will not be forgotten' by God (ch. 32; p. 80), Julian is more encouraged for her part 'to know all things in general than to take delight in any one thing in particular' (ch. 35; p. 83), and this involves learning what she is not to see. The exhortation at the end of one manuscript of the longer version—'take each thing along with everything else' (ch. 86; p. 165)—is more likely to be scribal than authorial, because Julian's work needs no such exhortation to convince any reader to regard everything in her text as unified by the integrity of a record of contemplative experience. A book reporting revelations makes an intrinsic claim to the special and exceptional, yet not the least wisdom of Julian's text is to chart how she learns that the authenticity of her experience is that vision can never be full, and accordingly that a text meditating upon revelations can never be complete.

Julian matters

The reception of Julian of Norwich during the twentieth century and since has been a story of rediscovery and renewal. If Julian's name is now widely known, the beginnings of her fame probably stem from the semi-modernized words of her thirteenth revelation—'Sin is Behovely, but | All shall be well, and | All manner of thing shall be well'—which appear in T. S. Eliot's *Little Gidding* (1942). Largely overlooked before the twentieth century, Julian's work is known to have been read by W. B. Yeats, May Sinclair, and Charles Williams, and is echoed in Iris Murdoch's novels, *Nuns and Soldiers* (1980) and *The Black Prince* (1999). When St Julian's Church was rebuilt in the early 1950s, following its destruction in the German bombing of Norwich on 27 June 1942, it included a reconstruction of Julian's anchorhold (lost since the Reformation), which is now a pilgrimage destination and something of a shrine, with an associated Julian Centre. The sixth centenary of Julian's revelations in 1973 was celebrated with an exhibition in Norwich with a published catalogue, and since 1980 Julian of Norwich has had her feast day on 8 May in the Church of England's calendar.

Julian's conviction that her revelations are not some private favour but are intended for all and everyone lends her work a sense of communality and sociality which affects its import at every level and has made it appear applicable to various causes. Unconcerned as she is to forbid or censure, and with nothing regulatory or hortatory in her writing, Julian has been recruited in support of ecumenism between different traditions of Christianity and enlisted as part of less traditional links between Eastern and Western spirituality. Not the least of Julian's appeal to the calamitous twentieth century was the serene hopefulness with which she understands Christ's incarnation to imply that there can be meaning in human suffering and indeed that humanity was worthy to be suffered for and saved. By contrast, Julian's retreat from the world as a recluse proves something of an embarrassment for modern admirers, who find the anchorhold hard to reconcile with social concern as they understand it.

One interpreter even imagines Julian in a tête-à-tête not with Margery Kempe but with the priest John Ball, a leading figure of the Peasants' Revolt, and finds much in common between the contemplative visionary and the preacher of social equality who reportedly began a sermon to the rebels with the question: 'When Adam dalf [dug] and Eve span [spun], | Who was then a gentleman?'[25] That Julian might be so otherworldly as to be a mystic, or that, as a visionary, her text claims an authority beyond her own authorship and accepts that many things may only be resolved beyond this world, are aspects of her writing sometimes downplayed.

Popularizations, selections, and devotional studies published by religious presses testify to Julian's continuing appeal to a devout readership,[26] although a wider audience evidently responds in Julian to what is interpreted as an implicitly humanist rewriting of humanity's fallenness, and one which liberatingly ignores the conventional burdens of original sin and tainted bodiliness, implying that most people were always going to be saved, and that the meaning of all things is to be found in love. Along with such general recognition has also come admiration for Julian as both a mystic and as a theologian, whose work presents an exceptional integration of visionary experience with theological reflection.[27] Julian's probing of the implications of a divine love which is without any beginning, and a God who stands outside our human experience of time, can speak challengingly on its own terms to modern cosmological enquiry into the origins of the universe. Her language of indwelling—whereby God is enclosed in the soul, yet the soul is enclosed in God—bursts the bounds of conventional spatiality and our capacity to conceive it. Julian's sense that much pain in the human condition arises essentially from our unwitting imperception and blindness implicitly holds out the hopeful possibility that an unimpeded vision may be retrieved by all in the end. Most special of all—to modern perceptions—her spiritually

---

[25] Kenneth Leech, 'Contemplative and Radical: Julian meets John Ball', in Robert Llewelyn (ed.), *Julian: Woman of Our Day* (London, 1985), 89–101.

[26] Robert Llewelyn, *With Pity Not with Blame: The Spirituality of Julian of Norwich and The Cloud of Unknowing for Today*, 3rd rev. edn. (London, 1994); Sheila Upjohn, *Why Julian Now? A Voyage of Discovery* (London, 1997).

[27] Rowan Williams, *The Wound of Knowledge*, 2nd rev. edn. (London, 1990), 142–3.

imaginative and movingly tender analysis of God as our mother has propelled Julian to celebrity as a daringly prophetic and pioneering woman writer who, as it is interpreted, had already re-gendered the Christian God long ago.

Yet confronted with what is unknown about Julian herself but known about her work's development, any devil's advocate would certainly ask whether it is not actually more likely that the book of this great 'foremother' was penned—at least to some degree—by a man? Margery Kempe's acknowledgement of her inability to write, and her description of dictating her text to an amanuensis, has misled some of her modern interpreters into crediting that man not so much with the transcription as the authorship of 'her' book. Julian describes herself as unlettered but has produced a profoundly original theological work, derived from her claim to have seen visions, yet presented so surefootedly as to be proof against narrowmindedly orthodox criticism. Might Julian not only have dictated her meditations but composed the polished longer text in collaborative interchange with some of the learned spiritual directors to whom she could have had access in contemporary Norwich? Could this explain the learnedness especially implicit in her longer text? Might this explain the transformation between the two versions in penetration of theological analysis as well as in rhetorical accomplishment and editorial textualization? It might indeed, and yet Kempe's account of her conversation with Julian is a precious witness to the authenticity of both women, in that Kempe's report catches something of the distinctive voice that can be heard in Julian's writing, which the illiterate Kempe is unlikely to have known. Those tantalizingly faint but precious echoes in *The Book of Margery Kempe* of Julian's reported conversation with her visitor on those days in 1413 suffice to testify that Julian of Norwich spoke much as her text is written—luminously, with compassionate wisdom, and inflected with scripture—and that her mind and her book as we have it were essentially one.

NOTE ON THE TEXT AND
TRANSLATION

Establishing the text of what Julian of Norwich actually wrote is exceptionally challenging, because of the interval between her lifetime and the likely dates of surviving copies of her work. Translating that text into modern English brings its own challenges in turn. The text of Julian's short text is least problematic, although it survives in a single copy (London: British Library MS Additional 37790) made decades after the likely date of Julian's death. Her complete long text survives in three manuscripts copied after the Reformation, probably by the communities of English nuns in exile on the Continent and perhaps from now-lost medieval manuscripts in their care or from copies of these. (Some extracts from the long text survive in a mid-fifteenth-century anthology, probably made for nuns, now London: Westminster Cathedral Treasury MS 4.) Julian's longer text is found in these three manuscripts:

MS P (Paris: Bibliothèque nationale de France, fonds anglais 40) is thought to be the earliest in date of the complete long text manuscripts, possibly from the later sixteenth century. It is a carefully written calligraphic exercise in imitation of a medieval script. The language of the text, however, has been sophisticated and modernized.

MS S1 (London: British Library MS Sloane 2499) is a seventeenth-century copy, possibly made by Dame Clementina Cary (d. 1671), founder of the Paris convent of English Benedictine nuns. The copyist of S1 or its parent appears to have copied what was in front of her and so preserves an East Anglian form of Middle English, although also making some careless omissions and other slips.

MS S2 (London: British Library MS Sloane 3705) is either copied from S1 or its parent, shares the omissions but modernizes some vocabulary and hence is of limited value as a witness to the text.

Julian's text therefore has to be reconstructed from the evidence of P and S1 (compared with the short text and the Westminster text where the text is common to both shorter and longer versions). MS P affects the appearance of a medieval manuscript, but the text it presents has been updated and modified. MS S1 makes no pretence to be other than of its date but evidently preserves more of the original language. Some modern editions have been based exclusively on one of these two manuscripts without reference to the other.

The present translation of the short and long texts is based on my forthcoming edition for Oxford University Press, where the short text is edited from the sole extant copy. The edited text of Julian's longer version has been based on S1, because it is more likely to retain more of Julian's language, but S1's mechanical omissions and other slips have been emended from P.

The short summaries before each chapter in MS S1 (also present in MS S2) are unlikely to derive from Julian—they give away her gender and refer to her in a way Julian would be unlikely to refer to herself—but their language points to an early date and they have been retained in this translation as a help to the modern reader as well as a symptom of past reception. In its sole manuscript the short text is divided into unnumbered sections rather than numbered chapters, and that arrangement is retained in this translation of the short text.

In 1670 the first printed edition of Julian's text was published, entitled *XVI Revelations of Divine Love, Shewed to a Devout Servant of our Lord, called Mother Juliana, and Anchorete of Norwich, Who lived in the Dayes of King Edward the Third*. This edition, based on MS P, was the work of Serenus Cressy (1605–74), a convert to Roman Catholicism who became a Benedictine monk and had been chaplain to the Paris house of English Benedictine nuns. It was in Cressy's edition that Julian's work would be known until well into the nineteenth century. Cressy declares his editorial policy in an address to the reader:

> I conceived it would have been a prejudice to the agreeable simplicity of the Stile, to have changed the dress of it into our Modern Language, as some advised. Yet certain more out of fashion Words or Phrases, I thought meet to explain in the Margine.

Cressy's policy of glossing the more obviously obsolete words while conforming Julian's English with modern spelling is the forerunner of what was to prove the practice of many later modernizations of Julian's text. One course of action is to modernize the spelling of that majority of words in Julian's text which are still used in some form in modern English, only replacing obviously obsolete words. This may appear to respect the original but is, of course, to overlook just how many words, although still in use, have shifted in meaning and register. This type of modernization produces versions which, although spelled like modern English, do not read like it and end up neither medieval nor modern. The other extreme is to turn Julian's English into the ordinariness of modern chat—so that her 'All shall be well' becomes 'Everything's going to be all right'—and not only her word choice and register but also her sentence structure are re-expressed in our contemporary idiom. The present version generally remains as faithful as is practical to the sentence structure of Julian's text, while translating that considerable part of Julian's diction which does need to be translated, rather than simply modernized in spelling. The aim has been to present a text that remains as close to the content and style of the original as is compatible with a readable modern English version.

Julian's English is on one level deceptively plain and unelaborate: she does not make use of a noticeably Latinate vocabulary, yet her simple diction succinctly expresses complex thought and deep feeling, often through the cumulative effect of the same simple words recurring and remembered. Few have said so much, and with such profound implication, in what appear to be such plain and simple words. Yet this is an art that conceals art, especially in the longer text, where a subtle patterning of words and clauses contributes to Julian's meaning. For the translator, this can make for difficult choices when those simple words have shifted in meaning and acquired distracting other associations in modern English. This is the case with some of Julian's much-used words like 'homely' and 'sensuality', or 'sweet', which have usually been replaced by translations in the present version. What Julian means by both her noun and adjective 'kind' corresponds to the modern 'nature' and 'natural', yet for Julian nature and the natural also carry an association with 'kindness' and 'kindly' which it has become difficult to express neatly and singly in modern English. Some of Julian's most frequently used words for pain and suffering ('peyne', 'travel', i.e. 'travail') often imply more in different contexts, and the same word in Julian's Middle English has sometimes been translated into different words in different places in this version, although attention has been paid overall to the cumulative effects which Julian achieves through repeating words throughout her text.

There can also be problems in translating Julian's use of syntax, because she often favours an extended accumulation of clauses which, to modern taste, may make for unusually, even excessively, long sentences. Punctuating into brisker, shorter sentences would fail to translate how Julian's meditative thinking works through extended associative patternings which may appear to circle their subject in building towards an accumulated understanding. Modern punctuation remains a blunt instrument for articulating Julian's concatenations of ideas, and a balance has had to be struck between modern norms and Julian's more capacious sense of just how much a sentence might include. All punctuation and paragraphing in this translation have been introduced by the translator and so remain a matter of interpretation. The capitalization of references to the Christian deity and doctrine follow recent conventions for less rather than more: nouns and titles tend to be capitalized in accordance with traditional practice ('Father', 'Lord', 'Passion', 'Second Person of the Trinity', 'Saviour'), but not second- or third-person pronouns. All biblical references are to the Authorized Version.

SELECT BIBLIOGRAPHY

Editions

Baker, Denise N. (ed.), *The Showings of Julian of Norwich*, Norton Critical Edition (New York, 2005).

Beer, Frances (ed.), *Julian of Norwich's Revelations of Divine Love: The Shorter Version, ed. From BL Add. MS 37790*, Middle English Texts 8 (Heidelberg, 1978).

Colledge, Edmund, and Walsh, James (eds.), *A Book of Showings to the Anchoress Julian of Norwich*, 2 vols., Pontifical Institute of Medieval Studies: Studies and Texts 35 (Toronto, 1978).

Crampton, Georgia Ronan (ed.), *The Shewings of Julian of Norwich*, TEAMS Middle English Texts Series (Kalamazoo, Mich., 1994).

Glasscoe, Marion (ed.), *Julian of Norwich: A Revelation of Love*, Exeter Medieval English Texts and Studies (Exeter, 1976; rev. edn. 1986; rev. edn. 1993).

Reynolds, Sister Anna Maria, and Bolton Holloway, Julia (eds.), *Julian of Norwich: Extant Texts and Translation* (Florence, 2001).

Watson, Nicholas, and Jenkins, Jacqueline (eds.), *The Writings of Julian of Norwich: A Vision Showed to a Devout Woman and A Revelation of Love* (Turnhout, 2006).

Windeatt, Barry (ed.), *English Mystics of the Middle Ages* (Cambridge, 1994).

—— (ed.), *Julian of Norwich: Revelations of Divine Love* (Oxford, 2015).

Translations

Beer, Frances (trans.), *Revelations of Divine Love, Translated from British Library Additional MS 37790* (Cambridge, 1998).

Colledge, Edmund, and Walsh, James (trans.), *Julian of Norwich: Showings* (New York, 1978).

Hudleston, Roger (trans.), *Revelations of Divine Love, Shewed to a Devout Ankress, by Name Julian of Norwich* (London, 1927; 2nd edn. 1952).

John-Julian, Father (ed. and trans.), *The Complete Julian of Norwich* (Brewster, Mass., 2009).

Reynolds, Anna Maria (trans.), *A Shewing of God's Love: The Shorter Version of Sixteen Revelations by Julian of Norwich* (London, 1958).

Spearing, Elizabeth (trans.), *Julian of Norwich: Revelations of Divine Love*, with an Introduction and Notes by A. C. Spearing (Harmondsworth, 1998).

lvi   *Select Bibliography*

Walsh, James (trans.), *The Revelations of Divine Love of Julian of Norwich* (London, 1961; repr. Wheathampstead, 1973).

Warrack, Grace (ed.), *Revelations of Divine Love, Recorded by Julian, Anchoress at Norwich, AD 1373* (London, 1901).

Studies

Abbott, Christopher, *Julian of Norwich: Autobiography and Theology* (Cambridge, 1999).

Aers, David, and Staley, Lynn, *The Powers of the Holy: Religion, Politics and Gender in Late Medieval English Culture* (Philadelphia, 1996).

Baker, Denise Nowakowski, *Julian of Norwich's Showings: From Vision to Book* (Princeton, 1994).

Bauerschmidt, Frederick Christian, *Julian of Norwich and the Mystical Body Politic of Christ* (Notre Dame, 1999).

Beer, Frances, *Women and Mystical Experience in the Middle Ages* (Woodbridge, 1992).

Bryan, Jennifer, *Looking Inward: Devotional Reading and the Private Self in Late Medieval England* (Philadelphia, 2008).

Bynum, Caroline Walker, *Holy Feast and Holy Fast: The Religious Significance of Food to Medieval Women* (Berkeley, 1987).

——, *Jesus as Mother: Studies in the Spirituality of the High Middle Ages* (Berkeley, 1982).

Cré, Marleen, *Vernacular Mysticism in the Charterhouse: A Study of London, British Library, MS. Additional 37790* (Turnhout, 2006).

Despres, D., *Ghostly Sights: Visual Meditation in Late-Medieval Literature* (Norman, Okla., 1989).

Erler, Mary, *Women, Reading and Piety in Late Medieval England* (Cambridge, 2002).

Gilchrist, Roberta, and Oliva, M., *Religious Women in Medieval East Anglia: History and Archaeology c.1100–1540* (Norwich, 1993).

Glasscoe, Marion, *English Medieval Mystics: Games of Faith* (Harlow, 1993).

Heimmel, Jennifer, *'God is our Mother': Julian of Norwich and the Medieval Image of Christian Feminine Deity* (Salzburg, 1982).

Hide, Kerrie, *Gifted Origins to Graced Fulfilment: The Soteriology of Julian of Norwich* (Collegeville, Minn., 2001).

Hill, Carole, *Women and Religion in Late Medieval Norwich* (Woodbridge, 2010).

Jantzen, Grace, *Julian of Norwich: Mystic and Theologian* (London, 1987).

Kamerick, Kathleen, *Popular Piety and Art in the Later Middle Ages: Image Worship and Idolatry in England 1350–1500* (London, 2002).

Karnes, Michelle, *Imagination, Meditation and Cognition in the Middle Ages* (Chicago, 2011).

Llewelyn, Robert (ed.), *Julian: Woman of Our Day* (London, 1985).

McAvoy, Liz Herbert, *Authority and the Female Body in the Writings of Julian of Norwich and Margery Kempe* (Cambridge, 2004).

—— (ed.), *A Companion to Julian of Norwich* (Cambridge, 2008).

McEntire, Sandra J. (ed.), *Julian of Norwich: A Book of Essays* (New York, 1998).

McNamer, Sarah, *Affective Meditation and the Invention of Medieval Compassion* (Philadelphia, 2010).

Magill, Kevin J., *Julian of Norwich: Mystic or Visionary?* (London, 2006).

Maisonneuve, Roland, *L'univers visionnaire de Julian of Norwich* (Lille, 1982).

Molinari, Paul, *Julian of Norwich: The Teaching of a 14th Century English Mystic* (London, 1958).

Mulder-Bakker, Anneke, *Lives of the Anchoresses* (Philadelphia, 2005).

Newman, Barbara, *From Virile Woman to Womanchrist: Studies in Medieval Religion and Literature* (Philadelphia, 1995).

——, *God and the Goddesses: Vision and Belief in the Middle Ages* (Philadelphia, 2003).

Nuth, Joan M., *Wisdom's Daughter: The Theology of Julian of Norwich* (New York, 1991).

Oliva, M., *The Convent and the Community in Late Medieval England: Female Monasticism in the Diocese of Norwich 1350–1540* (Woodbridge, 1998).

Palliser, Margaret Ann, *Christ, Our Mother of Mercy: Divine Mercy and Compassion in the Theology of the Shewings of Julian of Norwich* (Berlin, 1992).

Pelphrey, Brant, *Love was his Meaning: The Theology and Mysticism of Julian of Norwich* (Salzburg, 1982).

——, *Christ our Mother: Julian of Norwich* (London, 1989).

Rawcliffe, Carole, and Wilson, Richard (eds.), *Medieval Norwich* (London, 2004).

Renevey, Denis, and Whitehead, Christiania (eds.), *Writing Medieval Women: Female Spiritual and Textual Practices in Late Medieval England* (Cardiff, 2000).

Riehle, Wolfgang, *The Middle English Mystics* (London, 1981).

Ross, E. M., *The Grief of God: Images of the Suffering Jesus in the Later Middle Ages* (Oxford, 1997).

Salih, Sarah, and Baker, Denise N. (eds.), *Julian of Norwich's Legacy: Medieval Mysticism and Post-Medieval Reception* (London, 2009).

Tanner, Norman P., *The Church in Late Medieval Norwich 1370–1532* (Toronto, 1984).

Tugwell, Simon, *Ways of Imperfection: An Exploration of Christian Spirituality* (London, 1984).

Turner, Denys, *Julian of Norwich, Theologian* (New Haven, 2011).

Warren, Ann K., *Anchorites and their Patrons in Medieval England* (Berkeley, 1985).

REVELATIONS OF DIVINE LOVE

The Short Text

Here is a vision shown by the goodness of God to a devout woman and her name is Julian, and she is a recluse at Norwich and is still alive in the year of our Lord 1413; and in this vision are very many comforting and greatly moving words for all those who desire to be lovers of Christ.*

*　　*　　*

I ASKED for three graces by the gift of God. The first was to relive Christ's Passion in my mind;* the second was bodily sickness;* and the third was to receive three wounds, by the gift of God. The first came to my mind in my devotion; it seemed to me that I had great feeling for the Passion of Christ, but I still longed to have more, by God's grace. It seemed to me I wished that I had been there at that time with Mary Magdalene and with those who were lovers of Christ, so that I might have seen in the flesh our Lord's Passion which he suffered for me, and so that I could have suffered with him as others did who loved him.

Nonetheless, I firmly believed in all the sufferings of Christ as Holy Church reveals and teaches, and also in the paintings of crucifixes which are made by the grace of God in the likeness of Christ's Passion, according to the teaching of Holy Church, as far as human understanding can attain.*

Yet despite all this true faith, I longed for a vision of him in the flesh, so that I might have more knowledge of the bodily suffering of our Lord and Saviour, and of the fellow-suffering of our Lady, and of all those who truly loved him and who believed in his suffering at that time and since, for I wanted to be one of them and suffer with them. I never wished for any other vision of God or revelation until my soul were separated from the body, for I truly believed that I would be saved. And this was my intention because through that revelation I wanted to have afterwards a truer perception of the Passion of Christ.

The second gift came to my mind with contrition, freely and without any seeking: a willing desire to be given a bodily sickness by God. And I wanted this sickness to be severe enough as to seem mortal, so that in that illness I might receive all the rites of Holy Church, myself believing that I was going to die, and that all who saw me might suppose the same, for I wanted to have no hopes of any fleshly or earthly life. In this sickness I wanted to have every kind of suffering in body and spirit that I would have if I were to die, with all the terrors and tumults caused by devils,* and every other kind of pain, short of the soul's leaving the body. For I hoped that it might have been a benefit to me when I should die, because I longed to be soon with my God.

These two requests about the Passion and the sickness, I asked for them with a condition, for it seemed to me that this went beyond the usual practice of prayer. So I said, 'Lord, you know what I want. If it is your will that I should have it, grant it me; and if it is not your will, good Lord, do not be displeased, for I only want what you want.' I asked for this illness in my young days, that I should have it when I was thirty years old.

As for the third, I heard a man of Holy Church tell the story of Saint Cecilia,* from which account I understood that she had three wounds in the neck from a sword, through which she suffered death. Moved by this, I conceived a powerful longing, praying our Lord God that he would grant me three wounds in my lifetime: that is to say, the wound of contrition, the wound of compassion, and the wound of purposeful longing for God. Just as I asked for the other two with a condition, so I asked for the third without any condition.

These first two desires, just mentioned, passed from my mind, and the third remained with me continually.

*   *   *

AND when I was thirty and a half years old,* God sent me a bodily sickness in which I lay for three days and three nights; and on the fourth night I received all the rites of Holy Church and did not expect to live until morning. And after this I lingered on for two days and two nights. And on the third night* I often thought I was about to die, and so did those who were with me.

Yet at this time I felt very sorry and reluctant to die, but not because of anything on earth that I wanted to live for, nor because of anything I was afraid of, for I trusted in God. But it was because I wanted to live so as to have loved God better and for longer, in order that I might, through the grace of that living, have more knowledge and love of God in the bliss of heaven. For all the time that I could live here seemed so little and so brief to me in comparison with that ever-lasting bliss. So I thought, 'Good Lord, may my living no longer be to your glory!' And my reason told me, and my sensations of pain, that I was going to die. And with all the will of my heart I fully assented to be at God's will.

So I lasted till day, and by then my body was dead from the waist down, as it felt to me. Then I wanted to be propped up, leaning back with my head supported by bedclothes, so that my heart could have more freedom to be at God's will and so that I could think of God as long as my life would last. Those who were with me sent for the parson, my curate* to be present at my end. He came, and a boy along with him,* and brought a cross, and by then my eyes were fixed and I could not speak. The parson set the cross before my face and said, 'Daughter,* I have brought you the image of your Saviour. Look at it and take comfort from it, in reverence of him who died for you and me.'

It seemed to me that I was all right as I was, for my gaze was fixed upwards into heaven where I trusted I was going. But nevertheless I consented to fix my eyes on the face of the crucifix if I could, so as to hold out longer until the moment of my death; for it seemed to me that I could manage to look straight ahead of me for longer than I could look upwards. After this my sight began to fail, and it all grew dark around me in the room, as dark as though it had been night, except that in the image of the cross there remained a light for all mankind, and I never knew how. Everything other than the cross was ugly to me, as if much crowded with fiends.

After this I felt as if the upper part of my body were beginning to die. My hands dropped down on either side of me, and I also felt so weak that my head lolled to one side.* The greatest pain I felt was my shortness of breath and the ebbing away of my life. And then I truly believed that I was at the point of death. And suddenly, at that moment, all my pain left me and I felt as well, especially in the upper part of my body, as I ever felt before or after. I was astonished at this change, for it seemed to me a mysterious act of God, not of nature. And yet I had no more expectation that I would live because I felt this relief; nor did feeling more comfortable in this way fully comfort me, for I felt that I would rather have been released from this world, for my heart was willingly set upon that.

*   *   *

THEN it suddenly came to mind that I ought to wish for the second wound, as a gift and a grace from our Lord, so that he would fill my body with recollection of the feeling of his blessed Passion, as I had prayed before; for I wanted his pains to be my pains, with compassion, and then longing for God. So it seemed to me that, through his grace, I might have the wounds which I had wanted before. But in this I never asked for any bodily vision or any kind of revelation from God, but for compassion, such as it seemed to me a naturally sympathetic soul might feel for our Lord Jesus, who for love was willing to become a mortal man. And I longed to suffer with him, while living in my mortal body, as God would give me grace.

And at this, I suddenly saw the red blood trickling down from under the crown of thorns—hot and fresh, plentiful and lifelike—just how it seemed to me that it was when the crown of thorns was thrust on to his blessed head. Just so he who was both God and man suffered for me. I had a true and powerful perception that it was he himself who showed this to me without any intermediary.

And then I said, 'Blessed be thou, Lord!'* Meaning it reverently, I said this in a loud voice; and I was much stunned with the wonder and amazement I felt, that he was willing to be so friendly to a sinful being, living in this wretched flesh. So I took it that at that time our Lord Jesu, out of his courteous love, would show me comfort before the time of my temptation, for it seemed to me that by God's permission and with his safekeeping I might well be tempted by devils before I died. With this vision of his blessed Passion, along with the Godhead that I saw in my understanding, I saw that this was strength enough for me—yes, and for every living creature that is to be saved—against all the devils of hell and against all spiritual enemies.

*   *   *

AT the same time as I saw this bodily vision, our Lord showed me spiritually in a vision how intimately he loves us. I saw that he is everything that is good and comforting and helpful to us. He is our clothing that enwraps us and enfolds us, embraces us and wholly encloses us, surrounding us out of tender love, so that he can never leave us. And so in this vision, as I understand it, I saw truly that he is everything that is good.

And in this vision he also showed me a little thing, the size of a hazelnut, lying in the palm of my hand, and it was as round as a ball, as it seemed to me. I looked at it and thought, 'What can this be?' And the answer came to me in a general way, like this, 'It is all that is made.' I wondered how it could last, for it seemed to me so small that it might have disintegrated suddenly into nothingness. And I was answered in my understanding, 'It lasts, and always will, because God loves it; and in the same way everything has its being through the love of God.'

In this little thing I saw three properties: the first is that God made it; the second is that God loves it; the third is that God cares for it. But what is that to me? Truly, the maker, the lover, and the guardian. For until I am of one substance with him I can never have love, rest, nor true happiness; that is to say, until I am so joined to him that there is no created thing between my God and me. And who shall do this deed? Truly, himself, through his mercy and grace, for he has made me for this and blessedly restored me.

With this he brought to mind our Lady. I saw her in a spiritual manner but in her bodily likeness, a simple and humble girl, young in years, in the form that she was when she conceived. God also revealed to me in part the wisdom and the truth of her soul, and in this I understood the reverent contemplation with which she beheld our God who is her maker, marvelling with great reverence that he was willing to be born of her who was a simple creature of his own making. For it was this that she wondered at: that he who was her creator was willing to be born of her who was created. And this wisdom and faith, recognizing the greatness of her maker and the littleness of her created self, caused her to say humbly to the angel Gabriel, 'Behold me here, the handmaid of the Lord.'* In seeing this I truly understood that she is greater in worthiness and fullness of grace than everything which God created below her; for no created thing is above her except the blessed humanity of Christ.

This little thing that is made, that is beneath our Lady Saint Mary—God showed it me as small as if it had been a hazelnut— seemed to me as if it might have disintegrated into nothingness because of its smallness.*

In this blessed revelation God showed me three nothings,* of which nothings this is the first that was shown me. Every man and woman who longs to live contemplatively* needs to know this: that it should please them to count as nothing everything that is made, in order to have the love of God who is unmade. For this is the reason why those who deliberately occupy themselves in earthly business, and are constantly seeking worldly success,* find no peace from this in heart or soul: because they love and seek rest here in this thing which is so small and in which there is no rest, and do not know God, who is almighty, all wise, and all good, for he is true rest. God wishes to be known, and is pleased that we should rest in him; for all that is beneath him is not enough for us; and this is the reason why no soul is at rest until it counts as nothing all that is created. When a soul has made itself as nothing for love, in order to have him who is all that is good, then he is able to receive spiritual rest.

*   *   *

AND all the while that our Lord was revealing in spiritual vision what I have just described, I saw the continuing bodily vision of copious bleeding from Christ's head.* And as long as I saw this vision I kept saying, 'Blessed be thou, Lord!' From this first revelation of our Lord I understood six things. The first is the tokens of his blessed Passion and the copious shedding of his precious blood. The second is the Virgin who is his beloved mother. The third is the blessed Godhead that always was, is, and always shall be, almighty, all wisdom, and all love. The fourth is everything which he has made; for I well know that heaven and earth and all that is made is vast and beautiful, extensive and good, but the reason why it seemed to my eyes so small was because I saw it in the presence of him who is the creator. For to a soul who sees the maker of all things, all that is made seems very small. The fifth is that he has made everything that is made for love—and by the same love everything is sustained and will be without end, as has been said before. The sixth is that God is everything that is good, and the goodness that is in everything is God.

And all these things our Lord showed me in the first vision and gave me time and space to contemplate them. And the bodily vision ceased, and the spiritual vision remained in my understanding. And

I waited in reverent awe, rejoicing in what I saw, and wishing as much as I dared to see more if that were his will, or else to see the same vision for longer.

*   *   *

ALL that I say concerning myself, I mean on behalf of all my fellow Christians, for I was taught through the spiritual revelation of our Lord God that he intends it to be so. And therefore I beg you all for God's sake, and advise you for your own benefit, that you disregard the wretched, worldly, sinful creature* to whom it was shown, and with all strength, wisdom, love, and humility contemplate God, who in his courteous love and unending goodness wished to make this vision generally known, to the comfort of us all. And you who hear and see this vision and this teaching which is from Jesus Christ for the edification of your soul, it is God's will and my desire that you receive it with joy and delight as great as if Jesus had shown it to you, as he did to me.

I am not good because of the revelation unless I love God better; and so may and so should everyone do who sees it and hears it with good will and true intent. And so it is my desire that it should be the same benefit to everyone that I desired for myself, and to which I was moved by God the first time I saw it. For it is universal and in common, just as we are all one, and I am sure I saw it for the benefit of many others. For truly, it was not revealed to me because God loves me better than the least soul who is in a state of grace, for I am sure there are very many who never had a revelation or vision, but only the general teaching of Holy Church, who love God better than I do. For if I look at myself in particular, I am nothing at all; but in general I am in oneness of love with all my fellow Christians. For in this oneness of love depends the life of all humanity who will be saved. For God is all that is good, and God has made all that is made, and God loves all that he has made. And if any man or woman should withdraw their love from any of their fellow Christians, they do not love at all, because they do not love all; and so at that time they are not saved, because they are not at peace.* And whoever loves all fellow Christians in general loves all that is. For in those who will be saved, all is comprehended: that is to say, all that is made, and the maker of all; for in man is God, and so in man is all. And he who thus loves all his fellow Christians in general loves all.

And he who loves in this way is saved, and so I wish to love, and so I do love, and so I am saved—I am speaking on behalf of my fellow Christians—and the more I love in this way whilst I am here, the more I am as one with the bliss that I shall have in heaven without end, which is God, who in his endless love was willing to become our brother and suffer for us.* And I am sure that whoever considers it in this way will be truly taught and greatly comforted, if he should need comfort.

But God forbid that you should say, or take it, that I am a teacher, for I do not mean that, nor did I ever mean that, for I am a woman, ignorant, weak, and frail. But I know very well that what I am saying I have received through revelation from him who is the supreme teacher. But in truth, love moves me to tell you about it, for I want God to be known, and my fellow Christians to be helped, as I would wish to be myself, to the greater hating of sin and loving of God.*

But just because I am a woman, must I therefore believe that I should not tell you about the goodness of God, when I saw at the same time that it is his will that this be known? And you will see this clearly in the material which follows, if it be well and truly understood. Then you must quickly forget wretched me, and not let me hinder you, and contemplate Jesus, who is teacher of all.*

I speak of those who will be saved, for at this time God showed me no others. But in all things I believe as Holy Church teaches, for I perceived this whole blessed revelation of our Lord as unified in God's sight, and I never understood anything from it that bewilders me or keeps me from the true teaching of Holy Church.*

*   *   *

ALL this blessed teaching of our Lord God was shown to me in three ways: that is to say, by bodily sight, and by words formed in my understanding, and by spiritual vision. But I neither may nor can disclose the spiritual vision to you as openly and as fully as I would wish. But I trust in our Lord God almighty that he will, out of his goodness and for love of you, make you receive it more spiritually and more sweetly than I can or may tell it you—and so may it be, for we are all one in love.*

And in all this I was much moved by love for my fellow Christians, that they might all see and know the same as I was seeing, for I wanted it to be a comfort to them all as it is to me, for this vision was shown for all and not for any particular individual. Of everything that I saw, this was what comforted me most: that our Lord is so familiar with us and so courteous. And this was what most filled my soul with delight and assurance.

Then I said to the people who were with me, 'Today is Judgement Day for me', and I said this because I was expecting to die. For on that day that men or women die, they are judged as they will be eternally. I said this because I wanted them to love God more and set less store by the vanity of the world,* to make them mindful that this life is short, as they might see by my example, for during this whole time I was expecting to die.

* * *

AND after this I saw with my bodily sight in the face on the crucifix which hung before me—at which I was looking continuously—a part of his Passion: contempt, spitting which soiled his body, and blows to his blessed face, and many lingering pains and sufferings, more than I can tell, and frequent changes of colour, and all his blessed face covered for a time in dried blood. I saw this bodily and sorrowfully and obscurely, and I wished for more natural light to have seen more clearly. And I was answered in my reason that if God wanted to show me more, he would—but I needed no light but him.*

And after this I saw God in a point—that is to say, in my understanding—and by seeing this I saw that he is in everything. I looked attentively, knowing and recognizing in that vision that he does everything that is done. I marvelled at that sight with quiet awe, and thought, 'What is sin?' For I saw truly that God does everything, however small it may be, and nothing is done by chance or accident but by the eternal providence of God's wisdom. Therefore I had to grant that everything which is done is well done, and I was sure that God commits no sin. Therefore it seemed to me that sin is nothing, for sin was not shown me in all this.* And I had no wish to go on wondering over this any longer, but looked at our Lord to see what he would reveal to me. (And at another time God showed me the naked truth about what sin is in itself, as I shall recount later.)

And after this I saw, as I watched, the body bleeding profusely, hot and freshly and lifelike, just as I saw the head bleeding before. And I was shown this bleeding from the weals of the scourging, and this blood ran so abundantly in my vision that it seemed to me that if in its nature it had been the real thing at that time, it would have saturated the bed with blood and overflowed all around. God has created abundant waters on earth for our use and our bodily refreshment, out of the tender love that he has for us, yet it is more pleasing to him that we should fully accept his blessed blood to wash ourselves from sin; for there is no liquid created that it pleases him so much to give us; for it is so plentiful, and it shares our own nature.*

And afterwards, before God revealed any words to me, he allowed me to contemplate longer all that I had seen, and all that was in it. And then, without voice and without opening of lips, these words were formed in my soul: 'In this way the devil is overcome'. Our Lord said these words referring to his Passion, as he had shown me before.

In this our Lord brought into my mind and showed me a part of the devil's malice and all his powerlessness, and to do so he showed me that his Passion is the devil's defeat. God showed me that the fiend still has the same malice that he had before the incarnation and he works as hard, and just as continually he sees all those souls who will be saved escape him gloriously. And that is all his sorrow; for everything that God allows him to do turns into joy for us, and pain and shame for him. And he has as much sorrow when God gives him permission to work as when he is not working; and that is because he can never do as much evil as he would like, for all his power is held under lock and key in God's hand.

I also saw our Lord scorn his malice and discount him as nothing, and he wants us to do the same. At the sight of this I laughed heartily, and that made those who were around me to laugh, and their laughter was a pleasure to me. In my thoughts I wished that my fellow Christians had seen what I saw. Then they would all have laughed with me. But I did not see Christ laughing. Nevertheless it pleases him that we should laugh to comfort ourselves and rejoice in God because the devil is defeated.

And after this I grew serious and said, 'I see three things: a game, a scorning, and an earnestness. I see a game, that the devil is defeated. I see a scorning, that God scorns him, and he shall be scorned. And I see an earnestness, in that he is defeated by the blessed Passion and death of our Lord Jesus Christ, which was accomplished in great earnest and with steadfast suffering.'*

After this our good Lord said, 'I thank you for your service and your suffering, and especially in your youth.'

* * *

GOD showed me three degrees of bliss which every soul shall have in heaven who has willingly served God, whatever his degree here upon earth. The first is the glorious gratitude of our Lord God which he will receive when he is delivered from suffering. This gratitude is so exalted and so glorious that it seems to the soul that it is fulfilled, even if there were no greater bliss. For it seemed to me that all the pain and trouble that could be suffered by all those alive could not have deserved the gratitude that one shall have who has willingly served God. The second degree is that all the blessed in heaven will see that glorious gratitude of our Lord God, and God makes the soul's service known to all who are in heaven. And the third degree is that this will last eternally just as new and delightful as when it is first received.

I saw that this was said and revealed to me in a gracious and kindly way: that the age of everyone will be known in heaven* and be rewarded for willing service and time served; and especially, the age of those who willingly and freely offer their youth to God is surpassingly rewarded and wonderfully thanked.*

And after this our Lord revealed to me a supreme spiritual delight in my soul. In this delight I was filled full of everlasting certainty, powerfully sustained, without any fear. This feeling was so welcome to me and so excellent that I was at peace, at ease, and at rest, so that there was nothing on earth that could have distressed me.

This only lasted a while, and my mood turned right round and I was left to myself, feeling depressed, weary of myself and disgusted with my life, so that I could hardly have the patience to go on living. There was no ease or comfort, as I felt, except faith, hope, and charity, and these I had indeed but could feel them very little.

And immediately after this God again gave me comfort and rest in my soul, with pleasure and certainty so blissful and so powerful that no fear, no sorrow, no pain bodily nor spiritual that one might suffer could have troubled me. And then I felt this pain again revealed to me, and then the joy and the delight, now the one and now the other, at different times, I suppose about twenty times. And in the moments of joy I could have said with Saint Paul: 'Nothing shall separate me from the love of Christ.' And in the pain I could have said with Saint Peter: 'Lord, save me, I perish.'*

This vision was shown me to teach me—as I understand it—that it is necessary for everyone to feel in this way: sometimes to be comforted, and sometimes to feel failure and be left to oneself. God wants us to know that he keeps us equally safe in joy and in sorrow, and loves us as much in sorrow as in joy. And for the benefit of his soul a man is sometimes left to himself, although sin is not always the cause; for at this time I committed no sin for which I ought to be left to myself. Nor did I deserve to have the feeling of bliss. But our Lord gives freely when he wills, and sometimes allows us to be in sorrow—and both come from one love. For it is God's will that we keep ourselves in good spirits with all our might, for bliss lasts forever, and pain passes and will come to nothing. Therefore it is not God's will that we should be influenced by feelings of pain to sorrow and grieve over them, but quickly pass beyond them and hold on to the endless joy that is God almighty, who loves and safeguards us.*

* * *

AFTER this Christ showed me a part of his Passion, close to his death. I saw that dear face as if it were dry and bloodless with the pallor of death; and then more deathly pale in anguish, and then turning blue as death advanced, and afterwards a darker blue as death took more hold on his flesh. For all the pains that Christ suffered in his body were visible to me in the blessed face as far as I could see it,* and especially in the lips. There I saw these four colours, which before had appeared to me fresh and ruddy, full of life, and lovely to see.

This was a grievous change, to see this deep dying, and also, as it seemed to me, the nose shrivelled and dried up. This long torment made it seem to me as if he had been dead for a week,* continually suffering the last throes, and it seemed to me that the drying of Christ's flesh was the greatest pain, and the last, of his Passion.

And in this drying there came to my mind Christ's words: 'I thirst.'* For I saw in Christ a double thirst: one bodily, the other spiritual. In these words the bodily thirst was revealed to me, and I shall say later* what was revealed to me concerning the spiritual thirst. And I understood by its bodily thirst that the body had a lack of moisture, because the blessed flesh and bones were left alone, bereft of blood and moisture. The blessed body was left drying for a long time—with wrenching by the nails and the drooping of the head, and the weight of the body, with the blowing of the wind from outside which dried him and tormented him more with cold than my heart can imagine, and every other torment. But I saw such pains that all that I can describe or say of them is inadequate, for those pains cannot be described. But each soul, as Saint Paul says, should feel in himself what is in Christ Jesu.*

This revelation of Christ's pains filled me full of pains, for I was well aware that he only suffered once, but he wanted to show it to me and fill me with the recollection of it, as I had earlier wished. My mother, who was standing amongst other people and was watching me, held up her hand in front of my face to close my eyes, for she thought I was already dead, or else I had just died; and this greatly increased my sorrow, for despite all my sufferings I did not want to be hindered from seeing him, because of the love that I had for him.*

And yet in all this time that Christ was present to me, I felt no pain except for Christ's pains. Then I thought to myself, 'I little knew what pain it was that I asked for', because it seemed to me that my pains exceeded bodily death. I thought, 'Is any pain in hell like this pain?' And in my reason I was answered that despair is greater because that is spiritual pain, but there is no bodily pain greater than this. How could any pain be greater to me than to see him suffer who is my whole life, all my bliss, and all my joy? Here I truly felt that I loved Christ so much more than myself that I thought it would have been a great relief to me to have suffered bodily death.*

Here I saw part of the compassion of our Lady, Saint Mary, for Christ and she were so united in love that the greatness of her love caused the greatness of her pain, for in so much as she loved him more than anyone else, her sufferings surpassed those of all others. And so all his disciples, and all who truly loved him, suffered pains greater than their own bodily dying; for I am sure, from how I feel myself, that the least of them loved him more than they did themselves.

Here I saw a great affinity between Christ and us; for when he was in pain, we were in pain, and all creatures capable of suffering pain suffered with him. And this was the pain* of those who did not know him: that all created things, sun and moon, withdrew their service,* and so they were all left in sorrow at that time. And so those who loved him suffered pain for love, and those who did not love him suffered pain because the comfort of all creation failed them.

At this time I wanted to look away from the cross but I did not dare, for I well knew that while I looked at the cross I was safe and secure; therefore I would not agree to put my soul in danger, for apart from the cross there was no safety, but only the horror of fiends.

Then I thought my reason suggested to me, as if there had been said to me in a friendly way: 'Look up to heaven to his Father.' And then I saw clearly, with the faith that I felt, that there was nothing between the cross and heaven which could have distressed me. Either I must look up or else reply. I answered and said, 'No, I cannot, for you are my heaven.' I said this because I did not want to look up; for I would rather have remained in that pain until Judgement Day than have come to heaven in any other way than by him; for I well knew that he who redeemed me at such cost would unbind me when he wished.

* * *

So I chose Jesus for my heaven, whom I saw only in pain at that time. No other heaven pleased me but Jesus, who will be my bliss when I am there. And this has always been a comfort to me,* that I chose Jesus for my heaven in all this time of suffering and of sorrow. And that has been a lesson to me that I should do so for evermore and choose only Jesus for my heaven in both happiness and sorrow.

And so I saw my Lord Jesus lingering for a long time, because the union in him with the Godhead gave strength to his humanity to suffer for love more than all men could suffer. I do not mean only more pain than all men could suffer, but also that he suffered more pain than all those who ever existed from the very beginning until the last day. No tongue may tell nor heart fully think of the pains that our

Saviour suffered for us, considering the worth of the highest, most glorious king and the shameful, humiliating, and painful death; for he who was highest and noblest was brought most low and most utterly despised. But the love that made him suffer all this so far surpasses all his pain as heaven is above earth, for his suffering was a deed performed at one time through the working of love, but love was without beginning, and is and ever shall be without end.

And suddenly, as I was looking* at the same cross, he changed his expression into one of bliss. The change in his expression changed mine, and I was as entirely glad and happy as it is possible to be. Then our Lord brought to mind the happy thought, 'Is there any point now to your pain or your sorrow?' And I was very happy.

* * *

THEN our Lord spoke,* asking, 'Are you well pleased that I suffered for you?'

'Yes, good Lord,' I said. 'Thank you, good Lord, blessed may you be!'

'If you are pleased,' said our Lord, 'I am pleased. It is a joy and a bliss and an endless delight to me that I ever suffered my Passion for you, for if I could suffer more, I would suffer.'

In experiencing this my understanding was lifted up into heaven, and there I saw three heavens, and I was amazed at the sight, and I thought, 'I saw three heavens, and all are of the blessed humanity of Christ; and none is greater, none is less, none is higher, none is lower, but all are equal in bliss.'

For the first heaven Christ showed me his Father, not in any bodily likeness but in his nature and in his actions. This is the action of the Father: that he rewards his son, Jesus Christ. This gift and this reward is so blissful to Jesus that his Father could have given him no reward that could have pleased him better. The first heaven, which is the pleasing of the Father, appeared to me as a heaven, and it was full of bliss, for he is highly pleased with all the deeds that Jesus has done for our salvation; and therefore we are not only his through his redemption of us, but also, through his Father's courteous gift, we are his bliss, we are his reward, we are his glory, we are his crown! What

I am describing is such great joy to Jesus that he counts as nothing all his affliction, and his keen suffering, and his cruel and shameful death.

And in these words—'If I could suffer more, I would suffer more'— I truly saw that if he might die as often as for each individual who will be saved, as he once died for all, love would never let him rest until he had done it. And when he had done it, he would count it as nothing, out of love, for everything seems insignificant to him in comparison with his love. And he revealed that to me very gravely, saying these words, 'If I could suffer more.' He did not say, 'If it were necessary to suffer more',* but, 'If I could suffer more.' For even if it were not necessary, if he could suffer more, he would suffer more. This deed and this work for our salvation was as well done as God could order it. It was done as gloriously as Christ could do it. And here I saw complete joy in Christ, but this bliss could not have been complete if the deed might have been done any better than it was done.

And in these three sayings—'It is a joy, a bliss, and an endless delight to me'—were shown to me three heavens, as follows: by the joy, I understood the pleasure of the Father; by the bliss, the glory of the Son; and by the endless delight, the Holy Spirit. The Father is pleased, the Son is glorified, the Holy Spirit takes delight.

Jesus wishes us to pay heed to this delight that there is in the blessed Trinity about our salvation, and that we should have as much pleasure, through his grace, whilst we are here. And this was shown me in these words, 'Are you well pleased?' The other words that Christ said—'If you are pleased, then I am pleased'—he gave me to understand as if he had said, 'It is joy and delight enough to me, and I ask nothing else for my suffering but that I may please you.'

This was revealed to me abundantly and in full.

Think seriously too about the magnitude of these words, 'that I ever suffered my Passion for you', for in those words was revealed an exalted understanding of the love and the pleasure that he had in our salvation.

* * *

VERY happily and gladly our Lord looked into his side, and gazed, and said these words, 'Look how much I loved you', as if he had said,

'My child, if you cannot contemplate my Godhead, see here how I let my side be opened and my heart be split in two, and let flow out all the blood and water that was inside. And this is a delight to me, and I wish it to delight you too.' Our Lord revealed this to me to make us joyful and glad.*

And with this same expression and gladness he looked down on his right and brought to my mind where our Lady stood during his Passion, and said, 'Would you like to see her?' And I answered and said, 'Yes, good Lord, thank you, if it be your will.' I prayed for this often, and I expected to have seen her present bodily, but I did not see her like that. And with those words Jesus showed me a spiritual vision of her. Just as before I had seen her small and simple, so now he showed her high, and noble, and glorious, and pleasing to him above all other created beings. And so he wishes it to be known that all those who delight in him should delight in her, and in the delight that he has in her and she in him. And in these words that Jesus said—'Would you like to see her?'—it seemed to me that I had the greatest pleasure that he could have given me in the spiritual vision of her which he gave me. For our Lord gave me no revelation about any particular individual, except our Lady Saint Mary; and he showed her three times: the first was as she conceived, the second was as she was in her sorrows at the foot of the cross, and the third was as she is now, in delight, honour, and joy.*

And after this, as it seemed to me, our Lord showed himself yet more glorified than I had seen him before, and I learned from this that each contemplative soul to whom it is given to seek and look for God shall see Mary and pass on to God through contemplation. And after this teaching—friendly, courteous, and blessed and true life—our Lord Jesus often said to me:

'It is I who am highest. It is I you love. It is I you delight in. It is I you serve. It is I you long for. It is I you desire. It is I who am your purpose. It is I who am all. It is I that Holy Church preaches and teaches you. It is I who showed myself to you before.'

I record these words only so that each individual, according to the grace given by God in understanding and loving, may receive them as our Lord intended.*

And afterwards our Lord brought to mind the longing that I had for him before;* and I saw that nothing held me back but sin, and I saw that this is so with all of us in general. And it seemed to me that if there had been no sin, we should all have been pure and like our Lord, as he made us; and so, in my folly, I had often wondered before this time why, through the great foreseeing wisdom of God, sin was not prevented; for then, it seemed to me that all would have been well. I should have given up such thoughts, yet I grieved and sorrowed over this, unreasonably and without discretion, out of very great pride. Nevertheless, Jesu in this vision informed me of everything needful to me. I am not saying that I need no more teaching, for in revealing this to me our Lord has left me to Holy Church; and I am hungry and thirsty, and needy and sinful and frail, and willingly submit myself to the teaching of Holy Church, along with all my fellow Christians, until the end of my life.

He answered with these words and said, 'Sin is befitting.'* With this word 'sin', our Lord brought to mind everything in general which is not good: the shameful scorn and the utter humiliation that he bore for us in this life, and in his dying, and all the pains and sufferings in body and spirit of all his creatures—for we are all in part brought low, and we should be brought low, following our master Jesu's example, until we are fully purged: that is to say, until our mortal flesh is made as nothing, and all our inward inclinations which are not good. And in contemplating this, together with all the sufferings that ever were or ever shall be, all this was shown me in an instant and quickly turned into consolation; for our good Lord God did not wish the soul to be frightened by this ugly sight.

But I did not see sin, for I believe it has no kind of substance nor share of being, nor could it be recognized except by the sufferings it causes. And, as it seems to me, this suffering is something that exists for a while, because it purges us and makes us know ourselves and ask for mercy; for the Passion of our Lord is a comfort to us against all this, and that is his blessed will for all who shall be saved. He comforts us readily and sweetly by his words and says, 'But all shall be well, and all manner of things shall be well.'*

These words were revealed very tenderly, indicating no kind of blame for me or for anyone who will be saved. So it would be most unkind of me to blame or wonder at God because of my sin, since he does not blame me for sin.

So I saw how Christ has compassion on us because of sin; and just as I was previously filled with suffering and compassion at Christ's Passion, so now I was filled in part with compassion for all my fellow

Christians. And then I saw that each instance of kind compassion that a man feels for his fellow Christians out of love—it is Christ in him.

*   *   *

BUT I stayed contemplating this generally, sorrowfully, and mournfully, addressing our Lord in this way in my thoughts in very great awe, 'Ah, good Lord, how could all be well, in view of the great harm which has come upon your creatures through sin?' And I wished, as much as I dared, to receive some clearer explanation to set my mind at ease about this. And our blessed Lord answered to this very compassionately and in a very loving manner, and showed me that Adam's sin was the greatest harm that was ever done, or ever shall be, until the end of the world; and he also showed me that this is openly acknowledged throughout all Holy Church upon earth.

Furthermore, he taught me that I should contemplate the glorious atonement; for this atonement is incomparably more pleasing to the blessed Godhead and more glorious for the salvation of mankind than Adam's sin was ever harmful. So our blessed Lord's meaning in this teaching is that we should take heed of this: 'For since I have set right what was the greatest harm, it is my will that you should know by this that I shall set right all that is less harmful.'

He gave me to understand about the two parts of this. One is our Saviour and our salvation. This blessed part is open and clear, and fair and light and abundant, for all mankind who are or shall be of good will are comprehended in this part. We are bidden to this by God, and drawn and counselled and taught, inwardly by the Holy Spirit, and outwardly by Holy Church, through the same grace. Our Lord wants us to be occupied with this, rejoicing in him, for he rejoices in us. And the more abundantly that we draw on this, with reverence and humility, the more thanks we deserve from him and the more benefit to ourselves, and thus we may say, rejoicing, 'Our Lord is our portion.'*

The other part is hidden and barred to us: that is to say, everything which is over and above our salvation; for this is our Lord's private counsels, and it is fitting for the royal lordship of God to keep his private counsels undisturbed, and it is fitting for his servants, out of obedience and respect, not to wish to know his counsels. Our Lord has pity and compassion on us, because some people busy themselves so anxiously about this; and I am sure that if we knew how much we should please him and set our minds at rest by leaving it alone, we would do so. The saints in heaven wish to know nothing but what our Lord wishes to reveal to them, and also their love and their desires are governed according to our Lord's will; and so we ought to wish to be like them. And then we shall not wish nor desire anything except the will of our Lord, just as they do; for we are all one in God's purposes.

And here I was taught that we are to trust and rejoice only in our Saviour, blessed Jesu, for everything.

* * *

AND so our good Lord answered all the questions and doubts that I could raise, saying most comfortingly in this way, 'I may make all things well, I can make all things well, I will make all things well, and I shall make all things well; and you will see for yourself that all things shall be well.' Where he says he may, I understand this to apply to the Father; and where he says he can, I understand it to apply to the Son; and where he says 'I will', I understand it to apply to the Holy Spirit; and where he says 'I shall', I take it for the unity of the blessed Trinity, three persons in one truth; and where he says 'You will see for yourself', I understand it to refer to the union with the blessed Trinity of all mankind who shall be saved.

And with these five sayings God wishes us to be enclosed in rest and in peace; and so Christ's spiritual thirst will come to an end. For this is the spiritual thirst: the love-longing that lasts and ever shall, until we see the revelation on Judgement Day. For we who shall be saved, and shall be Christ's joy and his bliss, are still here, and shall be until that day. Therefore this is his thirst: the incompleteness of his bliss, that he does not have us in himself as wholly as he will have then.

All this was shown to me as a revelation of compassion, for that will cease on Judgement Day. So he has pity and compassion for us, and he longs to have us, but his wisdom and his love do not allow the end to come until the best time.

And in these same five sayings mentioned previously—'I may make all things well', etc.—I understand there to be great comfort concerning all the works of our Lord which are to come. For just as the blessed Trinity made all things from nothing, so the same blessed Trinity will make all well that is not well.

It is God's will that we should have great regard to all the deeds he has done, for he wants us to know from this all that he will do, and he revealed that to me in those words which he said, 'And you shall see yourself that all manner of things shall be well.'

I understand this in two ways: one is that I am well content that I do not know it; and the other is that I am glad and happy because I shall know it. It is God's will that we should know in general terms that all shall be well; but it is not God's will that we should know it now, except as it concerns us at the present time, and that is the teaching of Holy Church.

*   *   *

GOD showed me the very great pleasure that he takes in all men and women who strongly and humbly and willingly receive the preaching and the teaching of Holy Church. For he is Holy Church: he is the foundation, he is the substance, he is the teaching, he is the teacher, he is the goal, he is the reward for which every faithful soul strives; and he is known and will be known to every soul to whom the Holy Spirit makes it known. And I am sure that all those who seek in this way shall succeed, for they are seeking God.

All this that I have now said, and more of that I shall say later, gives comfort against sin; for first, when I saw that God does all that is done, I did not see sin, and then I saw that all is well. But when God gave me a revelation concerning sin, then he said, 'All shall be well.'

And when almighty God had shown me his goodness so abundantly and so fully, I wanted to know about a certain person I loved, and how it would be with her.* And in wishing this I held myself back, because I was not informed at this time. And then I was answered in my reason, as though by a friendly intermediary, 'Take this generally, and have regard to your Lord God's courtesy as he reveals it to you; for it honours God more to contemplate him in all things than in any particular thing.' I assented, and with that I learned that it honours God more to know all things in general than to take delight in any one thing in particular. And if I were to act wisely on this teaching,

I would neither be happy because of anything in particular, nor upset by anything of any kind, for 'All shall be well.'

God brought to mind that I would sin; and because of the delight that I had in contemplating him, I did not pay attention at once to that revelation. And our Lord very kindly waited until I would pay attention, and then our Lord brought to mind, along with my sins, the sins of all my fellow Christians, all in general and not in particular.

*   *   *

ALTHOUGH our Lord revealed to me that I would sin, by me alone I understood everyone. And at this I felt a quiet fear, and to this our Lord replied to me thus, 'I am keeping you very safe.' This was said to me with more love and assurance of spiritual safekeeping than I can or may tell. For just as it was revealed to me before that I would sin, so was the consolation revealed to me: assurance of safekeeping for all my fellow Christians. What can make me love my fellow Christians more than to see in God that he loves all who shall be saved as though they were all one soul?

And in every soul that shall be saved there is a godly will which never assented to sin nor ever shall. For just as there is an animal will in the lower part of our nature which cannot will anything good, so there is a godly will in the higher part of our nature, which, no less than the Persons of the blessed Trinity, can will no evil, but always good.* And our Lord revealed this to me in the completeness of love in which we stand in his sight—yes, that he loves us as much now while we are here as he will do when we are there before his blessed face.

God also revealed to me that sin is no shame to man, but his glory. For in this revelation my understanding was lifted up into heaven; and then there came truly to mind David, Peter and Paul, Thomas of India, and the Magdalene;* how they and their sins are known in the Church on earth to their glory. And it is no shame to them that they have sinned, any more than it is in the bliss of heaven,* for there the tokens of sin are turned into honours. In just this way our Lord God showed me them as an example of all the others who shall come there.

Sin is the sharpest scourge that any chosen soul can be struck with, a scourge which lashes men and women and utterly shatters them, and damages them in their own eyes to such an extent that they think themselves unworthy of anything except, as it were, to sink into hell. But when contrition seizes them through the inspiration of the Holy Spirit, then it turns the bitterness into hopes of God's mercy. And then their wounds begin to heal and the soul to revive, returned into the life of Holy Church. The Holy Spirit leads a man to confession to reveal his sins willingly, nakedly, and truly, with great sorrow and great shame that he has so besmirched the fair image of God. Then he receives penance for each sin imposed by his confessor, as is established in Holy Church through the teaching of the Holy Spirit.

By this medicine every sinful soul always needs to be healed, and especially of sins that are mortal. Even though he may be healed, his wounds appear before God not as wounds but as honours. And just as sin is punished here with sorrow and with penance, so by contrast sin will be rewarded in heaven by the courteous love of our Lord God almighty, who does not wish anyone who comes there to lose the rewards for his labours.

The reward that we will receive there will not be small, but it will be great, glorious, and full of honour. And so all shame will be turned into honour and into greater joy. And I am certain, from my own feeling, that the more that every well-natured soul sees this in the kind and courteous love of God, the more reluctant he is to sin.

* * *

BUT if you should be moved to say or to think, 'Since this is true, then it would be a good idea to sin, so as to gain the greater reward', beware of this prompting and despise it, for it comes from the enemy. For whatever soul that willingly follows this prompting may never be saved until he makes amends, as if for a mortal sin. For if all the suffering in hell and in purgatory and on earth were laid before me— death and all the rest—and sin, I would rather choose all that suffering than sin. For sin is so vile and so much to be hated that it can be compared to no suffering which is not the suffering of sin itself, for everything is good except sin, and nothing is evil except sin. Sin is neither action nor pleasure, but when a soul deliberately chooses the torment of sin in preference to his God, in the end he has nothing at all. That pain seems to me the hardest hell, for he does not have his God. A soul may have God in all sufferings except in sin.

And God is as willing to save man as he is powerful and wise; for Christ himself is foundation of all the laws of Christian people, and he has taught us to do good in return for evil. Here we can see that he is himself this love and acts towards us as he teaches us to do; for he wants us to be like him in oneness of unending love towards ourselves and towards our fellow Christians. No more than his love towards us is withheld because of our sin does he wish that our love be withheld from ourselves and our fellow Christians; but we must feel a naked hatred for sin and love the soul as God loves it without end. For these words which God said are an unending comfort: that he is keeping us very safe.

*   *   *

AFTER this our Lord gave me a revelation concerning prayer.* I saw two qualities in those who pray, according to what I have felt in myself. One is that they do not want to pray* for just anything that may be, but for that thing which is God's will and to his glory. The other is that they apply themselves powerfully and continually to pray for things that are his will and to his glory. And that is what I have understood from the teaching of Holy Church, for our Lord taught me the same in this: to have, as a gift from God, faith, hope, and charity, and to hold to them until the end of our lives. And so we say, 'Our Father', 'Hail Mary', and the creed,* with such devotion as God may grant. And so we pray for all our fellow Christians and for all kinds of people, as is God's will, for we wish that all kinds of men and women were in the same state of virtue and grace that we ought to desire for ourselves.

But yet our trust is often not complete in all this, for because of our unworthiness, as it seems to us, and because we are feeling nothing at all, we are not sure that God almighty hears us. For often we are as barren and dry after our prayers as we were before, and when we feel like this our folly is the cause of our weakness. For I have felt this way myself. And our Lord brought all this suddenly to mind, powerfully and vividly, comforting me against this kind of weakness in prayers, and said, 'I am the foundation of your prayers: first it is my will that you should have something, and then I make you want it, and then I make you pray for it. And if you pray, how then could it be that you should not have what you pray for?'

And so in his first statement, along with the three that follow subsequently, our Lord reveals something very comforting. And in the fifth statement, where he says, 'If you pray for it', he there reveals the very great delight and unending reward that he will give us for our prayer. And in the sixth statement, where he says, 'How then could it be that you should not have what you pray for?', there he issues a serious rebuke, for we do not trust as firmly as we should do.

So our Lord wants us both to pray and to trust, for the purpose of the statements previously reported is to strengthen us against weakness in our prayers. For it is God's will that we should pray, and he moves us to do so in these words reported before, because he wants us to feel sure that our prayers will be answered, for prayer pleases God. Prayer gives man pleasure with himself, and makes one who was previously contentious and in turmoil both calm and humble.*

Prayer unites the soul to God; for though the soul is always like God in nature and substance, it is often unlike him in condition, through sin on man's part. Then prayer makes the soul like God when the soul wills as God wills, and then it is like God in condition as it is in nature.* And so God teaches us to pray and firmly believe that we shall have what we pray for, because everything which is done would be done, even though we never prayed for it.* But the love of God is so great that he regards us as partners in his good work, and so he moves us to pray for what it pleases him to do, for he will reward us, and give us eternal recompense, for whatever prayer or good will that we receive through his gift. And this was revealed to me in these words, 'If you pray for it'.

With these words God revealed to me such great pleasure and such great delight, as if he were much beholden to us for each good deed that we do—even though it is he who does them—and because we pray him urgently to do whatever is pleasing to him, as if he said, 'How could you please me more than to pray me urgently, wisely, and willingly to do whatever I wish to do?'

And so prayer makes accord between God and man's soul, for while man's soul is at ease with God he does not need to pray, but reverently to contemplate what God says. For during the whole time of this revelation to me I was not moved to pray but always to bear this in mind as a comfort:* that when we see God, we have what we desire, and then we do not need to pray. But when we do not see God, then we need to pray, because of what we are lacking and so as to make ourselves fit for Jesus. For when a soul is tempted, troubled, and alone in its distress, then it is time to pray and make oneself compliant and submissive to God. But no kind of prayer makes God pliant to the soul, because God's love is always the same. But while man is in sin, he is so powerless, so unwise, and so unloving that he cannot love God or himself.

The greatest affliction that he has is blindness, for he does not see all this. Then the whole love of God almighty, ever one, gives him sight of himself,* and then he supposes that God is angry with him on account of his sin. And then he is moved to contrition and by confession and other good deeds to assuage God's anger until he finds rest of soul and ease of conscience. And then it seems to him that God has forgiven his sins, and it is true. And then, in the sight of the soul, God is moved to look upon the soul, as if it had been in pain or in prison, saying, 'I am glad that you have come to rest, for I have always loved you, and I love you now, and you love me.'

And so with prayers, as I have said before, and with other good works that are customary according to the teaching of Holy Church, the soul is united to God.*

*   *   *

BEFORE this time I often had a great longing and desired as a gift from God to be released from this world and from this life, so that I would be with my God in bliss, where I surely hope, through his mercy, to be without end. For I often considered the misery that is here, and the joy and the blessed existence that is there. And even if there had been no pain on earth except the absence of our Lord, it seemed to me sometimes more than I could bear; and this made me grieve and yearn intensely. Then, to encourage my patience and endurance, God said to me in this way:

'You shall suddenly be taken from all your suffering, from all your distress and from all your unhappiness. And you shall come up above, and you shall have me for your reward, and you shall be filled full of joy and bliss. And you shall never have any kind of suffering, any kind of sickness, anything displeasing, nor any disappointed desires, but always joy and bliss without end. Why then should it bother you to suffer for a while, since it is my will and my glory?'

And in these words 'You shall suddenly be taken', I saw how God rewards man for the patience that he shows in awaiting God's will in his time, and that man extends his patience over the course of his lifetime because he does not know when he will pass away. This is a great advantage, for if a man knew when his time was to be, he would not have patience over the time until then. God also wishes that, while the soul is in the body, it seems to itself that it is always on the point of being taken; for all this life and this distress that we have here is only a moment, and when we are suddenly taken out of suffering into bliss, then it will be nothing.*

And therefore our Lord said, 'Why should it then grieve you to suffer for a while, seeing that it is my will and my glory?' It is God's will that we accept his promises and his comfortings as generously and as fully as we can take them. And he also wants us to take our waiting and our distress as lightly as we can take them and count them as nothing; for the more lightly we take them—the less value we set on them out of love—the less pain we shall experience from feeling them, and the more thanks we shall have for them.

In this blessed revelation I was truly taught that any man or woman who willingly chooses God in this life may be sure that they are chosen.* Keep this faithfully in mind, for truly it is God's will that we all may be as certain in our hope of the bliss of heaven while we are here, as we shall be in certitude when we are there. And the more pleasure and joy that we take in this assurance with reverence and humility, the better God is pleased. For I am sure that if there had been none but me that should be saved, God would have done all that he has done for me. And so should every soul think, acknowledging that God loves him, forgetting if possible the rest of creation, and thinking that God has done for him all that he has done. And this, it seems to me, should move a soul to love and to please him, and fear nothing but him, for it is his will that we should know that all the power of our enemy is under lock and key in our friend's hand. And so a soul that knows this for sure shall fear none but him that he loves, and reckon all other fears along with passions and bodily illness and imaginings.

And therefore, if someone be in so much pain, in so much misery, and in so much distress that it seems to him that he can think of nothing at all but the state he is in or what he is feeling, let him, as soon as he can, pass over it lightly and count it as nothing. And why? Because God wants to be known. For if we knew him and loved him, we should have patience and be completely at rest; and all that he does should be a pleasure to us. And our Lord revealed this to me in these words that he uttered: 'Why then should it bother you to suffer for a while, since it is my will and my glory?' And this was the end of all that our Lord revealed to me that day.*

*   *   *

AND after this I soon came back to myself and to my bodily sickness, realizing that I would live, and like a wretch I grieved and mourned on account of the bodily pains that I felt, and thought how very irksome it was that I should go on living. And I felt as barren and dry as if I had only ever had little comfort before, because of the return of my pains and the disappearance of spiritual feeling.

Then a member of a religious order came to me and asked me how I was getting on. And I said that I had been raving that day, and he laughed loudly and heartily. And I said: 'The cross that stood at the foot of my bed—it was bleeding hard.'* And at these words the person to whom I was speaking was amazed and became very serious. And at once I felt very ashamed at my carelessness and I thought: 'This man takes seriously the least word that I say, and says nothing in reply.'

And when I saw that he took it so seriously and so very reverently, I became very greatly ashamed, and wanted to have been confessed; but I could not tell any priest about it, because I thought, 'How could a priest believe me? I did not believe our Lord God.' I believed this truly during the time that I was seeing him, and it was then my will and my intention to do so forever, without end, but like a fool I let it pass from my mind. Look what a wretch I was! This was a great sin and great ingratitude that I—through stupidity, because of feeling a little bodily pain—so foolishly lost for the time being the comfort of all this blessed revelation of our Lord God.

Here you can see what I am in myself; but our courteous Lord would not leave me like this. And I lay still till night, trusting in his mercy, and then I went to sleep. And as soon as I fell asleep, it seemed to me that the devil took me by the throat,* and would have strangled me, but he could not. Then I woke out of my sleep, barely alive.

The people who were with me were watching me and bathed my temples, and my heart began to take comfort. And straightaway a little smoke came in at the door with a great heat and a foul stench. I said, 'Blessed be the Lord! Is everything here on fire?' And I supposed it to have been an actual fire that would have burned us all to death. I asked those who were with me if they were aware of any stench. They said no, they did not notice anything. I said, 'Blessed be God!' because I knew very well that it was the devil that had come to assail me. And at once I accepted what our Lord had revealed to me that same day, together with all the faith of Holy Church, for I regarded them both as one, and had recourse to that as to my comfort. And immediately everything vanished away, and I was brought to a state of great rest and peace, without sickness of body or troubled conscience.

* * *

BUT I stayed awake and then our Lord opened my spiritual eyes and showed me my soul in the midst of my heart. I saw my soul as large as if it were a kingdom; and from the properties I saw in it, it seemed to me that it was a glorious city. In the midst of this city sits our Lord Jesu, true God and true man, a handsome person and of great stature—glorious, highest lord; and I saw him dressed splendidly in glories. He sits in the midst of the soul in peace and rest. And he rules and guards heaven and earth and all that is. The manhood sits at rest with the Godhead; the Godhead rules and guards without any instrument or effort; and my soul is blissfully occupied with the blessed Godhead which is supreme power, supreme wisdom, supreme goodness. Through all eternity Jesus will never vacate the place he takes in our soul; for in us is the home most familiar to him and the dwelling most pleasing.*

This was a delectable sight and a restful one, for it is truly so forever more. And to contemplate this while we are here is most pleasing to God and of the greatest advantage to us. And the soul that contemplates in this way makes itself like the one that is contemplated and unites itself in rest and peace. And this was a special joy and bliss to me that I saw him sitting; for the sight of this sitting revealed to me the certainty of his dwelling eternally. And I knew truly that it was he who had revealed everything to me before. And when I had considered this with much deliberation, then our good Lord revealed words to me very gently, voicelessly, and without opening his lips, just as he had done before, and said very gravely:* 'Be well aware that what you saw today was no delirium, but accept it and believe it, and hold to it, and you shall not be overcome.'

These last words were said in order to teach me true certainty that it is our Lord Jesu who revealed everything to me. For just as in the first words that our good Lord revealed to me, referring to his blessed Passion—'In this way the devil is overcome'*—just so he said the last words with the very greatest certainty, 'You shall not be overcome.'

And this teaching and this true comfort applies in general to all my fellow Christians, as I have said before, and it is God's will that it is so. And these words, 'You shall not be overcome', were said very firmly and very powerfully, for assurance and comfort against all the tribulations that may come. He did not say, 'You shall not be perturbed, you shall not be troubled, you shall not be distressed', but he said, 'You shall not be overcome.' God wants us to pay attention to his words and always to be strong in our certainty in good times and bad; for he loves us and is pleased with us, and so he wishes us to love him and be pleased with him and strongly trust in him; and all shall be well.

And soon afterwards everything was at a close, and I saw no more.

*   *   *

AFTER this the devil came back with his heat and his stench and preoccupied me: the stench was so foul and so unbearable, and the physical heat was frightening and troublesome too. I could also hear an audible jabbering and a talking, as though it were two people, and both, to my way of thinking, were jabbering away at once, as if they were busily debating something; and as it was all low muttering I understood nothing they said, but I thought all this was to drive me to despair.* And I put my trust firmly in God and comforted my soul by speaking out loud, as I would have done to another person than myself who had been afflicted in this way. I thought this preoccupation could not be compared to any other human anxiety. I fixed my bodily eyes on the same cross, in which I had seen comfort before, and I busied my tongue with speaking of Christ's Passion and rehearsing the faith of Holy Church, and I set my heart on God with all the trust and all the strength that was in me. And I thought to myself, 'Now you have plenty to do. If, from now on, you could always be so intent on keeping yourself from sin, that would be a supremely good way of occupying your time'; for I truly thought that if I were safe from sin I would be completely safe from all the fiends of hell and enemies of my soul.

And so they preoccupied me all that night and in the morning until it was just after sunrise. And then in a moment they were all gone, all disappeared, with nothing left but stench, and that still lingered for a while. And I scorned them, and so I was delivered from them by virtue of Christ's Passion, for through that the devil is overcome, as Christ said to me before.

Ah, wretched sin!* What are you? You are nothing! For I saw that God is everything—I did not see you. And when I saw that God has made everything, I did not see you. And when I saw that God is in everything, I did not see you. And when I saw that God does everything that is done, from the lesser to the greater, I did not see you. And when I saw our Lord Jesu seated in our soul so gloriously, loving and liking and ruling and guarding all that he has made, I did not see you. And so I am certain that you are nothing, and all those who love you and like you, and follow you, and willingly end in you, I am certain that they shall be brought to nothing with you, and eternally confounded. God protect us all from you. Amen, for the love of God.

And I want to say what baseness is, as I have been taught by the revelation of God. Baseness is everything which is not good: the spiritual blindness which we fall into by our first sin, and all that follows from that wretched condition: sufferings and pains, of spirit or body, and everything which is not good, on earth or in any other place. And then concerning this it may be asked: What are we? And to this I reply: If all that is not good were to be taken away from us, we should be good. When wretchedness is separated from us, God and the soul are all one, and God and man all one.

What is everything on earth that divides us from God? I answer and say: in that it serves us, it is good, and in that it shall perish, it is baseness, and in that a man sets his heart upon it in any other way than this, it is sin. And while a man or woman loves sin, if there be any such, he is in pain that surpasses all pains. And when he does not love sin, but hates it and loves God, all is well. And he who truly does this, though he may sometimes sin through frailty or ignorance in his will, he does not fall, for he wishes to rise again strongly and behold God, whom he loves with all his will. God has caused himself to be loved by him or her who has been a sinner, but he loves continually, and he longs continually to have our love. And when we love Jesu strongly and certainly, we are at peace.

All the blessed teaching of our Lord God was revealed to me in three ways as I have said before:* that is to say, by bodily sight, and by words formed in my understanding, and by spiritual vision. Concerning bodily sight, I have said what I saw as truly as I can; and as for the words formed, I have reported those words just as our Lord revealed them to me; and as for the spiritual vision, I have said something but I can never disclose it in full, and therefore I am moved to say more about this spiritual vision, if God will give me grace.

*   *   *

GOD showed me two kinds of sickness that we have, of which he wishes us to be cured: one is impatience,* because our trouble and our suffering are heavy for us to bear; the other is despair or doubting fear, as I shall explain later. And these are the two which most trouble and disturb us, according to what our Lord showed me, and the ones from which he is most pleased if we reform. I am talking of such men and women who for the love of God hate sin and dispose themselves to do God's will. Then these are two secret sins and most beset us.* Therefore it is God's will that they should be recognized, and then we shall reject them as we do other sins.

And so our Lord very humbly revealed to me what patience he had in his cruel Passion, and also the joy and the delight that he has in that Passion because of love. And he showed me this by way of example that we should bear our sufferings gladly and wisely, for that is greatly pleasing to him and eternal benefit to us. And the reason why we are troubled by them is because of our failure to recognize love.

Although the Persons in the blessed Trinity are all equal in attributes, love was revealed to me most of all—that it is closest to us all, and that we are most blind in recognizing this. For many men and women believe that God is almighty and may do everything, and that he is all wisdom and knows how to do everything, but that he is all love and is willing to do everything—there they stop short. And it is this ignorance that most hinders those who love God, for when they begin to hate sin, and to reform themselves according to the laws of Holy Church, there still persists a fear that moves them to dwell upon themselves and their sins committed in the past. And they take this fear for humility, but it is a reprehensible blindness and a weakness, and we cannot despise it, yet if we recognized it we should at once despise it, as we do any other sin that we recognize, for it comes from the enemy and it is contrary to truth.

For of all the attributes of the blessed Trinity, it is God's will that we find most certainty in delight and love. For love makes power and wisdom very humble towards us; for just as through his courtesy God forgets our sin from the time we repent, so he wishes us to forget our sin, and all our depression, and all our doubting fears.

*   *   *

FOR I saw four kinds of fear. One is the fear of attack, which comes to a person suddenly through weakness. This fear does good, for it helps to purify a person, as does bodily sickness or any other such suffering which is not sinful; for all such sufferings help people if they are patiently accepted.

The second is fear of punishment, through which someone is stirred and woken from the sleep of sin; for whoever is fast asleep in sin is unable at that time to receive the tender comfort of the Holy Spirit until he has experienced this fear of punishment, of bodily death, and of the fire of purgatory.* And this fear moves him to seek the comfort and mercy of God; and so this fear serves as an opening for him and enables him to be contrite through the blessed inspiration of the Holy Spirit.

The third is doubting fear, for though it is little enough in itself, if it be recognized, it is a kind of despair. For I am certain that God hates all doubting fears, and he wishes us to separate ourselves from them through a true knowledge of love.*

The fourth is reverent fear, for there is no fear in us which pleases God except reverent fear; and that is very sweet and gentle, through greatness of love. And yet this reverent fear and love are not one and the same, but they are different in nature and in way of working, and neither of them may be had without the other. Therefore I am sure that those who love also feel fear, though they may only feel it a little. Even though they may come under the guise of holiness, all fears which confront us, other than reverent fear, are not truly so, and this is how they can be recognized and distinguished one from another. For this reverent fear, the more we feel it, the more it softens and comforts, and pleases and relaxes us, and false fear troubles and disquiets and perturbs.*

This, then, is the remedy: to recognize them both and reject the false fear, just as we would do an evil spirit that appeared in the likeness of a good angel.* Even though he come in the guise and the likeness of a good angel, and however engaging his company and his actions may appear, an evil spirit first troubles, and disquiets, and perturbs the person he speaks to, and hinders him, and leaves him in complete turmoil, and the more that this spirit has to do with him, the more he perturbs him and the further he is from peace. Therefore it is God's will and to our advantage that we should know them apart. For God always wishes us to be secure in love, and peaceful and restful, as he is towards us. And just in the same way as he is towards us, so he wishes us to be towards ourselves and towards our fellow Christians. Amen.

Here concludes Julian of Norwich.

REVELATIONS OF DIVINE LOVE

The Long Text

I

An account of the chapters. This first chapter describes the sequence of revelations and numbers them.

THIS is a revelation of love which Jesus Christ, our endless bliss, made in sixteen showings or special revelations.*

The first* concerns his precious crowning with thorns; and by this was understood and specified the Trinity,* with the incarnation,* and the union between God and man's soul, with many lovely revelations of unending wisdom and teachings of love, in which all the revelations that follow are based and unified.

The second is the discolouring of his fair face, as a sign of his precious Passion.*

The third is that our Lord God—almighty, all wisdom, all love—just as he has truly made everything that is, so he truly does and brings about all that is done.*

The fourth is the scourging of his tender body, with plentiful shedding of his blood.*

The fifth is that the devil is overcome by the precious Passion of Christ.*

The sixth is the glorious gratitude of our Lord God with which he rewards his blessed servants in heaven.*

The seventh is frequent experience of joy and misery. To experience well-being is to be touched and encouraged by grace, with true certainty of unending joy. The experience of misery comes through temptation by the depression and irksomeness of our mortal lives, with spiritual understanding that we are sustained securely in love by the goodness of God, in misery just as much as in joy.*

The eighth is Christ's last sufferings and his cruel death.*

The ninth is the delight which the blessed Trinity takes in the cruel Passion of Christ and his piteous death; in which joy and delight he wishes us to be comforted and gladdened with him until we come to their fullness in heaven.*

The tenth is that our Lord Jesus displays his blessed heart riven in two for love, and rejoices.*

The eleventh is an exalted spiritual revelation concerning his dear mother.*

The twelfth is that our Lord is being itself in its noblest form.*

The thirteenth* is that our Lord God wishes us to have great regard for all the deeds he has done in the noble splendour of creating all things, and the excellence of man's creation (which is superior to all God's other works), and the precious atonement* which he has made for man's sin, turning all our blame into everlasting glory. Here our Lord also says, 'Behold and see, for by the same power, wisdom, and goodness I shall make well all that is not well, and you shall see it.'* And in this he wants us to keep to the faith and belief of Holy Church, not wishing to know his mysteries now, except as concerns us in this life.

The fourteenth is that our Lord is the foundation of our prayers. In this, two properties were seen: one is rightful prayer, the other is sure trust, and he wishes both to be equally ample. And so our prayers please him, and in his goodness he fulfils them.*

The fifteenth is that we shall suddenly be taken from all our suffering and from all our misery and, through his goodness, we shall come up above, where we shall have our Lord Jesus for our reward and be filled full of joy and bliss in heaven.*

The sixteenth is that the blessed Trinity our creator dwells eternally in our soul in Christ Jesus our Saviour, gloriously ruling and governing all things, strongly and wisely saving and protecting us out of love, and we shall not be overcome by our enemy.*

2

Concerning the time of these revelations, and how she made three petitions.

THESE revelations were shown to a simple, uneducated creature* in the year of our Lord 1373, on the eighth day of May.* This person had already asked for three gifts by the grace of God. The first was to relive his Passion in her mind;* the second was bodily sickness;* the third was that God would give her three wounds.

As for the first gift, it seemed to me that I had some feeling for the Passion of Christ but I still wanted more, by God's grace. It seemed to me I wished I had been there at that time with Mary Magdalene* and with others who loved Christ, so that I might have seen with my own eyes the Passion which our Lord suffered for me, and so that I might have suffered with him as others did who loved him. And so I longed for a vision of him in the flesh, by which I might have more knowledge of the bodily sufferings of our Saviour and of the fellow-suffering of our Lady and of all those who truly loved him and saw his sufferings at that time, for I wanted to be one of them and suffer with him. I never wished for any other vision or revelation from God until the soul was separated from my body, for I believed I would be saved by the mercy of God. This was what I intended, for because of that revelation I wanted to have afterwards a truer perception of Christ's Passion.

The second gift came to my mind with contrition, freely and without any seeking: a willing desire to be given a bodily sickness by God. I wanted that sickness to be severe enough as to seem mortal, so that in that illness I might receive all the rites of Holy Church, myself believing that I was to die, and that all who saw me might suppose the same, for I wanted to have no hopes of any fleshly or earthly life. In this sickness I wanted to have every kind of suffering in body and spirit that I would have if I were to die, with all the turbulent terrors and tumults caused by devils,* and every other kind of pain, short of the soul's leaving the body. And this was my intention because I wanted to be purged by the mercy of God, and afterwards live more to the glory of God because of that sickness. For I hoped that it might have been a benefit to me when I should die, because I longed to be soon with my God.

I expressed my two requests about the Passion and the sickness with a condition, for it seemed to me that this was not the usual practice of prayer. So I said, 'Lord, you know what I want, if it is your will that I should have it; and if it is not your will, good Lord, do not be displeased, for I only want what you want.'* I asked for this illness in my young days, that I should have it when I was thirty years old.*

As for the third gift, by the grace of God and the teaching of Holy Church, I conceived a strong desire to receive three wounds in my life:* that is to say, the wound of true contrition, the wound of kind compassion, and the wound of purposeful longing for God. Just as

I asked for the other two with a condition, so I asked for this third one urgently without any condition.

The first two of these desires just mentioned passed from my mind, and the third remained with me continually.

3

Concerning the sickness obtained from God by petition.

AND when I was thirty and a half years old, God sent me a bodily sickness in which I lay for three days and three nights; and on the fourth night I received all the rites of Holy Church and did not expect to live until morning. And after this I lingered on for two days and two nights. And on the third night I often thought I was about to die, and so did those who were with me.*

And being still young, I thought it was a great pity to die, but this was not because of anything on earth that I wanted to live for, nor because I was afraid of any pain, for I trusted in God's mercy. But it was because I wanted to live so as to have loved God better and for longer, in order that I might, through the grace of that living, have more knowledge and love of God in the bliss of heaven. For all the time that I had lived here seemed to me so little and so brief in comparison with that unending bliss—I thought it as nothing. So I thought, 'Good Lord, may my living no longer be to your glory!' And I understood in my reason and through the sensation of my pains that I was going to die. And with the will of my heart I fully assented to be at God's will.

So I lasted till day, and by then my body was dead from the waist down, as it felt to me. Then I wanted to be propped up, leaning back and supported, so that my heart could be more freely at God's will, and so that I could think of God while my life should last. My curate* was sent for to be present at my end, and by the time he came my eyes were fixed and I could not speak. He set the cross before my face and said, 'I have brought you the image of your maker and Saviour. Look at it and take comfort from it.'

It seemed to me that I was all right as I was, for my gaze was fixed upwards into heaven where I trusted I was going, by God's mercy. But nevertheless I consented to fix my eyes on the face of the crucifix if I could, and so I did, for it seemed to me that I could manage to look straight ahead of me for longer than I could look upwards. After this my sight began to fail, and all grew dark around me in the room, as though it had been night, except for the image of the cross in which I saw a light for all mankind—I did not know how. Everything apart from the cross was ugly to me, as if much crowded with fiends.

After this the upper part of my body began to die to such an extent that I hardly had any sensation. My greatest pain was my shortness of breath and the ebbing away of life. And then I truly believed that I was at the point of death. And suddenly, at that moment, all my pain was taken from me and I was as well, especially in the upper part of my body, as I ever was before. I was astonished at this sudden change, for it seemed to me a mysterious act of God, not of nature. And yet I had no more confidence that I would live because I felt this relief; nor did feeling more comfortable in this way fully comfort me, for it seemed to me I would rather have been released from this world, because my heart was willingly set upon that.

Then it suddenly came to mind that I ought to wish for the second wound, as a gift and a grace from our Lord, so that my body might be filled with recollection and feeling of his blessed Passion, as I had prayed before; for I wanted his pains to be my pains, with compassion, and then longing for God. So it seemed to me that, through his grace, I might have the wounds which I had wanted before. But in this I never asked for any bodily vision or any kind of revelation from God, but for compassion, such as it seemed to me a naturally sympathetic soul might feel for our Lord Jesus, who for love was willing to become a mortal man.* And I longed to suffer with him, while living in my mortal body, as God would give me grace.

4

Here begins the first revelation of the precious crowning of Christ, as set out in the first chapter; and how God fills the heart with the greatest joy; and of his great humility, and how the sight of Christ's Passion is strength enough against all the temptations of fiends; and of the great excellency and humility of the Blessed Virgin Mary.

AT this I suddenly saw the red blood trickling down* from under the crown of thorns, hot and fresh, plentiful and lifelike, just as though it were the moment in his Passion when the crown of thorns was pressed on to his blessed head, he who was both God and man, the same who suffered for me in this way. I had a true and powerful perception that it was he himself who showed this to me without any intermediary.

And in the same revelation the Trinity suddenly filled my heart full of the utmost joy, and I understood that it will be like that in heaven forever for all those who will come there. For the Trinity is God, and God is the Trinity; and the Trinity is our maker, the Trinity is our protector, the Trinity is our everlasting lover, the Trinity is our unending joy and bliss, through our Lord Jesus Christ and in our Lord Jesu Christ. And this was shown in the first revelation and in them all; for where Jesus appears, the blessed Trinity is to be understood, as it seems to me.*

And I said, 'Blessed be thou, Lord!'* I said this with a reverent intention in a loud voice; and I was much astounded at the wonder and amazement I felt, that he who is so much to be revered and so awesome was willing to be so friendly* to a sinful being, living in this wretched flesh. So I took it that at that time our Lord Jesus, out of his courteous love, would show me comfort before the time of my temptation, for it seemed to me that by God's permission and with his safekeeping I might well be tempted by devils before I died. With this vision of his blessed Passion, along with the Godhead that I saw in my understanding, I well knew that this was strength enough for me—yes, and for every creature living who is to be saved—against all the devils of hell and against all spiritual enemies.

With this he brought to mind our blessed Lady. I saw her in a spiritual manner but in her bodily likeness, a simple and humble girl, young in years and little more than a child, in the form that she was when she conceived.* God also revealed in part the wisdom and the truth of her soul, and in this I understood the reverent contemplation with which she beheld her God who is her maker, marvelling with great reverence that he was willing to be born of her who was a simple creature of his making. For it was this that she wondered at: that he who was her creator was willing to be born of her who was created. And this wisdom and faith, recognizing the greatness of her maker and the littleness of her created self, caused her to say very humbly to Gabriel, 'Behold me here, the handmaid of the Lord.' In seeing this I truly understood that she is greater in worthiness and grace than everything which God created

below her; for, as I see it, no created thing is above her except the
blessed humanity of Christ.

5

*How God is to us everything that is good, tenderly enfolding us; and
everything that is made is as nothing, compared with almighty God; and
how a man has no rest until he counts himself and everything as nothing
for the love of God.*

At the same time as I saw this vision of the head bleeding, our Lord
showed me spiritually in a vision how intimately he loves us. I saw that
he is to us everything that is good and comforting for our help. He is
our clothing that out of love enwraps us and enfolds us, embraces us
and wholly encloses us, surrounding us for tender love, so that he can
never leave us. And so in this vision I saw that he is everything that is
good, as I understand it.

And in this vision he also showed a little thing, the size of a hazelnut, lying in the palm of my hand, as it seemed to me, and it was
round as a ball.* I looked at it with my mind's eye and thought, 'What
can this be?' And the answer came in a general way, like this, 'It is
all that is made.' I wondered how it could last, for it seemed to me
so small that it might have disintegrated suddenly into nothingness.
And I was answered in my understanding, 'It lasts, and always will,
because God loves it; and in the same way everything has its being
through the love of God.'

In this little thing I saw three properties: the first is that God made
it; the second is that God loves it; the third is that God cares for it.
But what is that to me? Truly, the maker, the carer, and the lover. For
until I am of one substance with him I can never have complete rest
nor true happiness; that is to say, until I am so joined to him that there
is no created thing between my God and me. It seemed to me that
this little thing that is made might have disintegrated into nothing
because of its smallness. We need to know about this so as to delight in
setting at nought everything that is made in order to love and possess
God who is unmade.* For this is the reason why we are not entirely at
ease in heart and soul: because we seek rest here in these things which
are so small and in which there is no rest, and do not know our God
who is almighty, all wise, all good;* for he is true rest. God wishes to

be known,* and is pleased that we should rest in him; for all that is beneath him is not enough for us; and this is the reason why no soul is at rest until it counts as nothing all that is created. When a soul has willingly made itself as nothing for love, in order to have him who is all, then he is able to receive spiritual rest.

Our Lord God also revealed* that it is a very great pleasure to him that a simple soul should come to him in a bare, plain and homely way. For, according to my understanding of this revelation, this is the natural yearnings of the soul touched by the Holy Spirit: 'God, of your goodness, give me yourself; for you are enough for me, and I cannot ask for anything less that would fully honour you. And if I do ask for anything less, I shall always be in want, but in you alone I have everything.'*

And these words—'God, of your goodness'—are very dear to the soul and come very close to the will of God and his goodness; for his goodness includes all his creatures and all his blessed works and goes beyond them without end, for he himself is eternity. And he has made us only for himself, and restored us by his blessed Passion, and sustains us in his blessed love, and all this is out of his goodness.

6

How we should pray; of the great, tender love that our Lord has for man's soul—wishing us to be occupied in knowing and loving him.

THIS revelation was given, as I understand it, to teach our souls the wisdom of clinging to the goodness of God. And at the same time our habits of prayer were brought to mind: how we are accustomed, through our lack of understanding and knowledge of love, to make use of many intermediaries.* Then I saw indeed that it is more honour to God, and more true delight, if we pray faithfully to God himself in his goodness and cling to that by his grace, with true understanding and steadfast belief, than if we employ all the intermediaries that heart can devise; for if we use all these intermediaries, they fall short of fully honouring God; but in his goodness is everything, and nothing is lacking in that.

For what I am going to say came into my mind at the same time: we pray to God by his holy flesh and by his precious blood, his holy

Passion, his precious death and glorious wounds; and all the blessed kindness, the eternal life, that we receive from all this comes from his goodness. And we pray to him by the love of his sweet mother who bore him, and all the help we have from her is from his goodness; and we pray by his holy cross on which he died, and all the strength and help that we receive from the cross is from his goodness. And in the same way, all the help that we have from particular saints and all the blessed company of heaven, the precious love and the holy and unending friendship that we have from them, comes from his goodness. For in his goodness God has ordained many very lovely means to help us, of which the chief and principal means is the blessed human nature which he took from the Virgin, with all the means which went before and came afterwards, which are part of our redemption and of our eternal salvation.

Therefore it pleases him that we should seek him and worship him through these intermediaries, while understanding and knowing that he is the goodness of everything. For the highest prayer is to the goodness of God, and that comes down to us in our lowest need. It quickens our soul and gives it life, and makes it grow in grace and virtue. It is nearest in nature and readiest in grace; for it is the same grace which the soul seeks and always will until we truly know our God who has enclosed us all in himself. A man walks upright,* and the food* inside his body is shut up as if in a very fine purse; and when it is his time of necessity the purse is opened and shut again in a very decent way. And that it is God who does this is shown where he says that he comes down to us in our lowest need. For he does not despise what he has made,* nor does he disdain to serve us in the simplest task that is part of our bodily nature, for love of the soul which he has made in his own likeness. For as the body is clad in cloth, and the flesh in the skin, and the bones in the flesh, and the heart in the chest, so are we, soul and body, clad and enclosed in the goodness of God.* Yes, and more inwardly, for all these may decay and wear away.*

God's goodness is always complete, and incomparably closer to us, for truly our lover, God, wants our souls to cling to him with all their might, and always to be clinging to his goodness. For of all the things that the heart can think, this pleases God most and helps us soonest. For our soul is so especially loved by him who is highest that it surpasses the knowledge of all created beings—that is to say, there

. is no being made who can know how much and how sweetly and how tenderly our maker loves us.

And therefore with his grace and his help we can remain in spiritual contemplation, with endless wonder at this high, surpassing, inestimable love that almighty God has for us in his goodness. And therefore we may reverently ask all that we wish of our loving God;* for our natural wish is to have God, and God's good will is to have us.* And we can never stop wishing or longing until we possess him in the fullness of joy, and then we can wish for nothing more; for he wants us to be occupied in knowing and loving until the time comes when we shall attain fulfilment in heaven.

And that is why this lesson of love was revealed, with all that follows, as you will see. For the strength and foundation of everything was revealed in the first vision. For of all things, it is beholding and loving its maker that makes the soul seem least in its own eyes and most fills it with reverent awe and true humility, with abundance of love for its fellow Christians.

7

How our Lady, seeing the greatness of her maker, thought herself the least; and of the great drops of blood running from under the crown of thorns; and how man's greatest joy is that the most high and mighty God is the holiest and most courteous.

AND to teach us this, as I understand it, our Lord God showed our Lady Saint Mary at the same time, signifying the profound wisdom and faith which were hers in beholding her maker. This wisdom and faith made her behold her God as so great, so exalted, so mighty and so good. The greatness and nobility of this contemplation of God filled her full of reverent awe, and with this she saw herself so small and so humble, so simple and so poor in comparison with her Lord God that this reverent awe filled her with humility. And so, founded on this, she was filled with grace* and with every kind of virtue, and she surpasses all created beings.

And all the while he was revealing in spiritual vision what I have just described, I saw the continuing bodily vision of copious bleeding from Christ's head. The great drops of blood* fell down from under the crown of thorns like beads, looking as if they had come from the veins; and as they came out they were dark red, because the blood was very thick; and as it spread out it was bright red; and when it came to the brows, then it vanished;* and yet the bleeding continued until many things were seen and understood. The beauty and vividness is like nothing but itself. The profusion is like the drops of water which fall from the eaves after a heavy shower of rain and fall so thickly that it is beyond human wit to number them. And as for the roundness of the drops, they were like herring scales* as they spread out over the forehead. These three things came to mind at the time: beads, because of the roundness of the drops as the blood came out; herring scales, because of their roundness as they spread over the forehead; rain-drops from the eaves, because of their innumerable profusion. This vision was vivid and life-like, and horrifying and awesome, sweet and lovely. And what gave me most comfort in the whole revelation that I saw was that our God and Lord who is so much to be revered and so awesome is so familiar and so courteous. And this is what most filled me with delight and assurance in my soul.

And to help understand this, he gave me this clear example:* it is the highest honour that a majestic king or a great lord can show a poor servant if he is friendly with him, and especially if he makes it known himself, with true sincerity and a cheerful expression, both in private and in public. Then this poor creature thinks in this way, 'Ah! What greater honour and joy could this noble lord give me than to treat me, who am so humble, with this marvellous friendliness? This truly gives me more joy and pleasure than if he gave me great gifts and were himself distant in manner.'

This human example was shown so elevatedly that a man's heart could be ravished and almost forget itself for joy at this great friendliness. So it is with our Lord Jesus and with us. For truly it is the greatest possible joy, as I see it, that he who is highest and mightiest, noblest and worthiest, is lowest and humblest, the most friendly and the most courteous. And truly and indeed this marvellous joy will be revealed to us all when we see him. And this is our Lord's will: that we yearn and believe, rejoice and delight, take comfort and console ourselves as much as we can, with his help and his grace, until the time when we can see it truly for ourselves. For the greatest fullness of joy that we shall have, as I see it, is the marvellous courtesy and friendliness of our Father who is our maker, in our Lord Jesus Christ who is our brother and our Saviour.

But no one can know this marvellous intimacy in this life unless he receives it through a special revelation from our Lord, or through a great abundance of grace given inwardly by the Holy Spirit. But faith and belief with love deserve the reward, and so it is received by grace; for our life is founded on faith with hope and love. This revelation, given to whomever God wills, plainly teaches the same, made known and explained with many secret details which are part of our faith and which are glorious to know. And when the revelation, which is given at one time, is past and hidden, then faith maintains it by the grace of the Holy Spirit until the end of our life. And so the revelation is nothing other than the faith, neither less nor more, as may be seen by what our Lord means in this, by the time it is completed.

8

A recapitulation of what has been said, and how it was shown to her for everyone in general.

AND as long as I saw this vision of copious bleeding from the head I could never stop saying these words, 'Blessed be thou, Lord!' From this revelation I understood six things.

The first is the tokens of the blessed Passion and the copious shedding of his precious blood.

The second is the Virgin who is his beloved mother.

The third is the blessed Godhead that always was, is, and always shall be, almighty, all wisdom, all love.

The fourth is everything which he has made; for I well know that heaven and earth and all that is made is vast and extensive, beautiful and good, but the reason why it seemed so small in my eyes was because I saw it in the presence of him who is the creator of all things. For to a soul who sees the maker of all things, all that is made seems very small.

The fifth is that he has made everything that is made for love—and by the same love everything is sustained and will be without end, as has been said before.

The sixth is that God is everything that is good, as I see it, and the goodness that there is in everything, is God.

And all these things our Lord showed me in the first vision and gave me time and space to contemplate them. And the bodily vision ceased, and the spiritual vision remained in my understanding. And I waited in reverent awe, rejoicing in what I saw, and wishing as much as I dared to see more if that were his will, or else to see the same vision for longer.

In all this I was much moved with love towards my fellow Christians, that they might see and know the same as I saw; for I wanted it to be a comfort to them, for this whole vision was shown for everyone in general. Then I said to those who were around me, 'Today is Judgement Day for me.' And I said this because I expected to have died; for on that day that a man or woman dies he is judged as he will be judged eternally,* as I understand it. I said this because I wanted them to love God better, to make them mindful that this life is short, as they could see by my example. For all this time I was expecting to die, and I was surprised—and a little sad—because it seemed to me this vision was shown for those who would go on living.

And what I say about myself, I mean on behalf of all my fellow Christians, for I was taught through the spiritual revelation of our Lord God that he intends it to be so. And therefore I beg you all for God's sake, and advise you for your own benefit, that you disregard the wretch to whom it was shown, and with all strength, wisdom, and humility contemplate God, who in his courteous love and unending goodness wished to make it generally known, to the comfort of us all. For it is God's will that you receive it with joy and delight as great as if Jesus had shown it to you all.

9

Concerning the humility of this woman, which always keeps her in the faith of Holy Church, and how he who loves his fellow Christians for God's sake loves everything.

I AM not good because of the revelation unless I love God better; and in as much as you love God better, it is meant more for you than for me. I am not saying this to those who are wise, because they are well aware of this; but I am saying it to those of you who are uninformed, for your comfort and encouragement, for we are all as one in love. For truly it was not revealed to me that God loved me better than the least soul who is in a state of grace, for I am sure there are many who never had a revelation or vision, but only the common teaching of

Holy Church, who love God better than I do. For if I look at myself in particular, I am nothing at all; but in general I am, I hope, in oneness of love with all my fellow Christians. For in this oneness depends the life of all humanity who will be saved. For God is all that is good, as I see it, and God has made all that is made, and God loves all that he has made. And he who loves all his fellow Christians in general for God's sake loves all that is. For in those who will be saved, all is comprehended: that is to say, all that is made, and the maker of all; for in man is God, and God is in everything. And he who loves in this way loves everything. And I hope by the grace of God that he who regards it in this way will be truly taught and greatly comforted, if he needs comfort.

I speak of those who will be saved,* because at this time God showed me no others. But in everything I believe as Holy Church believes, preaches, and teaches.* For the faith of Holy Church which I had understood before and, as I hope, by God's grace willingly observed and practised, remained constantly before me, and I never wished nor intended to accept anything which might be contrary to it. And with this aim I contemplated the revelation with all care; for I considered this whole blessed revelation as one in God's meaning.

All this was shown in three ways: that is to say, by bodily sight, and by words formed in my understanding, and by spiritual vision.* But I neither can nor know how to disclose the spiritual vision as openly or as fully as I would wish. But I trust in our Lord God almighty that he will, out of his goodness and for love of you, make you receive it more spiritually and more sweetly than I can or may tell it.

10

The second revelation is of the discolouring of his face, of our redemption, and the discolouring of the Vernicle; and how it pleases God when we seek him diligently, awaiting him steadfastly, and trusting him greatly.

AND after this I saw with my bodily sight in the face on the crucifix which hung before me—at which I was looking continuously—a part of his Passion: contempt, spitting and soiling, and blows,* and many lingering pains, more than I can tell, and frequent changes of colour. And once I saw how half his face, beginning at the ear, was caked with dry blood until it covered to the middle of his face, and after that the other half was covered in the same way, and meanwhile it vanished in the first part just as it had come.*

I saw this bodily, sorrowfully and dimly, and I wished for better bodily sight to have seen more clearly. And I was answered in my reason, 'If God wishes to show you more, he will be your light*—you need none but him.' For I saw him and sought him: for we are now so blind and so unwise that we never seek God until out of his goodness he shows himself to us. And when we see anything of him by grace, then we are moved by the same grace to seek with great longing to see him more joyously. And so I saw him and sought him, and I had him and I wanted him. And this is, and should be, our usual way of proceeding in this life, as I see it.

At one time my understanding was guided down to the bottom of the sea,* and there I saw green hills and valleys, seeming as if overgrown with moss, with seaweed and gravel. Then I understood this: that if a man or woman were under the broad waters, if he could have sight of God (just as God is constantly with us), he would be safe in body and soul, and come to no harm and, furthermore, he would have more comfort and consolation than all this world can tell. For God wants us to believe that we see him continually, even though it seems to us that we see only a little, and through this belief he makes us to be gaining in grace continually; for he wants to be seen, and he wants to be sought; he wants to be awaited, and he wants to be trusted.

This second revelation was so humble and so small and so simple that my spirits were greatly troubled as I contemplated it, grieving, fearful, and longing; for I was doubtful for a while whether it was a revelation.* And then at various times our good Lord gave me more insight, so that I truly understood that it was a revelation. It was an emblem and likeness of our foul, black, mortal covering, which our fair, bright, blessed Lord bore for our sins. It made me think of the holy Vernicle in Rome,* which he imprinted with his own blessed face while he was in his cruel Passion, willingly going to his death, and often changing colour. Many marvel how it could be—the brownness and blackness, the pitifulness and leanness of this image—considering that he imprinted it with his blessed face, which is the fairness of heaven, the flower of earth, and the fruit of the Virgin's womb.* Then how could this image be so discoloured and so far from fair? I would like to say what I have understood by the grace of God.

We know by our faith, and believe through the teaching and preaching of Holy Church that the blessed Trinity made mankind in its image* and in its likeness. In the same way we know that when man fell so deeply and so wretchedly through sin, no other help was forthcoming to restore man except through him who made man. And he who made man for love, by the same love would restore man to the same blessedness and surpassingly more. And just as we were made like the Trinity in our first creation, our creator wished that we should be like Jesus Christ our Saviour, in heaven without end, by virtue of our remaking.

Then between these two he wanted, for the love and honour of man, to make himself as like man in this mortal life, in our vileness and our wretchedness, as a man without sin could be.* This is the meaning of what was said before: it was the image and likeness of our foul, black, mortal covering, within which our fair, bright, blessed Lord God is hidden.* But I dare say most confidently, and we ought to believe, that there was never so fair a man as he,* until the time when his fair colour was changed by trouble and sorrow, and suffering and dying. This is spoken of in the eighth revelation,* where more is said about the same likeness. And as concerns the Vernicle in Rome, it moves through various changes in colour and expression, sometimes more comfortingly and animated, and sometimes more pitiful and deathly, as may be seen in the eighth revelation.

And this vision was a lesson to my understanding that the soul's continual seeking pleases God very much; for it can do no more than seek, suffer, and trust, and this is accomplished by the Holy Spirit in the soul that is so moved; and the illumination of discovery comes by his special grace when it is his will. The seeking with faith, hope, and charity* pleases our Lord, and the finding pleases the soul and fills it full of joy. And so I was taught in my understanding that seeking is as good as beholding during the time that he will allow the soul to be at labour. It is God's will that we seek to behold him, for through that he will show himself to us by his special grace when it is his will. And God will teach himself how a soul shall behave in contemplating him; and that is the most honour to him and benefit to the soul, and it receives the greatest humility and virtues by the grace and guidance of the Holy Spirit. For a soul that cleaves to God alone with true trust, either by seeking or in beholding does him the greatest honour that he can, as I see it.

There are two actions that may be seen in this vision: the one is seeking, the other is beholding. The seeking is common to all; every soul can have that by his grace and ought to have that discernment and teaching from Holy Church. It is God's will that, as gifts from him, we have three objects in our seeking: the first is that we seek willingly and diligently, without laziness, as it may be through his grace, gladly and cheerfully, without unreasonable depression and pointless unhappiness; the second is that for love of him we await him steadfastly, without grumbling and contending against him, until the end of our lives, for life will only last a while; the third is that we should greatly trust in him, in fully certain faith, for that is his will. We know that he will appear suddenly and joyously to all who love him; for he works secretly, and he wishes to be perceived, and his appearing will be very sudden; and he wishes to be trusted, for he is most gracious, approachable, and courteous—blessed may he be!

11

The third revelation. How God does everything except sin, never changing his purpose without end, for he has made everything in perfection of goodness.

AND after this I saw God in a point*—that is to say, in my understanding—and by seeing this I saw that he is in everything. I looked attentively, seeing and recognizing in that vision that he does everything that is done. I marvelled at that sight with quiet awe, and thought, 'What is sin?' For I saw truly that God does everything, however small it may be. And I saw truly that nothing is done by chance or accident but everything by God's prescient wisdom. If it seems to be chance or accident in our eyes, our blindness and lack of foresight is the cause, for those things that are in the foreseeing wisdom of God from without beginning*—which he justly and gloriously and continually guides to the best conclusion as they happen—come upon us suddenly and unawares; and so, in our blindness and our lack of foresight, we say these things are chance or accident. So I understand in this revelation of love, because I well know that in the sight of our Lord God there is no chance or accident.

Therefore I had to grant that everything which is done is well done,* because our Lord God does everything; at this time the actions of human beings were not shown, but only those of our Lord God in human beings; for he is at the mid-point of everything,* and he does everything, and I was sure that he does no sin.* And here I saw truly that sin is no kind of deed,* for sin was not shown me in all this. And I had no wish to keep wondering over this any longer, but looked at our Lord to see what he would reveal. And so, as far as it could be at that time, the rightfulness of God's actions was shown to the soul. Rightfulness has two excellent properties: it is just and it is complete*—and so are all the works of our Lord God—and there is no need for the operation of mercy or grace, for it is wholly rightful and lacking in nothing. (And at another time, as I shall describe,* he disclosed the naked truth about sin in a vision, where he did employ the operation of mercy and grace.)

And this vision was shown to my understanding because our Lord wants to have the soul truly turned to the contemplation of him and of all his works in general. For they are all wholly good, and all his doings are sweet and comforting, bringing great comfort to the soul which is turned from regarding the blind judgement of man to the fair, sweet judgement of our Lord God. For a man regards some deeds as well done and some deeds as evil, but our Lord does not regard them so; for as everything that exists in nature is of God's making, so everything that is done is an aspect of God's doing. For it is easy to understand that the best deed is well done;* and the least deed is done as well as the best and the most exalted; and all in the manner and order that our Lord has ordained from without beginning, for there is no doer but he.

I saw most certainly that he never changes his purpose in any kind of thing, nor ever shall, eternally. For nothing was unknown to him in his just ordinance from without beginning, and therefore, before anything was made, everything was set in order* as it would remain without end; and nothing of any kind falls short in that regard; for he made everything in fullness of goodness; and therefore the blessed Trinity is always completely satisfied with all his works.*

And he showed all this most blessedly with this meaning,* 'See, I am God. See I am in everything. See, I do everything. See, I never lift my hands from my works, nor ever shall, without end. See, I guide everything to the end to which I ordained it from without beginning by the same power, wisdom, and love with which I made it. How should anything be amiss?'

Thus powerfully, wisely, and lovingly was the soul tested in this vision. Then I saw truly that I must give my assent with great reverence, rejoicing in God.

12

The fourth revelation. How it is more pleasing to God to wash ourselves from sin in his blood rather than in water, for his blood is most precious.

AND after this I saw, as I watched, the body bleeding profusely in weals from the scourging,* like this: the fair skin was broken very deeply into the tender flesh* through sharp blows all over the precious body;* the hot blood ran out so abundantly that neither skin nor wound was to be seen, but it seemed as if it were all blood. And when it came to where it should have fallen down, then it vanished; nevertheless, the bleeding continued for a while, so that it could be observed with deliberation. And it was so abundant to my way of seeing that it seemed to me that if it had been the real thing in nature and essence* at that time, it would have saturated the bed with blood and overflowed all around.

And then it came into my mind that God has created abundant waters on earth* for our use and our bodily refreshment, out of the tender love that he has for us, yet it is more pleasing to him that we should very simply take his blessed blood to wash ourselves from sin; for there is no liquid created that it pleases him so much to give us; for it is most abundant as it is most precious, and that is so by virtue of his blessed Godhead.* And it shares our nature and washes most blissfully over us by virtue of his precious love.

The beloved blood of our Lord Jesus Christ is as truly most precious as it is truly abundant. Behold and see!* The precious plenty of his beloved blood descended down into hell and broke their bonds and delivered all those who were there who belonged to the court of heaven.* The precious plenty of his beloved blood overflows the whole earth and is ready to wash from sin all who are, have been, and shall be of good will. The precious plenty of his beloved blood ascended up into heaven* to the blessed body of our Lord Jesus Christ, and is in him there, bleeding and praying for us to the Father*—and is and shall be for as long as it is needed. And it flows through all heaven for ever more, rejoicing in the salvation of all mankind who are there and shall be there, making up the number that is lacking.*

13

The fifth revelation is that the temptation of the devil is overcome by the Passion of Christ, to the increase of our joy and to the pain of the devil, eternally.

AND afterwards, before God revealed any words, he allowed me to contemplate him for a suitable time, and all that I had seen, and all the significance in it, as far as the simplicity of my soul could take it in. Then he, without voice or opening of lips, formed in my soul these words: 'In this way the devil is overcome.'* Our Lord said these words referring to his blessed Passion, as he had shown it before.

In this our Lord revealed a part of the devil's malice and all his powerlessness, for he showed that his Passion is the devil's defeat. God showed that the devil still has the same malice that he had before the incarnation* and he works as hard, and just as continually he sees all those souls who will be saved escape him gloriously through the power of Christ's precious Passion. And that is his sorrow, and very badly humiliates him; for everything that God allows him to do turns into joy for us and to shame and misery for him. And he has as much sorrow when God gives him permission to work as when he is not working; and that is because he can never do as much evil as he would like, for all his power is under lock and key in God's hand.* But there can be no anger in God, as it seems to me, for our good Lord has regard eternally for his own glory and the benefit of all who shall be saved. With power and justice he withstands the reprobates who, out of malice and malignity, busy themselves to scheme and to act against God's will.*

I also saw our Lord scorn his malice and discount his powerlessness, and he wants us to do the same. At the sight of this I laughed heartily,* and that made those who were around me to laugh, and their laughter was a pleasure to me. In my thoughts I wished that all my fellow Christians had seen what I saw, and then they would all have laughed with me. But I did not see Christ laughing,* although I was very aware that the vision he showed me made me laugh. For

I understood that we may laugh to cheer ourselves and to rejoice in God because the devil is defeated. And when I saw him scorn the devil's wickedness, it was through my understanding being led into our Lord; that is to say, an inward revelation of truth, without any change in his demeanour; for, as it seems to me, this is a glorious quality in God, that he is without change.

And after this I became serious and said, 'I see three things: a game, a scorning, and an earnestness. I see a game, that the devil is defeated. I see a scorning, that God scorns him, and he shall be scorned. And I see an earnestness, in that he is defeated by the blessed Passion and death of our Lord Jesus Christ, which was accomplished in great earnest and with steadfast suffering.'

And when I said 'He is scorned', I mean that God scorns him: that is to say, because God sees him now as he will do without end. For in this God revealed that the devil is damned. And I meant this when I said, 'He shall be scorned': for I saw that he will be generally scorned at the Last Judgement by all those who will be saved, whose consolation he greatly envies. For then he will see that all the sorrow and tribulation that he has caused them will be turned into the increase of their eternal joy, and all the misery and tribulation that he would have liked to bring upon them shall go with him forever to hell.*

14

The sixth revelation is of the glorious gratitude with which he rewards his servants, and it has three joys.

AFTER this our good Lord said, 'I thank you for your service and your suffering, and especially in your youth.'*

And with this my understanding was lifted up into heaven, where I saw our Lord as a lord in his own house, who has called all his beloved servants and friends* to a splendid feast.* Then I saw the Lord take no seat in his own house, but I saw him reign royally in his house, and he filled it full of joy and delight, himself eternally gladdening and comforting his beloved friends most friendlily and most courteously, with marvellous melody of endless love in his own fair, blessed face, which glorious face of the Godhead fills heavens full of joy and bliss.*

God showed three degrees of bliss which every soul shall have in heaven who has willingly served God, whatever his degree upon earth. The first is the glorious gratitude* of our Lord God, which he will receive when he is delivered from suffering. This gratitude is so exalted and so glorious that it seems to the soul that it is fulfilled, even if there were nothing more. For it seemed to me that all the pain and trouble that could be suffered by all those alive might not deserve the glorious gratitude that one shall have who has willingly served God. The second degree is that all the blessed in heaven will see that glorious gratitude, and God makes the soul's service known to all who are in heaven. And at this time this example was shown: if a king thanks his servants it is a great honour for them, and if he makes it known to the whole kingdom, then their honour is much increased.* The third degree is that this will last eternally just as new and delightful as when it is first received.

And I saw that this was revealed in a gracious and kindly way: that the age of everyone will be known in heaven* and will be rewarded for willing service and time served; and especially, the age of those who willingly and freely offer their youth to God is surpassingly rewarded and wonderfully thanked. For I saw that whenever or how long a man or woman be truly turned to God, for one day's service and for his willingness to serve without end, he shall have all these three degrees of bliss. And the more the loving soul sees this courtesy in God, the gladder it is to serve God all the days of its life.*

15

The seventh revelation concerns frequent feelings of joy and sorrow, etc., and how it is expedient that a person sometimes be left without comfort, even though sin is not the cause.

AND after this he revealed a supreme spiritual delight in my soul. In this delight I was filled full of everlasting certainty, powerfully sustained, without any fear to pain me. This feeling was so joyful and so spiritual that I was wholly at peace, at ease, and at rest, so that there was nothing on earth that could have distressed me.

This only lasted a while,* and my mood turned right round and I was left to myself, feeling depressed, weary of my life and disgusted with myself, so that I could hardly have the patience to go on living. There was no ease or comfort, as I felt, except faith, hope, and charity, and these I had indeed, but could feel them very little.

And immediately after this our blessed Lord again gave me comfort and rest in my soul, with pleasure and certainty so blissful and so powerful that no fear, no sorrow, no pain bodily nor spiritual that one might suffer could have troubled me. And then I felt this pain again revealed to me, and then the joy and the delight, now the one and now the other, at different times, I suppose about twenty times. And in the moments of joy I could have said with Saint Paul: 'Nothing shall separate me from the love of Christ.'* And in the pain I could have said with Saint Peter: 'Lord, save me, I perish.'*

This vision was shown me to teach me—as I understand it—that it is helpful for some souls to feel in this way: sometimes to be comforted, and sometimes to feel failure and be left to themselves. God wants us to know that he keeps us equally safe in sorrow and in joy. And for the benefit of his soul a man is sometimes left to himself, although sin is not always the cause;* for at this time I committed no sin for which I ought to be left to myself, for it was all so sudden. Nor did I deserve to have the feeling of bliss. But our Lord gives freely when he wills, and sometimes allows us to be in sorrow—and both come from one love. For it is God's will that we keep ourselves in good spirits with all our might, for bliss lasts forever, and pain passes and will come to nothing for those who are to be saved.* And therefore it is not God's will that we should be influenced by feelings of pain to sorrow and grieve over them, but quickly pass beyond them and hold on to the endless joy that is God.

16

The eighth revelation is of the piteous final sufferings of Christ when dying, and of the discolouring of his face and drying of his flesh.

AFTER this Christ showed part of his Passion, close to his death. I saw his dear face as it was dry and bloodless with the pallor of death; and then more deathly pale, in anguish, and then turning blue as death advanced, and afterwards a darker blue* as death took more hold on his flesh. For his Passion was revealed to me most distinctly in his blessed face, and especially in his lips. There I saw these four colours, which before had appeared fresh and ruddy, full of life and lovely to see.

This was a grievous change, to see this deep dying, and also, as it seemed to me, the nose shrivelled and dried up, and the dear body was brown and black, completely transformed from his fair living colour as it dried out in death. For at that same time that our Lord and blessed Saviour was dying on the cross, it seemed to me that there was a dry, keen wind and terribly cold;* and it was revealed that when all the precious blood that could bleed from the dear body had bled from it, there still remained some moisture in Christ's dear flesh. Loss of blood and pain drying him inside, and the blowing of the wind and cold coming from outside, met together in the dear body of Christ. And these four, two externally, and two internally, dried up Christ's flesh over the process of time. And though this pain was bitter and sharp, it seemed to me that it lasted for a very long time and painfully dried out all the vitality* in Christ's flesh.

So I saw the dear flesh dying, seemingly bit by bit, drying up with astonishing suffering. And as long as any vital spirit remained in Christ's flesh, he went on suffering pain. This protracted torment made it seem to me as if he had been dead for a week, dying, at the point of passing away, continually suffering the last throes. And when I said it seemed to me as if he had been dead for a week, that means that the dear body was as discoloured, as dry, as shrivelled, as deathly, and as pitiful as if he had been dead for a week, yet continually dying.* And it seemed to me that the drying of Christ's flesh was the greatest pain, and the last, of his Passion.*

17

Concerning Christ's grievous bodily thirst, caused in four ways; and of his piteous crowning; and of the greatest pain to one who loves kindly.

AND in this drying there came to my mind Christ's words: 'I thirst.'* For I saw in Christ a double thirst:* one bodily, the other spiritual (of which I shall speak in the thirty-first chapter). For in these words the bodily thirst was revealed, and I shall say later what was revealed concerning the spiritual thirst. And I understood by its bodily thirst that the body had a lack of moisture, because the blessed flesh and bones were left all alone, bereft of blood and moisture. The blessed body was left alone to dry for a long time, being wrenched by the nails and the weight of the body. For I understood that because of the tenderness of the dear hands and the dear feet, and because the nails were so big, hard, and rough, the wounds grew wider and the body sagged under its own weight* through hanging there for a long time, along with the piercing and twisting of the head and the binding of the crown of thorns, all baked with dry blood, with the dear hair and the dry flesh clinging to the thorns, and the thorns to the dying flesh.

And at the beginning, while the flesh was fresh and bleeding, the continual pressure of the thorns made the wounds wide. And furthermore I saw that the dear skin and the tender flesh, with the hair and the blood, was all lifted and loosened away from the bone by the thorns with which it had been slashed in many places, like a sagging cloth, as if it would soon have fallen off because it was so heavy and loose while it retained its natural moisture. And that caused me great sorrow and fear, for I thought I would sooner have died than see it fall. How this was done I did not see, but I understood it was caused by the sharp thorns, and the rough and agonizing imposition of the crown of thorns, pitilessly and unsparingly.

This continued for a while and soon it began to change, and I watched and marvelled at how it could be. And then I saw that it was because it began to dry and lose part of its weight and congeal around the garland of thorns.* And so it encircled his head all around, as if it were garland upon garland. The garland of thorns was dyed with the blood, and this other garland and the head were all one colour, like congealed blood when it is dry. Where it showed, the skin of the flesh on his face and body was fine, wrinkled, with a tanned colour* like a dry board which has aged; and the face darker than the body.

I saw four ways in which the body dried: the first was loss of blood; the second was the consequent torment; the third, being hung up in the air as a cloth is hung up to dry;* the fourth, that his bodily nature required fluids, and no kind of comfort was offered to him in all his distress and pain. Ah, cruel and grievous was his pain, but it was much more cruel and grievous when the moisture ran out and everything began to dry and shrivel in this way. These were the sufferings that were revealed in the blessed head: the first caused by the drying while the body was still moist; and the other was slow, with shrinking as it dried,* and with the blowing of the wind from outside which dried him and tormented him more with cold than my heart can imagine; and then other pains, but I saw that all that I can say of them is inadequate, for those pains cannot be described.

The revelation of Christ's pains filled me full of pain, for I was well aware that he only suffered once,* but he wanted to show it to me and fill me with the recollection of it, as I had earlier wished. And in all this time that Christ was present to me, I felt no pain except for Christ's pains. Then I thought to myself, 'I little knew what pain it was that I asked for',* and like a wretch I regretted it, thinking, 'If I had known what it would be like, I would have been reluctant to pray for it',* for it seemed to me that my pains exceeded bodily death. I thought, 'Is any pain in hell like this?'* And in my reason I was answered, 'Hell is a different pain, for despair is there. But of all the pains which lead to salvation, this is the greatest: to see your love suffer.'* How could any pain be greater to me than to see him suffer who is my whole life, all my bliss, and all my joy? Here I truly felt that I loved Christ so much more than myself that there was no pain that could be suffered like that sorrow I felt to see him in pain.

18

Concerning the spiritual martyrdom of our Lady and other lovers of Christ, and how all things suffered with him, good and bad.

HERE I saw part of the compassion of our Lady, Saint Mary, for Christ and she were so united in love that the greatness of her love caused the greatness of her pain. For in this I saw the essence of natural love, maintained by grace, which all creatures have for him. This natural love was most abundantly and surpassingly shown in his dear mother, for in so much as she loved him more than anyone else, her sufferings surpassed those of all others. For the higher, the stronger, the dearer the love is, the greater the sorrow it is to the lover to see in pain the body that is loved. And all his disciples, and all who truly loved him, suffered pains greater than their own bodily dying; for I am sure, from how I feel myself, that the least of them loved him so far above themselves that it surpasses all that I can say.

Here I saw a great affinity between Christ and us, as I understand it; for when he was in pain, we were in pain. And all creatures capable of suffering pain suffered with him; that is to say, all the creatures that God has created to serve us. The firmament and the earth failed out of sorrow in their very nature at the moment of Christ's death;* for it is natural to them to recognize him as their God, in whom all their powers have their foundation. When he failed, then their natures obliged them to fail with him as much as they could, out of sorrow at his sufferings. And so those who were his friends suffered pain because of love. And everyone in general—that is to say, including those who did not know of him—suffered from a failure of every kind of comfort, except for the mighty and mysterious safekeeping of God. I have in mind two kinds of people,* as may be understood by the example of two individuals: one was Pontius Pilate,* and the other was Saint Dionysius of France,* who at that time was a pagan. For when he saw the marvellous and wonderful sorrows and terrors which happened at that time, he said, 'Either the world is coming to an end, or else he who is the creator of nature is suffering.' Therefore he had written upon an altar: 'This is the altar of the unknown God.' God who in his goodness makes the planets and the elements function in their nature for the blessed and for the damned withdrew that goodness from both at that time. So it was that those who did not know him were in sorrow at that time.

So was our Lord Jesus set at nought for us, and we all remain in this way as if set at nought with him, and shall do until we come to his bliss, as I shall say later.

19

Concerning the comforting contemplation of the crucifix; and how desire of the flesh without consent of the soul is no sin; and the flesh must be in pain, suffering, until both flesh and spirit be united in Christ.

AT this time I wanted to look up from the cross and I did not dare, for I well knew that while I contemplated the cross I was safe and secure; therefore I would not agree to put my soul in danger, for apart from the cross there was no safety against the horror of fiends.

Then I thought my reason suggested to me, as if there had been said to me in a friendly way:* 'Look up to heaven to his Father.' And then I saw clearly, with the faith that I felt, that there was nothing between the cross and heaven which could have distressed me. Either I must look up or else reply. I answered inwardly with all my soul's strength and said, 'No, I cannot, for you are my heaven.'* I said this because I did not want to look up; for I would rather have remained in that pain until Judgement Day than come to heaven in any other way than by him; for I well knew that he who held me bound so sorely would unbind me when he wished.

So I was taught to choose Jesus for my heaven, whom I saw only in pain at that time. No other heaven pleased me but Jesus, who will be my bliss when I come there. And this has always been a comfort to me, that I chose Jesus for my heaven, through his grace, in all this time of suffering and sorrow. And that has been a lesson to me that I should do so for evermore: to choose only Jesus for my heaven in both happiness and sorrow.

And though, like a wretch, I felt regret—I said before, if I had known what pain there would be, I would have been reluctant to pray as I did—I now saw truly that this was the grumbling and cursing of the flesh, without the soul's agreement, to which God attributes no blame. Regret and conscious choice are two opposites, which I felt both together at that time; and these are in two parts: one outward, and the other inward. The outward part is our mortal flesh, which is now in pain and sorrow, and will be in this life, and I felt this a great deal at this time, and this was the part of me that felt regret. The inward part is an exalted and blessed life which is all peace and love, and this was more mysteriously experienced; and this is the part in which I strongly, certainly, and willingly chose Jesus for my heaven.

And in this I truly saw that the inward part is master and ruler of the outward part, neither heeding nor attaching any weight to what the outward part may want, but fixing all intention and desire on being united with our Lord Jesus forever. It was not revealed to me that the outward part would lead the inward part to conform; but that the inward part leads the outward part, through grace, and that both shall be united in bliss without end through the power of Christ—this was revealed.

20

Concerning the indescribable Passion of Christ, and three things about the Passion to be always remembered.

AND so I saw our Lord Jesus lingering for a long time; because the union in him with the Godhead gave strength to his humanity to suffer for love more than all men could suffer. I do not mean only more pain than all men could suffer, but also that he suffered more pain than could be expressed or fully imagined by all those who are to be saved who ever existed from the very beginning until the last day, considering the worth of the highest, most glorious king and his shameful, humiliating, and painful death; for he who is highest and noblest was brought most low and most utterly despised.* For the most fundamental implication to consider in the Passion is to recognize and comprehend what he is who suffered, also bearing in mind two lesser considerations: one is what he suffered, and the other is for whom he suffered.

And in this he brought to mind some part of the exaltedness and nobility of the glorious Godhead, along with the preciousness and the tenderness of the blessed body, which are united together, and also the reluctance in our human nature to suffer pain. For just as he was most tender and pure, so he was strongest and most mighty to suffer. And he suffered for the sins of everyone who shall be saved; and he saw everyone's sorrow and desolation and sorrowed out of kindness and love. For in as much as our Lady sorrowed over his sufferings, he suffered as much for her sorrows,* and more, in as much as his precious humanity was of its nature more excellent. For as long as he was liable to suffer, he suffered for us and sorrowed for us; and now he is risen again and no longer liable to suffering, he still suffers with us.

And I, contemplating all this through his grace, saw that his love for our souls was so strong that he chose to suffer willingly, and with great longing for that, and meekly suffered with great satisfaction. For the soul that contemplates in this way, when touched by grace, shall truly see that the pains of Christ's Passion surpass all pains; that is to say, those pains will be turned into surpassing and everlasting joys* by virtue of Christ's Passion.

21

Concerning three ways of regarding the Passion of Christ, and how we are now dying on the cross with Christ, but his countenance dispels all pain.

IT is God's will, as I understand it, that we should have three ways of contemplating his blessed Passion.* The first is that we should contemplate with contrition and compassion the cruel pain that he suffered; and our Lord revealed that at this time and gave me the power and grace to see it. And I watched with all my might for the moment of his passing away and expected to see the body quite dead, but I did not see him so. And just at the very moment when, to all appearances, it seemed to me that life could last no longer and there must be a revelation of his end, suddenly, as I was looking at the same cross, his blessed countenance changed.* The change in his blessed expression changed mine, and I was as glad and happy as it is possible to be. Then our Lord brought to mind the happy thought, 'Is there any point now to your pain or your sorrow?' And I was very happy.

I understood that we are now—in our Lord's intention—dying on his cross with him in our pain and our sufferings;* and if we remain willingly on the same cross with his help and his grace until the last moment, he will suddenly change his expression towards us, and we will be with him in heaven. Between one moment and the next there will be no time, and then everything will be turned to joy; and this is what he meant in this revelation, 'Is there any point now to your pain or your sorrow?' And we shall be wholly blessed.

And here I truly saw that if he showed us now his blessed countenance there is no pain on earth, nor in any other place, that could afflict us, but everything would be joy and bliss for us. But because he shows us a time of suffering such as he bore in this life and on his cross, we are therefore in distress and hardship with him, as our human frailty demands. And the reason why he suffers is because he wishes, in his goodness, to raise us the higher with him in his bliss; and for this little pain which we suffer here we shall have an exalted, endless knowledge in God, which we could never have without that. And the harder our sufferings have been with him on his cross, the greater will be our glory with him in his kingdom.

22

The ninth revelation is of Christ's being pleased, etc.; of three heavens, and of the infinite love of Christ, willing to suffer for us every day if he could, although it is not necessary.

THEN our good Lord Jesus Christ spoke, asking, 'Are you well pleased that I suffered for you?'

I said, 'Yes, good Lord, thank you. Yes, good Lord, blessed may you be!'

Then Jesus, our kind Lord, said, 'If you are pleased, I am pleased. It is a joy, a bliss, an endless delight to me that I ever suffered my Passion for you; and if I could suffer more, I would suffer more.'*

In experiencing this my understanding was lifted up into heaven, and there I saw three heavens,* and was amazed at the sight. And though I saw three heavens, and all are of the blessed humanity of Christ, none is greater, none is less, none is higher, none is lower, but all are equal in bliss.

For the first heaven Christ showed me his Father, in no bodily likeness but as he is in his nature and in his actions; that is to say, I saw in Christ what the Father is.* This is the action of the Father: that he rewards his son, Jesus Christ. This gift and this reward causes Jesus such joy that his Father could have given him no reward that could have pleased him better. The first heaven, which is the pleasing of the Father, appeared to me as a heaven, and it was full of bliss, for he is highly pleased with all the deeds that Jesus has done with regard to our salvation;* and therefore we are not only his through his redemption of us, but also through his Father's courteous gift* we are his bliss, we are his reward, we are his glory, we are his crown*—and this was an especial marvel and a most delectable vision, that we are his crown! What I am describing is such great joy to Jesus that he counts as nothing all his affliction and his keen suffering and his cruel and shameful death.

And in these words—'If I could suffer more, I would suffer more'— I truly saw that he was willing to die just as often as he was able to die, and love would never let him rest until he had done it. And I watched very attentively to know how often he would die if he could, and truly, the number so far exceeded my understanding and my intelligence that my reason had neither power nor knowledge to comprehend it. And when he had died, or would die, so often, he would still think nothing of it, out of love; for everything seems insignificant to him in comparison with his love. For though the precious humanity of Christ could only suffer once, the goodness in him can never cease from offering to do so; he is ready to do the same every day, if that might be. For if he said that, for love of me, he would make new heavens and a new earth,* that would only be small in comparison, for he could do this every day if he wished, without any effort. But to die for love of me so often that the number passes human understanding, that is the noblest offer that our Lord God could make to man's soul, as I see it. This, then, is his meaning, 'How could it then be that I should not do all I could for love of you? To do so does not grieve me, since I would die so often for love of you, without regard to my cruel pains.'

70 *Revelations of Divine Love*

And this I saw as the second way of contemplating this blessed Passion: the love that made him suffer surpasses all his pains as far as heaven is above earth; for the suffering was a noble, glorious deed performed at one time through his action of love. And love was without beginning, is, and shall be without end. On account of this love he very lovingly said these words, 'If I could suffer more, I would suffer more.' He did not say, 'If it were necessary to suffer more',* but, 'If I could suffer more.' For even if it were not necessary, if he could suffer more, he would. This deed and this work for our salvation was ordered as well as God could order it. It was done as gloriously as Christ could do it. And here I saw complete joy in Christ, for his bliss could not have been complete if the deed might have been done any better than it was done.

23

How Christ wishes us to rejoice greatly with him in our redemption and to long for his grace that we may do so.

AND in these three sayings—'It is a joy, a bliss, an endless delight to me'—were shown three heavens, as follows: by the joy, I understood the pleasure of the Father; and by the bliss, the glory of the Son; and by the endless delight, the Holy Spirit. The Father is pleased, the Son is glorified, and the Holy Spirit takes delight.

And here I saw* the third way of contemplating his blessed Passion: that is to say, the joy and the bliss that cause him to take pleasure in it. For our courteous Lord showed me his Passion in five ways: the first is the bleeding of the head, the second is the discolouring of his face, the third is the copious bleeding of the body in weals from the scourging, the fourth is the deep drying—these four have already been described as the pains of the Passion—and the fifth is what was revealed about the joy and the bliss of the Passion.

For it is God's will that we take true delight with him in our salvation, and in this he wants us to be greatly comforted and strengthened, and through his grace he wishes our souls to be happily occupied in this; for we are his bliss; he delights in us without end, and so shall we in him, through his grace. And all that he has done for us, and does, and always shall, was never a cost nor burden to him, nor ever could be; only excepting what he did in our humanity, beginning at the precious incarnation and lasting until the blessed resurrection on Easter morning. So long indeed endured his cost and burden concerning our redemption, in which deed he eternally rejoices, as has been said before.

Jesus wishes us to pay heed to the delight that there is in the blessed Trinity about our salvation, and that we should long to have as much spiritual pleasure, through his grace, as has been said before:* that is to say, that our pleasure in our salvation should be like the joy that Christ has in our salvation, as much as that may be whilst we are here. All the Trinity was at work in the Passion of Christ, ministering abundance of virtues and plenitude of grace to us through him, but only the Virgin's son suffered; and at this the whole blessed Trinity rejoices eternally.* And this was shown in these words, 'Are you well pleased?', and by the other words that Christ said, 'If you are pleased, then I am pleased'—as if he said, 'It is joy and delight enough to die, and I ask nothing else from you for my suffering but that I may please you.'*

And in this he brought to mind the character of a glad giver:* a glad giver pays little attention to what he is giving, but his whole desire and his whole intention is to please and comfort the one to whom he is giving it; and if the recipient accepts the gift appreciatively and gratefully, then the courteous giver thinks nothing of all his expense and all his trouble because of the joy and delight that he feels at having pleased and comforted the one that he loves. This was revealed to me abundantly and in full.

Think seriously too about the magnitude of this word 'ever';* for in that was revealed an exalted understanding of the love that he shows in our salvation, with the manifold joys that follow from the Passion of Christ. One is that he rejoices that he has indeed done it, and he will suffer no more; another, that he brought us up into heaven and made us his crown and endless bliss; another is that with this he has redeemed us from endless torments in hell.

24

The tenth revelation is that our Lord Jesus lovingly reveals his blessed heart riven in two, and rejoices.

THEN with a glad expression our Lord looked into his side and gazed, rejoicing; and with his dear gaze he led his creature's understanding through the same wound into his side within.* And then he revealed a beautiful and delightful place, large enough for all mankind that will be saved to rest there in peace and in love.* And with that he brought to mind his beloved blood and precious water which he let pour all out for love. And with the precious vision he showed his blessed heart quite riven in two.

And with this sweet rejoicing* he revealed in part to my understanding the blessed Godhead, as far as he would at that time, strengthening then the poor soul to understand, as far as it may be expressed: that is to say, the meaning of the endless love which was without beginning, and is, and always shall be. And with this our good Lord said most blessedly, 'Look how I loved you', as if he had said, 'My darling, look and see your Lord, your God, who is your maker and your endless joy. My darling, look and see your own brother, your sovereign. My child, look and see your Lord God, your creator and your endless joy. See what delight and bliss I have in your salvation, and for my love rejoice with me now.'

And also, for my greater understanding, these blessed words were said, 'Look how I loved you', as if he had said, 'Look and see that I loved you so much before I died for you, that I was willing to die for you; and now I have died for you, and willingly suffered what I could. And now all my bitter pain and all my hard labour is turned into endless joy and bliss for me and for you. How could it now be that you could pray to me for anything that pleased me which I would not very gladly grant you? For my delight is your holiness* and your endless joy and bliss with me.'

This is my understanding, as simply as I can express it, of these blessed words, 'Look how I loved you.' Our good Lord revealed this to make us glad and joyful.

25

The eleventh revelation is an exalted spiritual revelation concerning his mother.

AND with this same expression of gladness and joy our good Lord looked down on his right side* and brought to my mind where our Lady stood during his Passion, and he said, 'Would you like to see her?' as if he had said, with these sweet words, 'I well know you would like to see my blessed mother, for after myself she is the highest joy that I could show you, and the greatest delight and honour to me; and it is she that my blessed creatures most desire to see.' And because of the exalted, marvellous, special love that he has for this sweet virgin, his blessed mother, our Lady Saint Mary, he showed her highly rejoicing, which is the meaning of these sweet words, as if he had said, 'Would you like to see how I love her, so that you can rejoice with me in the love that I have for her and she for me?'

And also, for greater understanding of these sweet words, our Lord God speaks to all mankind who will be saved as though to one person, as if he said, 'Would you like to see in her how you are loved? For love of you I made her so exalted, so noble, and of such worth; and this delights me, and I want it to delight you.' For after himself she is the most blessed sight. But I was not taught by this to long to see her bodily presence* while I am here, but the virtues of her blessed soul: her truth, her wisdom, her love, through which I may learn to know myself and reverently fear my God.

And when our good Lord had revealed this and said these words—'Would you like to see her?'*—I answered and said, 'Yes, good Lord, thank you. Yes, good Lord, if it be your will.' I prayed for this very often, and I expected to see her present bodily, but I did not see her like that. And with those words Jesus showed me a spiritual vision of her. Just as I had seen her small and simple before, so now he showed her high, and noble, and glorious,* and pleasing to him above all other created beings. And he wishes it to be known that all those who delight in him should delight in her, and in the delight that he has in her and she in him.

And for greater understanding he gave this example: if a man loves someone uniquely above all other creatures, he wants to make all creatures love and delight in that creature whom he loves so much. And these words that Jesus said—'Would you like to see her?'—seemed to me the most pleasing words about her that he could have conveyed to me with the spiritual vision of her which he gave me. For our Lord gave me no revelation about any particular individual, except our Lady Saint Mary; and he showed her three times:* the first was as she conceived, the second was as she was in her sorrows at the foot of the cross, and the third was as she is now, in delight, honour, and joy.

26

The twelfth revelation is that the Lord our God is supreme being.

AND after this our Lord showed himself yet more glorified, as it seemed to me, than I had seen him before, and I learned from this that our soul will never find rest* until it comes to him, recognizing that he is the fullness of joy, familiar and courteous, full of bliss, and true life itself.

Our Lord Jesus often said, 'It is I.* It is I. It is I who am highest. It is I you love. It is I you delight in. It is I you serve. It is I you long for. It is I you desire. It is I who am your purpose. It is I who am all. It is I that Holy Church preaches and teaches you. It is I who showed myself to you here.'

The number of words transcended my wits and all my understanding, and all my powers, for they are the most exalted, as it seems to me, for I cannot tell what they comprehend; but the joy that I saw when they were revealed surpasses all that heart may wish and soul may desire.* And therefore the words are not explained here; but may everyone, according to the grace that God gives him in understanding and loving, receive them as our Lord intended.

27

The thirteenth revelation is that our Lord God wishes us to have great regard to all his deeds that he has done in creating all things with great nobility; and how sin is only recognized by the suffering.

AFTER this, the Lord brought to mind the longing that I had for him before;* and I saw that nothing held me back except sin, and I saw that this is so with all of us in general. And it seemed to me that if there had been no sin, we should all have been pure and like our Lord, as he made us; and so, in my folly, I had often wondered before this time why, through the great foreseeing wisdom of God, the beginning of sin was not prevented; for then, it seemed to me, all would have been well. I should have given up such thoughts, yet I grieved and sorrowed over this, unreasonably and without discretion.* But Jesus, who in this vision informed me of everything needful to me, answered with these words and said, 'Sin is befitting,* but all shall be well, and all shall be well,* and all manner of things shall be well.'

In this unadorned word 'sin', our Lord brought to mind everything in general which is not good, and the shameful scorn and the uttermost abnegation that he bore for us in this life, and his dying, and all the pains and sufferings in body and spirit of all his creatures—for we are all in part set at nought,* and we shall be set at nought, following the example of our master Jesus, until we are fully purged: that is to say, until our mortal flesh is made as nothing, and all our inward feelings which are not truly good. And in contemplating this, together with all the sufferings that ever were or ever shall be, I understand Christ's Passion as the greatest and most surpassing suffering. And all this was shown in an instant and quickly turned into consolation; for our good Lord did not wish the soul to be frightened by this ugly sight.

But I did not see sin, for I believe it has no kind of substance nor share of being, nor could it be recognized except by the suffering it causes.* And, as it seems to me, this suffering is something that exists for a while, because it purges us and makes us know ourselves and ask for mercy, for the Passion of our Lord is a comfort to us against all this, and that is his blessed will. And because of the tender love which our good Lord has for all who shall be saved,* he comforts us readily and sweetly, meaning this, 'It is true that sin is cause of all this suffering, but all shall be well, and all shall be well, and all manner of things shall be well.'

These words were said very tenderly, indicating no kind of blame* for me or for anyone who will be saved. So it would be most unkind to blame God or marvel at him because of my sin, since he does not blame me for sin.

And in these same words I saw a marvellous and exalted mystery hidden in God,* a mystery which he will make openly known to us in heaven, in which knowledge we shall truly see the reason why he allowed sin to come about; and in the sight of this we shall rejoice in our Lord God forever.*

28

How the children of salvation shall be shaken by sorrows, but Christ rejoices with compassion; and a remedy against tribulation.

So I saw how Christ has compassion on us because of sin. And just as I was previously filled with suffering and compassion at Christ's

Passion, so now I was filled in part with compassion for all my fellow Christians;* for these beloved people who will be saved—that is to say, God's servants, Holy Church—will be shaken by sorrows and anguish and tribulation in this world, as a cloth is shaken in the wind.* And concerning this, our Lord responded in this way, 'I shall make a great thing out of this in heaven, a great thing of endless glories and everlasting joys.'

Yes, I was able to see as much as this: that our Lord rejoices with pity and compassion over the tribulations of his servants.* To bring to his bliss each person whom he loves, he lays on them something which is no defect in his sight, on account of which they are disparaged and despised in this world, scorned, abused, and rejected. And he does this to prevent the damage that they would receive from the pomp and vainglory of this wretched life, and to prepare their way to come to heaven, and raise them to his everlasting bliss. For he says, 'I shall completely break you* of your empty passions and your vicious pride; and afterwards I shall gather you together and make you humble and meek, pure and holy, through union with me.'

And then I saw that each instance of kind compassion that a man feels for his fellow Christians out of love—it is Christ in him.* That same humbling which was revealed in his Passion was revealed again here in this compassion, in which there were two ways of understanding our Lord's meaning. One was the bliss to which we are brought, in which he wants us to rejoice. The other is for comfort in our suffering; for he wants us to know that it will all be turned to glory and advantage by virtue of his Passion, and to know that we do not suffer alone but with him, and to see in him our foundation, and to see that his pains and his self-abnegation so far surpass all that we may suffer that it cannot be fully comprehended. And to contemplate this will save us from grumbling and despair when we experience our suffering; and if we truly see that our sins deserve it, his love still excuses us, and out of his great courtesy he sets aside all our blame, and he regards us with compassion and pity as children, innocent and guileless.

29

Adam's sin was the greatest, but the reparation for it is more pleasing to God than the sin was ever harmful.

BUT I stayed contemplating this generally, sorrowfully, and mournfully, addressing our Lord in this way in my thoughts in very great awe, 'Ah, good Lord, how could all be well, in view of the great harm which has come upon your creatures through sin?' And in this I wished, as much as I dared, to receive some clearer explanation to set my mind at ease about this. And our blessed Lord answered to this very compassionately and in a very loving manner, and showed that Adam's sin was the greatest harm that was ever done,* or ever shall be, until the end of the world; and he also showed that this is openly acknowledged throughout all Holy Church upon earth.

Furthermore, he taught that I should contemplate the glorious atonement; for this atonement is incomparably more pleasing to the blessed Godhead and more glorious for the salvation of mankind than Adam's sin was ever harmful. So our blessed Lord's meaning in this teaching is that we should take heed of this: 'Since I have set right what was the greatest harm, it is my will that you should know by this that I shall set right all that is less harmful.'

30

How we should rejoice and trust in our Saviour Jesus, not presuming to know his secret counsels.

HE gave me to understand about the two parts of this.* One is our Saviour and our salvation. This blessed part is open and clear, and fair and light and abundant, for all mankind who are and shall be of good will are comprehended in this part. We are bound to this by God, and drawn and counselled and taught, inwardly by the Holy Spirit, and outwardly by Holy Church, through the same grace. Our Lord wants us to be occupied with this, rejoicing in him for he rejoices in us. And the more abundantly that we draw on this, with reverence and humility, the more thanks we deserve from him and the more benefit to ourselves, and thus we may say, rejoicing, 'Our Lord is our portion.'*

The other part is hidden and barred to us: that is to say, everything which is over and above our salvation; for this is our Lord's private counsels,* and it is fitting for the royal lordship of God to keep his private counsels undisturbed, and it is fitting for his servant, out of obedience and respect, not to wish to know his counsels. Our Lord has pity and compassion on us, because some people busy themselves so anxiously about this; and I am sure that if we knew how much we should please him and set our minds at rest by leaving it alone, we would do so. The saints in heaven wish to know nothing but what our Lord wishes to reveal to them, and their love and their desires are governed according to our Lord's will; and so we ought to wish to be like them. Then we shall not wish nor desire anything except the will of our Lord, just as they do; for we are all one in God's purposes.

And here I was taught that we are to trust and rejoice only in our Saviour, blessed Jesus, for everything.

31

Concerning the longing and the spiritual thirst of Christ, which lasts and shall last until Judgement Day; and because of his body he is not yet fully glorified; nor is he yet entirely beyond the possibility of suffering.

AND so our good Lord answered all the questions and doubts that I could raise, saying most comfortingly, 'I may make all things well; I can make all things well, and I will make all things well, and I shall make all things well; and you will see for yourself that all manner of things shall be well.' Where he says 'I may', I understand this to apply to the Father; and where he says 'I can', I understand it to apply to the Son; and where he says 'I will', I understand it to apply to the Holy Spirit; and where he says 'I shall', I take it for the unity of the blessed Trinity, three persons and one truth; and where he says 'You will see for yourself', I understand it to refer to the union with the blessed Trinity of all mankind who shall be saved.

And with these five sayings God wishes us to be enfolded in rest and in peace; and so Christ's spiritual thirst will come to an end.* For this is the spiritual thirst of Christ: the love-longing that lasts and ever shall, until we see that revelation on Judgement Day. For some of us who shall be saved, and shall be Christ's joy and his bliss, are still here, and some are yet to come, and so will some be until that day.* Therefore this is his thirst: a love-longing* to have us all together wholly in him to his delight, as it seems to me; for we are not now so fully, so wholly, in him as we shall be then.

For we know through our faith, and it was also revealed in all this, that Christ Jesus is both God and man. And as regards the Godhead, he is himself the highest bliss, and was from without beginning, and shall be without end; and this endless bliss may never be heightened nor diminished in itself. For this was abundantly seen in every revelation, and especially in the twelfth, where he says, 'It is I who am highest.'* And as regards Christ's humanity, it is known through our faith, and also revealed, that he, through the power of the Godhead, to bring us to his bliss for love, underwent pains and sufferings, and died. And these are the deeds of Christ's humanity, in which he rejoices, and he revealed that in the ninth revelation, where he says, 'It is a joy, a bliss, an endless delight to me that I ever suffered my Passion for you.'* And this is the bliss of Christ's deeds, and this is what he means where he says in the same revelation: we are his bliss, we are his reward, we are his glory, we are his crown.

For regarding Christ as our head,* he is glorified and no longer liable to suffering; but with respect to his body, in which all his members are joined,* he is not yet fully glorified or beyond being liable to suffer. For the same thirst and longing which he had on the cross—a thirst, yearning, and longing which, as it seems to me, were in him from without beginning—the same he still has, and will do until the last soul which is to be saved has come up to his bliss.

For as truly as there is a property of compassion and pity in God, so truly there is a property of thirst and longing. And because of the power of this longing in Christ, it is for us to long for him in return, and without this no soul comes to heaven. And this property of thirst and longing comes from the endless goodness of God, just as the property of pity comes from his endless goodness, although longing and pity are two different properties, as it seems to me; and in this goodness consists the essence of the spiritual thirst, which lasts in him as long as we are in need, drawing us up to his bliss.*

And all this was seen in the revelation of compassion, for that will cease on Judgement Day. So he has pity and compassion for us, and he longs to have us, but his wisdom and his love do not allow the end to come until the best time.

32

How all things shall be well, and scripture fulfilled; and we must keep ourselves steadfastly in the faith of Holy Church, as is the will of Christ.

AT one time our good Lord said, 'All things shall be well'; and another time he said, 'You will see for yourself that all manner of things shall be well'; and from these two the soul derived different understandings. One was this: that he wants us to know that he takes heed not only of noble and great things, but also of the little and small, the humble and simple, both the one and the other. And this is what he means when he says, 'All manner of things shall be well.' For he wants us to know that the smallest thing will not be forgotten. This is another understanding: we see evil deeds done and such great harm inflicted that it seems impossible to us that any good could ever come out of this. And we witness this, sorrowing and grieving over it, so that we cannot repose in the blessed contemplation of God as we should do. And this is the cause: that our use of our reason is now so blind, so base, and so uninformed, that we cannot recognize the high, marvellous wisdom, the power, and the goodness of the blessed Trinity. And this is what he means where he says, 'You will see for yourself that all manner of things shall be well', as if he said, 'Take heed now, faithfully and trustingly, and on the last day you will truly see it in fullness of joy.' And so in these same five sayings mentioned previously*—'I may make all things well', etc.—I understand there to be great comfort concerning all the works of our Lord God which are to come.

There is a deed which the blessed Trinity will do on the last day, as it seems to me, and when the deed will be, and how it will be done, is unknown to all creatures under Christ,* and will be until it is done. The goodness and the love of our Lord God wishes us to know that it will be; and his power and wisdom, through the same love, wishes to conceal and hide from us what it will be and how it will be done. And the reason he wants us to know is because he wants us to be the more at ease in our souls and at peace in love, rejoicing in him and disregarding all the stormy tumults that might keep us from the truth. This is the great deed ordained by our Lord God from without beginning, treasured and hidden in his blessed breast, known only to himself, and through this deed he will make all things well.* For just as the blessed Trinity made all things from nothing, so the same blessed Trinity will make all well that is not well.

And I wondered a great deal about this revelation and reflected on our faith, wondering in this way: our faith is founded on God's word,* and it is part of our faith that we believe that God's word will be kept in all things.* And one article of our faith is that many will be damned*—such as the angels who fell out of heaven because of pride, who are now devils; and those on earth who die outside the faith of Holy Church (that is to say, those who are heathens, and also those who have received baptism and live an unchristian life and so die excluded from the love of God)—all these will be condemned eternally to hell, as Holy Church teaches me to believe. And considering all this, it seemed impossible to me that all manner of things should be well, as our Lord revealed at this time. And to this I received no other answer by way of revelation from our Lord God except this: 'What is impossible to you is not impossible to me. I shall keep my word in all things, and I shall make all things well.'*

So I was taught by the grace of God that I should hold steadfastly to the faith as I had previously understood, and at the same time that I should firmly believe that all things shall be well, as our Lord revealed at that time. For this is the great deed that our Lord shall do, and in this deed he will keep his word in all things, and he will make well all that is not well. But what the deed will be, and how it will be done, there is no creature under Christ that knows it, or shall know it, until it is done, according to the understanding which I formed of our Lord's meaning at this time.

33

All damned souls are despised in the sight of God as the devil is; and these revelations do not detract from the faith of Holy Church but support it; and the more anxious we are to know God's secrets, the less we know.

AND yet in all this I desired, as far as I dared, to have had a full view of hell and purgatory. But it was not my intention to put to the test anything that pertains to our faith—for I truly believed that hell and purgatory are for the same purpose as Holy Church teaches—but my intention was to have seen them in order to learn everything that pertains to my faith, so that I could live more to God's glory and to my benefit spiritually. But however much I might wish, I could see nothing at all about this, except what has already been said in the fifth revelation, where I saw that the devil is scorned by God and damned forever.* Through this revelation I understood that all those who are of the devil's condition in this life and end in that state are no more mentioned before God and his holy ones than the devil is,* despite their being of humankind, whether they have been baptized or not.

For though the revelation was of goodness, in which there was little mention of evil, I was still not drawn away by it from any article of the faith that Holy Church teaches me to believe. For I had sight of Christ's Passion in various revelations*—in the first, in the second, in the fourth, and in the eighth—as has been said before,* in which I felt in part the sorrow of our Lady and of his true friends who saw him suffering. But I did not see indicated so particularly the Jews who put him to death,* even though I knew from my faith that they were eternally accursed and damned, except for those who were converted by grace. And I was fortified and generally instructed to hold to every article of the faith, and to everything as I had previously understood it, hoping that I was within that faith with God's mercy and grace, longing and praying that I might continue in it until the end of my life, as I intended.

And it is God's will that we should have great regard to all the deeds that he has done, for by doing so he wants us to know, trust, and believe all that he will do. But we always need to stop ourselves considering what the deed will be. And let us wish to be like our brethren who are saints in heaven, who wish for nothing at all but God's will.* Then we shall rejoice only in God and be well pleased both with what is hidden and with what is revealed. For I truly saw our Lord's intention: the more we busy ourselves to know his secrets in this or anything else, the further we shall be from knowing.

34

God reveals the mysteries needful for those who love him; and how they greatly please God who diligently receive the preaching of Holy Church.

OUR Lord God revealed two kinds of mystery.* One is this great mystery, along with all the secret details relating to it, and these mysteries he wants us to acknowledge as hidden until the time when he wishes to reveal them to us clearly. The other kind are the mysteries which he himself revealed openly in this revelation, for these are mysteries which he wants to make openly known to us; for he wants us to know that it is his will that we know them. They are mysteries to us not only because he wants them to be mysteries to us, but they are mysteries to us because of our blindness and our ignorance; and he feels great pity because of this, and therefore he himself wishes to make them more open to us, so that we may know him, and love him, and cling to him. For everything helpful for us to know and understand, our Lord will most courteously show us, and what it is, through all the preaching and teaching of Holy Church.

God showed the very great pleasure that he takes in all men and women who strongly and humbly and willingly receive the preaching and teaching of Holy Church. For he is Holy Church: he is the foundation, he is the substance, he is the teaching, he is the teacher, he is the goal, he is the reward for which every naturally well-disposed soul strives; and this is known and will be known to every soul to whom the Holy Spirit makes it known. And I truly expect that all those who seek in this way shall prosper, for they are seeking God.

All this that I have now said, and more that I shall say later, gives comfort against sin; for in the third revelation,* when I saw that God does all that is done, I did not see sin, and then I saw that all is well. But when God gave me a revelation concerning sin, then he said, 'All shall be well.'

35

How God does all that is good, and nobly tolerates everything in his mercy,
which will come to an end when sin is no longer tolerated.

AND when almighty God had shown me his goodness so abundantly and so fully, I wanted to know whether a certain person I loved would continue to lead a good life,* which I hoped had been begun by God's grace. And in this specific request it seemed that I held myself back, because I was not informed at this time. And then I was answered in my reason, as though by a friendly intermediary, 'Take this generally, and have regard to the Lord God's courtesy as he reveals it to you; for it honours God more to contemplate him in all things than in any particular thing.' I assented, and with that I learned that it honours God more to know all things in general than to take delight in any one thing in particular. And if I were to act wisely on this teaching, I would neither be happy because of anything in particular, nor greatly upset by anything of any kind, for 'All shall be well.'

For the fullness of joy is to see God in everything;* for by the same blessed power, wisdom, and love with which he made all things, our good Lord is continually leading them to the same end, and he himself will accomplish this; and when it is the right time we shall see it. And the foundation of this was shown in the first revelation, and more openly in the third,* where it says, 'I saw God in a point.'

All that our Lord does is rightful, and all that he tolerates is laudable; and in these two good and evil are comprehended; for our Lord does all that is good, and our Lord tolerates what is evil. I am not saying that any evil is laudable, but I am saying that our Lord God's tolerance of it is laudable, and through this his goodness will be recognized without end and his wonderful meekness and compassion, through the working of mercy and grace. Righteousness is that thing which is so good that it cannot be better than it is; for God himself is true righteousness, and all his deeds are performed righteously as they are ordained from without beginning* by his supreme power, his supreme wisdom, his supreme goodness. And just as he ordained for the best, so he works continually and leads everything to the same end; and he is always fully satisfied with himself and with all his works.* And to see this blessed accord is very sweet to the soul who sees it by grace. All the souls which will be saved in heaven without end are made righteous in the sight of God and through his own goodness; and in this righteousness we are endlessly and marvellously protected, above all other creatures.

And mercy is a working of God's goodness, and it will continue operating as long as sin is allowed to pursue righteous souls. And when sin no longer has permission to pursue, then the operation of mercy will cease; and then all will be brought to righteousness and remain so forever. And by his permission, we fall; and in his blessed love we are kept safe by his might and his wisdom; and through mercy and grace we are raised to manifold greater joys. And so in righteousness and in mercy he wishes to be known and loved, now and forever. And the soul that wisely sees this through grace is well pleased with both, and rejoices without end.

36

Concerning another excellent deed that our Lord will do, which may be known here in part by grace; and how we should rejoice in the same; and how God still performs miracles.

OUR Lord God revealed that a deed will be done, and he himself will do it, and it will be glorious and marvellous and bounteous; and it will be done with regard to myself and he himself will do it.* And this is the supreme joy that the soul understood: that God himself will do it, and I shall do nothing but sin, and my sin will not prevent his goodness from working. And I saw that to contemplate this is a heavenly joy to a reverent soul, who naturally by grace always longs for God's will to be done. This deed will be begun here, and it will be to the glory of God and abundantly beneficial to those on earth who love him; and whenever we come to heaven we will see it in marvellous joy, and it will go on working in this way until the last day; and the glory and the bliss of that will last in heaven before God and all his holy ones without end. In this way this deed was seen and understood in our Lord's intention, and the reason why he revealed it is to make us rejoice in him and in all his works.

When I saw that his revelation continued, I understood that it was revealed on account of a great thing that was to come, a thing which God revealed that he himself would do; and this deed has the properties already described; and this he revealed very blessedly, with the intention that I should take it wisely, faithfully, and trustingly. But what this deed would be was kept secret from me. And in this I saw that he does not want us to be afraid to know the things that he reveals; he reveals them because he wants us to know them, and through this knowledge he wants us to love him and take delight and endlessly rejoice in him. And because of the great love which he has for us, he reveals to us everything which at the time is to his glory and our benefit. And the things which he wants to keep secret for now, he still, out of his great goodness, reveals them without full disclosure, and in this revelation he wants us to believe and understand that we shall see them indeed in his eternal bliss. Then we ought to rejoice in him for all that he reveals and all that he conceals; and if we do this willingly and humbly we shall find great comfort in it, and we shall have endless thanks from him for it.

And this is how these words are to be understood: that it will be done for me (that is, mankind in general; that is to say, all who shall be saved); it will be glorious and marvellous and bounteous, and God himself will do it. And this is the highest joy there may be, to see the deed that God himself shall do, and yet man will do nothing at all except sin. So what our good Lord means is this, as if he said, 'Look and see. Here you have cause for humility; here you have cause for love; here you have cause to make yourself as nothing; here you have cause to rejoice in me. And for love of me, rejoice in me, for of all things you could please me most by that.'

And as long as we are in this life, whenever in our folly we incline to consider the damned, our Lord God touches us tenderly and blessedly calls us, saying in our soul, 'Let me be your whole love, my precious child. Attend to me—I am enough for you*—and rejoice in your Saviour and in your salvation.' And I am sure that this is how our Lord works within us; the soul that is informed of this through grace will see it and feel it. And even though this deed is truly understood to apply to mankind in general, it still does not exclude the individual; for what our good Lord will do for his poor creatures is now unknown to me. But this deed and the one mentioned before are not both the same but two separate ones. But this deed will be done sooner, and that will be when we come to heaven; and by those to whom our Lord gives it, this may be known here in part. But the great deed previously mentioned shall be known neither in heaven nor in earth until it is done.

And moreover he gave special understanding and instruction about the working of miracles, as follows, 'It is known that I have performed miracles before now, many and manifold, high and marvellous, glorious and great; and as I have done, so I now do continually, and shall do in times to come.' It is known that sorrow and anguish and tribulation come before miracles; and this is so that we should recognize our own weakness and the troubles that we have fallen into through sin, to humble us and make us fear God, crying for help and grace. Miracles come after that, from the great power, wisdom, and goodness of God, showing his excellence and the joys of heaven, as far as this is possible in this transitory life, and in order to strengthen our faith and to increase our hope, in love; and because of this it pleases him to be known and honoured through miracles. Then this is what he intends: he does not want us to be too cast down on account of the sorrows and upheavals that befall us; for it has always been so before the coming of a miracle.

37

God keeps his chosen ones very safely, even though they sin, for in them is a godly will that never assented to sin.

GOD brought to mind that I would sin;* and because of the delight that I had in contemplating him, I did not at once pay attention to that revelation. And our Lord very kindly waited and gave me grace to pay attention. And I took this revelation to apply particularly to myself, but through all the consolations of grace which ensue, as you will see,* I was taught to apply it to all my fellow Christians in general and not to anyone in particular.* Although our Lord revealed to me that I would sin, by me alone is understood everyone. And at this I began to experience a quiet fear, and to this our Lord replied, 'I am keeping you very safe.' This was said with more love and assurance of spiritual safekeeping than I can or may tell. For just as it was revealed that I would sin, so was the consolation revealed:* assurance of safekeeping for all my fellow Christians. What can make me love my fellow Christians more than to see in God that he loves all who shall be saved as though they were all one soul?

For in every soul that shall be saved there is a godly will which never assented to sin nor ever shall.* Just as there is an animal will in the lower part of our nature which cannot will anything good, so there is a godly will in the higher part of our nature, and this will is so good that it can never will evil, but always good. And because of this we are those whom he loves, and we do what pleases him forever. And our Lord revealed this in the completeness of love in which we stand in his sight—yes, that he loves us as much now while we are here as he will do when we are there before his blessed face. All our difficulty is because of a failure of love on our part.

38

The sins of the chosen shall be turned into joy and glory; the examples of David, Peter, and John of Beverley.

GOD also revealed that sin shall be no shame to man, but his glory. For just as for every sin there is a corresponding punishment in truth, so for every sin the same soul is given a joy by love. Just as various sins are punished with various penalties according to how serious they are, in the same way they will be rewarded with various joys in heaven, according to how painful and sorrowful the sins have been to the soul on earth. For the soul that will come to heaven is precious to God, and the place so glorious, that God's goodness never allows any soul to sin which is to come there, unless the sin is rewarded; and this is made known without end, and blissfully restored by surpassing glories.*

For in this revelation my understanding was lifted up into heaven; and then God brought joyfully into my mind David* and innumerable others of the Old Law,* and in the New Law he brought to mind first Mary Magdalene, Peter and Paul, and Thomas of India,* and Saint John of Beverley,* along with innumerable others: how they and their sins are known to the church on earth, and this is no shame to them, but everything is turned to their glory. And therefore our courteous Lord gives a partial revelation about them here of what will be in perfection in heaven; for there the sign of sin is turned into an honour.

And our Lord showed Saint John of Beverley most exalted, so as to encourage us with his familiarity, and brought to mind how he is a near neighbour and well-known to us; and God called him 'Saint John of Beverley' simply as we do, and that in a very happy and loving manner, showing that he is in God's sight a very great and blessed saint in heaven. And at the same time God made mention that in his youth and in his tender years he was a beloved servant of God, greatly loving and fearing God. And nevertheless God allowed him to fall, mercifully protecting him so that he did not perish nor forfeit any time; and afterwards God raised him to many times more grace; and, for the contrition and humility that he showed in his life, God has given him manifold joys in heaven, surpassing what he would have had if he had not fallen. And on earth God shows that this is true by continually performing abundant miracles around his body. And all this was to make us glad and cheerful in love.

39

Concerning the sharpness of sin and the goodness of contrition, and how our kind Lord will not want us to despair over our frequent falls.

SIN is the sharpest scourge that any chosen soul can be struck with, a scourge which lashes men and women and utterly shatters them, and damages them so much in their own eyes that sometimes they think themselves unworthy of anything except, as it were, to sink into hell, until contrition seizes them through the inspiration of the Holy Spirit and turns the bitterness into hopes of God's mercy. And then the wounds begin to heal and the soul to revive, returned into the life of Holy Church. The Holy Spirit leads a man to confession to reveal his sins willingly, nakedly, and truly, with great sorrow and great shame that he has besmirched the fair image of God. Then he receives penance for each sin imposed by his confessor, as is established in Holy Church through the teaching of the Holy Spirit.

And this is one form of humility which greatly pleases God, as does meekly accepting bodily sickness sent by God, as also sorrow and outward shame, and the reproof and scorn of this world, with all kinds of afflictions and temptations that are thrown at us, both physically and spiritually. Our Lord takes care of us very lovingly when it seems to us that we are almost forsaken and abandoned because of our sin and because we have deserved it. And because of the humility which we gain through this, we are raised very high in God's sight by his grace. And also our Lord in his special grace visits whomever he wishes with such great contrition, and also with compassion and a true longing for God. Then they are suddenly freed from sin and from pain, and taken up into bliss, and made equal with exalted saints. By contrition we are made pure, by compassion we are made ready, and by true longing for God we are made worthy. These are the three means, as I understand it, by which all souls come to heaven—that is to say, those who have been sinners on earth and are to be saved.*

For every soul must be healed by these medicines.* Although he may be healed, his wounds appear before God not as scars but as honours. And just as we are punished here with sorrow and with penance, so by contrast we shall be rewarded in heaven by the courteous love of our Lord God almighty, who does not wish anyone who comes there to lose the rewards for his labours in any way. For he regards sin as sorrow and suffering for those who love him, to whom he attributes no blame, out of love.*

The reward that we will receive will not be small, but it will be great, glorious, and full of honour. And so shame will be turned into honour and greater joy.* For our courteous Lord does not want his servants to despair because they fall often and grievously; for our falling does not prevent him from loving us. Peace and love are always in us, being and working, but we are not always in peace and love. But he wants us to pay attention to this: that he is the foundation of our whole life in love,* and furthermore, that he is our everlasting protector and defends us powerfully against our enemies, who are very cruel and fierce towards us; and our need is so much the greater because we give them occasion when we fall.

40

We need to long for love with Jesus, avoiding sin for love; the vileness of sin surpasses all punishments, and God loves us very tenderly whilst we are in sin, and we need to love our neighbour likewise.

THIS is a supreme act of friendship by our courteous Lord, that he looks after us so tenderly while we are in our sins; and furthermore he touches us very inwardly and shows us our sin by the sweet light of mercy and grace. But when we see ourselves to be so loathsome, we think God is angry with us because of our sins, and then the Holy Spirit moves us through contrition to prayer and a longing with all our might to amend our life, so as to abate God's anger until the time that we find peace of soul and ease of conscience. And then we hope that God has forgiven us our sins; and it is true. And then our courteous Lord reveals himself to the soul, very joyfully and with an expression of gladness and a friendly welcome, as if the soul had been in pain and in prison, saying this sweetly, 'My darling, I am glad you have come to me. In all your misery I have always been with you, and now you see how I love you, and we are united in bliss.' So sins are forgiven by mercy and grace, and our soul is gloriously received in joy, just as it will be when it comes to heaven, whenever this comes about through the working by grace of the Holy Spirit and the power of Christ's Passion.

Here I truly understood that all manner of things are made ready for us by the great goodness of God, so much so that when we are ourselves in peace and charity we are truly safe. But because we cannot have this fully while we are here, it is fitting for us therefore always to live with our Lord Jesus in sweet prayer and in loving longing. For he always longs to bring us to the fullness of joy, as has been said before, where he reveals his spiritual thirst.

But now, if any man or woman—on account of all this spiritual comfort just described—should be moved by folly to say or to think, 'If this is true, then it would be a good idea to sin, so as to have a greater reward', or else to give less weight to sin, beware of this impulse, for truly, if it arises, such an impulse is false and derives from the enemy of that same true love which teaches us about all this comfort.* The same blessed love teaches us that we should hate sin only because of love.* And I am sure, from my own feeling, that the more that every naturally well-disposed soul sees this in the courteous love of our Lord, the more reluctant he is to sin and the more he is ashamed. For if all the sufferings in hell and in purgatory and on earth were laid before us—death and all the rest—and sin, we would rather choose all that suffering than sin. For sin is so vile and so much to be hated that it can be compared to no suffering which is not the suffering of sin itself. And no harder hell than sin was revealed to me, for a well-natured soul hates no hell but sin, for everything is good except sin, and nothing is evil except sin. And when we give our minds to love and humility, we are made all fair and spotless through the working of mercy and grace.

And God is as willing to save man as he is powerful and wise; for Christ himself is foundation of all the laws of Christian people, and he taught us to do good in return for evil.* Here we can see that he is himself this love* and acts towards us as he teaches us to do;* for he wants us to be like him in completeness of unending love towards ourselves and towards our fellow Christians. He does not wish our love for ourselves and our fellow Christians to be discontinued, any more than he discontinues his love for us on account of our sin; but we must feel a naked hatred for sin, and love the soul as God loves it without end. Then we shall hate sin just as God hates it, and love the soul as God loves it. For these words which God said are an unending comfort: 'I am keeping you very safe.'

41

The fourteenth revelation concerns the aforesaid, it is impossible that we should pray for mercy and be without it; and how God wants us always to pray although we may be dry and barren, because prayer is acceptable and pleasing to him.

AFTER this our Lord gave a revelation concerning prayer, in which revelation I saw two attributes in what our Lord was conveying: one is rightful prayer, another is sure trust. But yet our trust is often not complete, for it seems to us that, because of our unworthiness and because we feel nothing at all, we are not sure that God hears us. For often we are as barren and dry after our prayers as we were before, and when we feel like this our folly is the cause of our weakness. For I have felt this way myself. And our Lord brought all this suddenly to mind and revealed these words and said, 'I am the foundation of your prayers: first, it is my will that you should have something, and then I make you desire it, and then I make you pray for it. And if you pray for it, how then could it be that you should not have what you pray for?'

And so in his first statement, along with the three that follow, our good Lord reveals something very comforting, as can be seen in the same words. And in the fifth statement, where he says, 'If you pray for it', he there reveals the very great delight and unending reward that he will give us for our prayer. And in the sixth statement,* where he says, 'How then could it be . . . ?', this was said as an impossibility; for it is quite impossible that we should pray for mercy and grace and not have them. For everything which our good Lord makes us pray for, he himself has ordained for us from without beginning.* Here we can see that our prayer is not the cause of the goodness and grace which he gives us, but his own goodness. And he revealed that truly in all those precious words when he says, 'I am the foundation.' And our good Lord wishes this to be known by those on earth who love him, and the more we know, the more we should pray, if we take this wisely; and this is our Lord's intention.

Prayer is a true, gracious, lasting will of the soul united and joined to the will of our Lord by the precious and mysterious working of the Holy Spirit. Our Lord himself is the primary recipient of our prayers,* as it seems to me, and accepts them most gratefully, and highly rejoicing; and he sends them up above and sets them in a treasury where they will never perish.* They are there before God and all his holy ones, received continually, always furthering us in our needs. And when we receive our bliss, they will be given to us as a measure of our joy, with endless and glorious thanks from him.

Our Lord is very glad and happy because of our prayers, and he expects them and wants to have them. For through his grace he makes us like himself in condition as we are in nature, and this is his blessed will, for he says, 'Pray with all your heart, even if it seems to give you no pleasure, because it is helpful, even though you may not feel it. Pray with all your heart, even though you may feel nothing, though you may see nothing—yes, even though you may think you cannot.

For in dryness and in barrenness, in sickness and in weakness, then your prayers are most pleasing to me, even though it seems to you that they give you almost no pleasure. And so it is in my sight with all your faithful prayers.'

On account of the reward and the eternal thanks that he wishes to give us, God is therefore eager to have us pray continually in his sight.* God accepts the good will and the effort of his servants, however we are feeling; and for this reason he is pleased when we work at our prayers and at living well, with his help and his grace, preserving our strength for him with reason and discretion, until we possess him whom we seek in the fullness of joy: that is, Jesus. And he revealed that in the fifteenth revelation, above all in these words, 'You will have me as your reward.'*

And thanksgiving is also an aspect of prayer.* Thanksgiving is a true, inward awareness, applying ourselves with all our might, and with great reverence and loving fear, to the work to which our Lord moves us, rejoicing and giving thanks inwardly. And sometimes thanksgiving is overflowing and breaks out into words and says, 'Good Lord, thank you; blessed may you be!' And sometimes when the heart is dry and feels nothing, or else through temptation by our enemy, then it is driven by reason and by grace to cry out to our Lord aloud,* recounting his blessed Passion and his great goodness. And the power of our Lord's word enters the soul and gives life to the heart, and through his grace causes it to work truly, making it pray very blessedly and truly to rejoice in our Lord. This is a most blessed thanksgiving in his sight.

42

Concerning three things that are part of prayer, and how we should pray; and about the goodness of God which continually makes up for our imperfections and feebleness when we do what it is for us to do.

OUR Lord God wants us to have true understanding, and especially of three things which are part of our prayers. The first is through whom and how our prayers originate; he reveals through whom when he says, 'I am the foundation'; and he reveals how, through his goodness, because he says, 'First it is my will.' The second thing is in what manner and how we should pursue our prayers; which is that our will should be turned into the will of our Lord, rejoicing; and he means this when he says, 'I make you desire it.' The third thing is that we should know the fruit and the end of our prayers: that is, to be one with and like our Lord in all things. And to this purpose and to this end was all this loving lesson revealed; and he will help us and he will make it so, as he says himself—blessed may he be!

For this is our Lord's will: that both our prayers and our trust should be equally ample. For if we do not trust as much as we pray, we do not fully honour our Lord in our prayers, and we also delay and harm ourselves; and the reason, I believe, is because we do not truly know that our Lord is the foundation from which our prayers arise, and also because we do not know that this is given us by the grace of his love. For if we knew this, it would make us trust to have everything that we desire, through our Lord's gift. For I am sure that no one asks for mercy and grace with true intent unless mercy and grace are given to him first.

But sometimes it comes into our minds that we have prayed for a long time and yet, as it seems to us, that we do not have what we asked for. But we should not be heavy-hearted over this, for I am sure that, through our Lord's intention, we are waiting either for a better time, or more grace, or a better gift. He wants us to have true knowledge that he himself is being; and he wants our understanding to be founded in this knowledge with all our might, and all our purpose, and all our intention; and upon this foundation he wants us to take our place and make our home. And through the light of himself, by grace, he wants us to understand the three following things: the first is our noble and excellent creation; the second, our costly and precious redemption; the third, everything beneath us which he has created to be of service to us and which for love of us he sustains. So this is what he means, as if he said, 'Behold and see that I have done all this before your prayers, and now you have your being and are praying to me.' And so he means that it is for us to know that the greatest deeds have been done, as Holy Church teaches. And in contemplating this with thanksgiving we ought to pray for the deed which is now being done: and that is that he may rule us and guide us to his glory in this life, and bring us to his bliss; and he has done everything to this end.

So this is his meaning then: that we see that he is doing it, and we pray for it; for the one is not enough. For if we pray and do not see that he is doing it, it makes us depressed and doubting, and that is not to God's glory. And if we see that he is doing it and we do not pray, we are not doing what we owe; and it cannot be like that, which is to say, it is not how God regards it. But to see that he is doing it and to pray for it, in this way he is glorified and we are advantaged. It is our Lord's will that we pray for everything which he has ordained to do, either specifically or in general. And the joy and bliss that this is to him, and the gratitude and the glory that we shall have for this, is beyond the understanding of any creature, as it seems to me.

For prayer is a right understanding of the fullness of joy which is to come, with great longing and certain trust. Lack of that bliss for which we are ordained by nature makes us feel longing; true understanding and love, with sweet recollections of our Saviour, by grace makes us trust. And so by nature we are to long, and by grace we are to trust. And our Lord watches us continually in these two actions; for this is what we owe, and his goodness cannot assign any less to us. Then it is for us to do our utmost; and when we have done that, it will still seem to us that it is nothing—and this is true. But if we do what we can, and truly ask for mercy and grace, we shall find in him all that we lack. And this is what he means where he says, 'I am the foundation of your prayers.' And so in these blessed words, with the revelation, I saw all our weakness and all our doubting fears completely overcome.

43

What prayer does, when ordained according to God's will; and how the goodness of God takes great delight in the deeds that he does through us, as though he were beholden to us, doing everything most lovingly.

PRAYER unites the soul to God;* for though the soul is always like God in nature and substance, restored by grace, it is often unlike him in condition, through sin on man's part. Then prayer is a witness that the soul wills as God wills, and eases the conscience and fits man to receive grace.* And so God teaches us to pray and firmly to trust that we shall have what we pray for; because he regards us with love and wants to make us partners in his good work. And so he moves us to pray for what it pleases him to do; and for such prayers and our good will that he wishes to have, he will reward us and give us eternal recompense. And this was revealed in these words, 'If you pray for it'. In these words God revealed such great pleasure and such great delight, as though he were much beholden to us for every good deed that we do—and yet it is he who does them—and because we pray him with all our might to do everything that is pleasing to him, as if he said, 'Then what could please me more than to be prayed to with all your might, wisely, and willingly to do what I shall do?' And so the soul, through prayer, is of one accord with God.*

But when our courteous Lord shows himself to our soul through his grace, we have what we desire, and for a while we do not see what we should pray for, but our whole aim and all our strength is set entirely on the contemplation of him. And this is an exalted, imperceptible prayer, as it seems to me; for the whole reason why we pray is to be at one with the sight and contemplation of him to whom we pray, experiencing a marvellous rejoicing, with reverent fear and such great sweetness and delight in him that we can only pray as he moves us at the time. And I am very well aware that the more the soul sees of God, the more it longs for him, through his grace.

But when we do not see him in this way, then we feel a need and reason to pray, out of a sense of lack, and so as to make ourselves fit for Jesus. For when the soul is in turmoil, troubled, and alone in its distress, then it is time to pray, to make itself compliant and submissive to God. But no kind of prayer makes God compliant to the soul, because God's love is always the same.

And so I saw that when we see something we need to pray for, then our good Lord follows us, helping us in our desire. And when through his special grace we behold him clearly, seeing no need for anything else, then we follow him and he draws us into him by love.* For I saw and felt that his marvellous and abundant goodness is the fulfilment of all our powers; and then I saw that his continued working in every kind of thing is done with such goodness, so wisely, and so powerfully, that it surpasses all our imagining and all that we can think or expect. And then we can do no more than contemplate him, rejoicing, with a great and powerful longing to be wholly united into him, entered into his dwelling-place, and rejoice in his love and delight in his goodness.

And then we shall, by his precious grace, in our own humble and continued prayers, come into him now in this life through many mysterious touches of precious spiritual revelations and feelings, apportioned to us as our simplicity can bear it; and this is done and shall be done by the grace of the Holy Spirit, until we shall die in longing

for love.* And then we shall all enter into our Lord, knowing ourselves clearly and possessing God in full; and we will be unendingly
and wholly possessed in God, seeing him truly and feeling him fully,
hearing him spiritually, and smelling him delectably, and swallowing
him sweetly.* And then we shall see God face to face, intimately and
fully. The creature that is made shall see and endlessly contemplate
God, who is the maker; for no one can see God in this way and live
on afterwards, that is to say, in this mortal life.* But when through his
special grace God wishes to reveal himself here, he gives the created
being more than its own strength, and he apportions the revelation
according to his own will, as much as it is helpful at the time.

44

*Concerning the attributes of the Trinity; and how man's soul, God's
creation, has the same attributes in doing what it was made for: seeing,
contemplating, and marvelling at its God, so that, in comparison, the soul
seems as nothing to itself.*

GOD showed frequently in all the revelations* that man always works
his will, and to his glory, enduringly and unceasingly. And what this
work is, was shown in the first revelation,* and that on a wonderful basis, for it was shown in the working of the soul of our blessed
Lady Saint Mary—truth and wisdom. And how this was shown,
I hope, by the grace of the Holy Spirit, I shall tell as I saw. Truth sees
God, and wisdom contemplates God, and from these two comes the
third, which is a holy, marvellous delight in God, which is love. Where
truth and wisdom truly are, there is love, truly coming from them
both, and all of God's making. For he is endless supreme truth, endless supreme wisdom, endless supreme love, uncreated; and man's
soul is a creature in God, which has the same properties, but created;
and it always does what it was made for: it sees God, it contemplates
God, and it loves God: and so God rejoices in the creature, and the
creature in God, endlessly marvelling; in which marvelling he sees his
God, his Lord, his maker, so high, so great, and so good in comparison with him who is made that the creature seems scarcely anything
to himself; but the clarity and the purity of truth and wisdom make
him see and recognize that he is made for love, in which God endlessly sustains him.

45

*Concerning the constant and deep judgement of God, and the variable
judgement of man.*

GOD judges us according to the essence of our human nature, which
is always kept united in him, whole and safe without end; and this
judgement derives from his righteousness. And man judges on the
basis of our changeable sensory being, which seems now one thing
and now another, according to how it is variously influenced and
appears outwardly. And this judgement is mixed, for sometimes it
is good and tolerant, and sometimes it is harsh and severe. And in
as much as it is good and tolerant it pertains to God's righteousness;
and in as much as it is harsh and severe our good Lord Jesus reforms
it by mercy and grace through the power of his blessed Passion, and
so brings it into righteousness. And although these two are thus rec-
onciled and united, yet both shall be known in heaven without end.

The first judgement, which is from God's righteousness, is from
his exalted, endless love, and this is that lovely, gentle judgement that
was shown throughout the whole lovely revelation, in which I saw
him attribute to us no kind of blame.* And though this was sweet
and delectable, I could still not be completely reassured simply by
contemplating this, and that was on account of the judgement of Holy
Church, which I had understood before and was constantly before
me. And according to this judgement it seemed to me that I had to
acknowledge myself a sinner, and on account of this same judgement
I understood that sinners at some time deserve blame and anger; and
I could not see these two things in God, and therefore my longing was
greater than I can or may tell. For God revealed the higher judgement
himself at the same time, and therefore I had to accept it, necessarily; and the lower judgement had been taught to me previously by
Holy Church, and therefore I could in no way disregard the lower
judgement.

This, then, was what I wanted so much: that I might see in God
how what the judgement of Holy Church teaches here is true in his
sight and how it is for me to know it truly, so that both judgements
might be maintained, in such a way as were to the glory of God
and the right way for me.* And I had no other answer to all this
than a wonderful parable of a lord and a servant, as I shall report

later—and that was revealed very ambiguously.* And I am still longing—and will until the end of my life—to understand by grace these
two judgements as they apply to me; for all heavenly things—and all
earthly things that belong to heaven—are comprehended in these
two judgements. And the more understanding that we have of these
two judgements—by the gracious guidance of the Holy Spirit—the
more we shall see and recognize our failings. And all the more that
we see them, the more naturally, through grace, we shall long to be
filled with endless joy and bliss, for we are created for that, and our
natural substance is now blessed in God, and has been since it was
made, and shall be without end.

46

*We cannot know ourselves in this life except through faith and grace, but
we must know ourselves to be sinners; and how God is never angry, being
nearest to the soul, protecting it.*

BUT our fleeting life that we lead here in our sensory being does not
know what our self is, except through our faith. And when we know
and see truly and clearly what our self is, then we shall truly and
clearly see and know our Lord God in fullness of joy. And so it has
to be that the nearer we are to our bliss, the more we shall be longing, both through nature and through grace. We may have knowledge
of ourselves in this life through the continuing help and strength of
our higher nature, and in this knowledge we may increase and grow
through the furtherance and assistance of mercy and grace, but we can
never fully know ourselves until the last moment—at which moment
this passing life and every kind of pain and misery shall have an end.
And therefore it is proper for us, both through nature and through
grace, to long and desire with all our might to know ourselves, and
in this full knowledge we shall truly and clearly know our God, in
fullness of endless joy.

And yet during all this time, from the beginning to the end,
I experienced two kinds of perception: one was endless, continuing
love with certainty of safekeeping and blessed salvation, for the whole
revelation was about this; the other was the general teaching of Holy
Church, in which I was previously instructed and had my grounding,
and had willingly observed and understood. And the awareness of this

never left me; for I was not moved nor led away from that by the revelation in any detail, but in it I received teaching to love it and like it, through which I might, by the help of our Lord and his grace, grow and rise to more heavenly knowledge and a higher loving.

And so in all this contemplation it seemed necessary to me to see and to recognize that we are sinners and do many evil things that we ought to avoid, and leave many good deeds undone that we ought to do, and for this we deserve pain, blame, and anger. And in spite of all this, I saw truly that our Lord was never angry, nor ever shall be, for he is God:* he is good, he is truth, he is love, he is peace; and his power, his wisdom, his charity, and his unity do not permit him to be angry. For I saw truly that it is against the nature of his power to be angry, and against the nature of his wisdom, and against the nature of his goodness. God is the goodness that cannot be angry, for he is nothing but goodness. Our soul is united to him, unchangeable goodness, and between God and our soul is neither anger nor forgiveness in his sight, for through his own goodness our soul is completely united to God, so that nothing at all may come between God and the soul.

And to this understanding the soul was led by love and powerfully drawn in every revelation. That this is so, and how it is so, our good Lord revealed truly in his great goodness; and he wants us to long to know—that is to say, as far as it is appropriate for a creature of his to know it. For everything that the simple soul* understood, God wishes to be revealed and known; for the things that he wishes to keep secret, he powerfully and wisely hides them himself out of love; for I saw in the same revelation that many mysteries remain hidden,* which may never be known until the time when God, of his goodness, has made us worthy to see them. And I am well satisfied with this, awaiting our Lord's will in this great marvel. And for now I submit myself to my mother, Holy Church,* as a simple child ought to do.

47

We must reverently marvel and meekly suffer, always rejoicing in God; and how our blindness—in that we do not see God—is the cause of our sin.

Two things are an obligation for our soul. One is that we reverently wonder; the other is that we meekly suffer, always rejoicing in God;

for he wants us to know that in a short time we shall see clearly in him all that we desire. And in spite of all this, I contemplated and wondered very much what the mercy and forgiveness of God is; for according to the teaching that I received earlier, I understood that the mercy of God would be the remission of his anger after occasions when we have sinned. For it seemed to me that to a soul whose intention and desire is to love, the anger of God would be harder than any other pain, and therefore I took it that the remission of his anger would be one of the principal features of his mercy. But however much I might look and long I could not see this anywhere in the entire revelation. But, as God will give me grace, I will say something of what I saw and understood of the works of mercy.

I understood this: man is changeable in this life, and falls into sin through frailty and being overcome; in himself he is weak and foolish, and also his will is overwhelmed, and during this time he is in turmoil, and in sorrow and misery, and the cause is blindness—because he does not see God; for if he saw God continually he would have no harmful feelings, nor any sort of prompting to the craving that is conducive to sin. I saw and felt this at the same time, and it seemed to me that the sight and the feeling were exalted and abundant and full of grace in comparison with what are our usual feelings in this life, but yet I thought they were only mean and petty compared with the great desire that the soul has to see God. For I felt in myself five kinds of reaction, which are these: rejoicing, mourning, desire, fear, and sure hope; rejoicing, because God gave me understanding and knowledge that it was he himself that I saw; mourning, for lack of him; desire, and that was so that I might see him always more and more, understanding and acknowledging that we shall never be completely at rest until we see him truly and clearly in heaven; the fear was because during all that time it seemed to me that the vision would cease, and I would be left to myself; the certain hope was in the endless love, in which I saw I should be protected by his mercy and brought to his bliss. And the rejoicing in his sight with this certain hope of his merciful protection caused me to have understanding and comfort, so that the mourning and fear were not greatly painful.

And yet in all this I perceived through the revelation of God that this kind of sight of him cannot be continuous in this life—and that is for his own glory and for the increasing of our endless joy. And therefore we often lack the sight of him, and at once we fall back upon ourselves, and then we find no feeling of anything but the contrary spirit that is in us, and that stems from the ancient root of our first sin, with all that follows of our own contriving, and in this we are troubled and shaken with the feeling of sin and of suffering in many different ways, both spiritually and bodily, as this is known to us in this life.

48

Concerning mercy and grace and their properties; and how we shall rejoice that we ever endured sorrow patiently.

BUT our good Lord, the Holy Spirit, who is endless life dwelling in our soul, protects us most securely, and effects a peace in the soul, and gives it comfort by grace, and accords it to God, and makes it compliant. And this is his mercy and the path on which our Lord continually leads us, as long as we are here in this changeable life. For I saw no anger except on man's part, and he forgives that in us; for anger is nothing else but a resistance and contrariness to peace and to love, and it comes either from lack of strength, or from lack of wisdom, or from lack of goodness—and this lack is not in God, but it is on our part; for through sin and wretchedness we have in us a wretched and continual resistance to peace and to love, and he revealed this very often in his loving expression of pity and compassion; for the foundation of mercy is love, and the operation of mercy is to safeguard us in love; and this was revealed in such a way that I could not discern any aspect of mercy other than in love alone—that is to say, as it appeared to me.

Mercy works sweetly through love by grace, mingled with abundant pity; because mercy works for our safekeeping, and mercy works by turning everything to good for us. Through love, mercy lets us fail to some degree: and in as much as we fail, by so much we fall, and in as much as we fall, so much we die; for we have to die, in as much as we fail in sight and feeling of God, who is our life. Our failing is full of fear, our falling is full of shame, and our dying is full of sorrow; but throughout all this the sweet eye of pity and love never looks away from us,* nor does the operation of mercy cease. For I saw the property of mercy and I saw the property of grace, which have two ways of working within one love. Mercy is a compassionate property which belongs to motherhood in tender love,* and grace is an honourable property which belongs to royal lordship in the same love. Mercy works—protecting, tolerating, reviving, and healing, and all through the tenderness of love; and grace works: raising, rewarding, and endlessly exceeding what our love and our efforts deserve, distributing far and wide and displaying the high and abundant largesse of God's royal lordship through his marvellous courtesy. And this stems from the abundance of love; for grace transforms our fearful failing into abundant and unending solace, and grace transforms our shameful falling into a high and honourable rising; and grace transforms our sorrowful dying into holy, blessed life; for I saw most certainly that just as our contrariness brings us pain, shame, and sorrow here on earth, so, on the contrary, grace brings us solace, honour, and bliss in heaven—and to such an extent that when we come up and receive the sweet reward which grace has created for us, then we shall thank and bless our Lord, rejoicing without end that we ever suffered sorrow. And that will be on account of a property of blessed love that we shall recognize in God, which we might never have known without sorrow coming before. And when I saw all this, I had to admit that the mercy and the forgiveness of God is in order to abate and dispel our anger.

49

Our life is grounded in love, and without that we perish; yet God is never angry, but in our anger and sin he mercifully sustains us and causes us to find peace, rewarding our tribulations.

FOR this was a great marvel to the soul, continually shown in everything and regarded very attentively: that our Lord God, with regard to himself, cannot forgive,* because he cannot be angry—that would be impossible. For this was revealed: that our life is all grounded and rooted in love,* and without love we cannot live. And therefore to the soul which through his special grace sees so much of the great and wonderful goodness of God—and that we are endlessly united to him in love—it is the greatest impossibility there could be that God should be angry, for anger and friendship* are two opposites. It must necessarily be so that he who dispels and destroys our anger and makes us meek and mild is himself always constant in love, meek and mild, which is the opposite of anger. For I saw very clearly that where our Lord appears, peace reigns,* and anger has no place; for I saw no kind of anger in God, neither for a short time nor for long; for truly, as it seems to me, if God could be angry even for an instant we should never have life, nor place, nor being; for as truly as we have our being from the endless power of God, and from the endless wisdom, and from the endless goodness, so truly we have our safekeeping in the endless power of God, in the endless wisdom, and in the endless goodness; for though we feel anger, argument, and contention in ourselves, we are still all mercifully enclosed in the compassion of God and in his gentleness, in his kindliness and in his favour; for I saw most certainly that all our eternal friendship, our dwelling place, our life, and our being are in God; for the same endless goodness that protects us when we sin so that we do not perish, that same endless goodness continually effects a peace in us to set against our anger and our perverse falling, and makes us see our need, with a true fear, to entreat God with all our strength that we may have forgiveness, with a grace-given longing for our salvation; for we cannot be blessedly saved until we are truly in a state of peace and love; for that is our salvation.

And though we, through the anger and contrary spirit that is within us, are now in tribulation, distress, and misery, as befits our blindness and weakness, yet we are certainly safe through the merciful protection of God, so that we do not perish. But we are not blessedly safe in the possession of our endless joy until we are all in peace and in love: that is to say, in full contentment with God, and with all his works, and with all his judgements, and loving and at peace with ourselves and with our fellow Christians and with all that God loves, as is pleasing to love. And God's goodness does this in us.

So I saw that God is our true peace,* and our sure protector when we are not at peace in ourselves, and he works continually to bring us into endless peace. And so when we, through the working of mercy and grace, are made humble and gentle, we are completely safe. Suddenly the soul is united to God when it is truly at peace in itself, for no anger is to be found in God. And so I saw that when we are all in peace and in love we find no contrariness, nor any kind of hindrance through that contrary spirit which is in us now. In his goodness our Lord makes this very beneficial to us; for this contrariness is the cause of all our tribulation and all our misery, and our Lord Jesus takes them and sends them up to heaven, and there they are made more sweet and delectable than heart can think or tongue can tell, and when we come there we shall find them ready, all turned into very lovely and unending glories. So God is our sure foundation, and he shall be our whole bliss and make us as unchanging as he is, when we are there.

50

How the chosen soul was never dead in the sight of God; and concerning her amazement at this; and three things emboldened her to ask God how to understand it.

AND mercy and forgiveness are our way in this mortal life and continually lead us to grace. And, through the tumult and the sorrow that we fall into for our part, we are often dead according to human judgement on earth, but in the sight of God the soul that shall be saved was never dead,* nor ever shall be. But still I did wonder and marvel at this with all the diligence of my soul, thinking to myself in this way: 'Good Lord, I see that you are very truth, and I know truly that we sin grievously all the time* and are greatly to blame. And I can neither stop being conscious of this truth nor see you blame us in any way. How may that be?' For I knew by the common teaching of Holy Church, and by my own feeling, that the blame for our sins weighs upon us continually, from the first man until the time that we come up into heaven. Then it was this that I marvelled at, that I saw our Lord God blaming us no more than if we were as pure and as holy as angels are in heaven. And between these two contrary things my reason was greatly afflicted by my blindness, and could have no rest for fear that his blessed presence should pass from my sight and I would be left not knowing how he regards us in our sin. For either I needed to see in God that sin was completely done away with, or else I needed to see in God how he sees it, so that I might truly know how I ought to see sin and what sort of blame is ours. My longing endured—contemplating him continually—and yet I could not be patient, because of great fear and perplexity, thinking, 'If I take it in this way—that we are not sinners nor blameworthy—it seems as though I should be in error and fail to recognize this truth. And if it be so that we are sinners and to blame, good Lord, how may it be then that I cannot see this truth in you, who are my God, my creator, in whom I desire to see all truths? For three things embolden me to ask. The first is because it is such a paltry thing, for if it were something elevated I would be afraid. The second is that it is so universal, because if it were special and secret I should also be afraid. The third is because I need to know, as it seems to me, if I am to live here, in order to recognize good and evil, so that through reason and grace I can tell them apart more clearly, and love goodness and hate evil, as Holy Church teaches.' I cried inwardly with all my might, seeking into God for help, thinking in this way, 'Ah, Lord Jesus, king of bliss, how am I to be comforted? Who shall teach me and tell me what I need to know, if I may not see it in you at this time?'

51

The answer to her earlier doubt, in the form of a marvellous parable of a lord and a servant; and God wishes to be waited for, because it was nearly twenty years later before she fully understood this parable; and how it is to be understood that Christ sits on the right hand of the Father.

AND then our courteous Lord answered by showing in a mysterious, veiled way* a wonderful parable* of a lord who has a servant, and gave me insights towards my understanding of both. This insight was shown doubly in the lord, and doubly in the servant: one part was shown spiritually but in bodily form, and the other part was shown more spiritually without bodily likeness.

So, for the first, I saw two persons in bodily likeness, that is to say, a lord and a servant; and with that God gave me spiritual understanding. The lord sits in solemn state, in rest and in peace; the servant stands by respectfully in front of his lord, ready to do his lord's will. The lord looks at his servant very lovingly and kindly, and he gently sends him to a certain place to do his will. The servant does not just walk but suddenly springs forward and runs in great haste to do his lord's will out of love. And at once he falls into a hollow* and receives very severe injury. And then he groans and moans, and wails and writhes, but he cannot rise nor help himself in any way. And the greatest harm of all that I saw him in was a lack of comfort; for he could not turn his face to look at his loving Lord,* who was very close to him and in whom is all comfort; but, like someone who was weak and foolish for the moment, he was intent on his own feelings and went on suffering in misery.

In this misery he suffered seven great pains. The first was the severe bruising* which he received in his fall, which caused him to feel pain.

The second was the sheer weight of his body.

The third was the weakness consequent upon these first two.

The fourth, that he was blinded in his reason and dazed in his mind, to such an extent that he had almost forgotten his own love.

The fifth was that he could not rise.

The sixth was most astonishing to me, and it was that he lay alone; I looked all around and scanned far and near, high and low, but I did not see any help for him.*

The seventh was that the place in which he lay was narrow, hard, and comfortless.

I marvelled at how this servant could meekly suffer all that misery there. And I watched carefully to discover if I could perceive any fault in him, or if the lord would apportion any blame to him; and in truth there was none to be seen; for his good will and the greatness of his longing were the only cause of his fall; and he was as willing and as inwardly good as when he stood before his lord, ready to do his will.

And so his loving lord continually regards him most tenderly in this way, and now with a double aspect:* one outward, most gently and kindly, with great compassion and pity, and this was the first aspect; the other was inward, more spiritual, and this was revealed through my understanding being led into the lord, when I saw him greatly rejoicing over the honourable restoring and nobility to which he would and must bring his servant through his abundant grace. This belonged to the other, second kind of insight; and now my understanding led me back to the first kind, while keeping both in mind.

Then this courteous lord speaks in the following sense: 'See, see, my beloved servant,* what harm and distress he has received in my service for love of me, yes, and because of his good will! Is it not reasonable that I should recompense him for his fright and his dread, his hurt and his injury and all his misery? And not only this, but would it not be proper for me to give a gift that would be better for him and more honourable than if he had stayed entirely uninjured? And otherwise it seems to me that I would be ungracious to him.'

And in this an inward, spiritual revelation of the lord's purpose came down into my soul, in which I saw that, considering his greatness and his own glory, it must needs be that his beloved servant whom he loved so much should be truly and blissfully rewarded forever, above what he would have been if he had not fallen; yes, and so much so that his fall and the misery that he received from that will be transformed into great and surpassing glory, and endless bliss.

And at this point the showing of the parable vanished, and our good Lord guided my understanding in the seeing and in showing of the revelation to the end. But despite all this guidance, my feeling of puzzlement at the parable never left me; for it seemed to me that it had been given me as an answer to what I yearned to know, and yet at that time I could not understand it fully to my satisfaction; for in the servant who represented Adam, I saw, as I shall explain, many different characteristics which in no way could be attributed to Adam alone. And so at that time I remained in a state of ignorance; for full understanding of this marvellous parable was not given me at that time.

In this mysterious parable three aspects of the revelation are still largely hidden; and despite this I saw and understood that every revelation is full of secrets, and so it is for me now to describe three aspects through which I have been somewhat consoled. The first is the initial teaching which I understood from it at the time; the second is the inner teaching that I have understood from it since then; the third is the whole revelation from the beginning to the end—that is to say, of this book—which our Lord God in his goodness often brings freely to my mind's eye. And these three are so united in my understanding that I neither can nor may separate them.

And through these three, united as one,* I have been taught how I ought to believe and trust in our Lord God who—out of the same goodness and for the same purpose that he revealed it—will make it clear to us when he wishes, with exactly the same goodness and for the same purpose that he revealed it. For three months short of twenty years after the time of the revelation,* I received teaching inwardly as I shall tell: 'You need to pay attention to all the particular properties and attributes that were shown in the parable, though they may seem to you mysterious and indeterminate in your eyes.' I willingly agreed with great eagerness, looking inwardly with careful consideration at all the details and characteristics that were shown at the time, as far as my wits and understanding would serve. I began by looking intently at the lord and at the servant, and the way the lord was sitting, and the place where he sat, and then the colour of his clothing and how it fitted, and his outward appearance and his inner nobility and goodness; at the way the servant was standing and where and how, at his kind of clothing and its colour and fit, at his outward behaviour, and at his inner goodness, and his alacrity.

The lord who sat in solemn state, in rest and in peace, I understood to be God. The servant who stood in front of the lord I understood to represent Adam, that is to say, one man and his fall was shown at that time so as to make it understood through that how God regards any man and his fall; for in the sight of God all men are one man, and one man is all men.* This man was injured in strength and much enfeebled; and he was confused in his understanding, for he turned away from looking at his lord. But his will was preserved intact in the sight of God; for I saw our Lord commend and approve his will,* but he himself was hindered and blinded from the knowledge of this will, and this is a great sorrow and grievous distress to him; for he neither sees clearly his loving lord, who is most meek and kind to him, nor does he truly see what he is himself in the sight of his loving lord. And I am sure that when these two things are wisely and truly seen, we shall gain rest and peace here in part and the fullness in the bliss of heaven, through his abundant grace. And this was a beginning to the teaching revealed to me at this time, through which I might come to know how he regards us in our own sin. And then I saw that only suffering blames and punishes, and our courteous Lord comforts and succours; he is always gladly regarding the soul, loving and longing to bring us to bliss.

The place where our Lord sat alone in a wilderness was plain, barren, and deserted ground. His clothing was full and flowing and most becoming, as befits a lord; the colour of the cloth was as blue as azure, most sober and beautiful. His expression was merciful, the colour of his face was a beautiful brown, with most handsome features; his eyes were black, most beautiful and becoming, his looks all full of loving pity; and within him there was a lofty sanctuary, long and broad, all full of endless heavens. And the loving regard with which he looked continually at his servant, and especially when he fell—it seemed to me that it could melt our hearts for love and break them in two for joy. This lovely regard displayed a becoming mixture, which was wonderful to look at: part was compassion and pity, part was joy and bliss. The joy and bliss so far surpass compassion and pity as heaven is above earth. The pity was earthly and the bliss was heavenly. The compassion in the Father's pity was for the fall of Adam, who is his most loved creature; the joy and bliss was for his dearly beloved son, who is equal with the Father. The merciful gaze of his loving expression filled the whole earth and descended down with Adam into hell, and by this continuing pity Adam was kept from endless death. And this mercy and pity remain with mankind until the time when we come up into heaven. But man is blinded in this life, and therefore we cannot see our Father, God, as he is. And when he, out of his goodness wishes to show himself to man, he shows himself in a familiar fashion, like a man, even though I saw truly that we ought to recognize and believe that the Father is not man.

But his sitting on the barren and deserted ground signifies this: he made man's soul to be his own city and his dwelling place,* which is most pleasing to him of all his works; and once man had fallen into sorrow and pain he was not entirely fit to fulfil that noble office, and therefore our kind Father would prepare no other place for himself but sit upon the earth waiting for mankind, which is mixed with earth,* until the time when, through his grace, his beloved son had redeemed his city back into its noble beauty by his hard labour.*

The blue of his clothing betokens his steadfastness.* The brown of his handsome face, with the pleasing darkness of the eyes, was most appropriate to signal his holy gravity. The fullness of his clothing, which was beautiful, and shining radiantly around him,* signifies that he has enclosed within himself all heavens and all joy and bliss. And this was shown in a brief glimpse, where I said, 'My understanding was led into the lord',* when I saw him greatly rejoicing because of the glorious restoration to which he wishes to bring, and shall bring, his servant through his abundant grace.

And yet I was amazed in contemplating the lord and the servant as previously mentioned. I saw the lord sitting in solemn state, and the servant standing respectfully before his lord, and in this servant there is a double significance, one outward and another inward. Outwardly he was simply dressed like a labourer ready for work, and he stood very near the lord, not right in front of him but a little to one side, on the left. His clothing was a white tunic, unlined, old, and all worn, stained with the sweat of his body, tight-fitting and short on him, as if only a hand's breadth below the knee, threadbare, looking as though it would soon be worn out, about to go to rags and tatters. And I was greatly astonished about this, thinking, 'Now this is unsuitable clothing* for so greatly loved a servant to wear before so honoured a lord.'

And inwardly there was revealed in him a depth of love, and this love which he had for the lord was just like the love which the lord had for him. The wisdom of the servant saw inwardly that there was one thing to be done which would be to the honour of the lord.* And the servant, for love, having no regard for himself or for anything that might happen to him, jumped up quickly and ran at his lord's command to do the thing which was his will and to his glory. For it seemed by his outer clothing as if he had been a labourer continuously for a long time; and through the inward perception that I had, both of the lord and of the servant, it seemed that he was fresh to the task. That is to say, newly beginning to labour—a servant who had never been sent out before.*

There was a treasure in the earth which the lord loved.* I was astonished and wondered what it could be. And I was answered in my understanding, 'It is a food which is delightful and pleasing to the lord.'* For I saw the lord sit like a man, and I saw neither food nor drink to serve him with—this was one surprise. Another surprise was that this majestic lord had only one servant, and him he sent forth. I watched, wondering what kind of labour it could be that the servant was to do. And then I understood that he was to do the greatest labour and the hardest toil that there is—he was to be a gardener,* digging and ditching, toiling and sweating, and turning the earth upside down, and digging down deeper, and watering the plants in a timely way. And he was to continue to toil at this and to cause sweet streams to flow,* and noble and plentiful fruits to grow, which he was to bring before the lord and serve him with to his liking. And he was never to return until he had prepared this food entirely as he knew it pleased the lord; and then he was to take this food, and the drink with the food, and carry it most reverently before the lord. And all this time the lord was to sit in the same place, awaiting his servant whom he sent out.

And still I puzzled where the servant came from; for I saw in the lord that he has within himself eternal life and every kind of goodness, except for that treasure which was in the earth—and that was grounded in the lord in marvellous depths of endless love—but it was not altogether to his glory until this servant had prepared it so nobly and brought it before him, into his presence; and without the lord there was nothing but wilderness. And I did not understand all that this parable meant, and therefore I wondered where the servant came from.

In the servant is comprehended the Second Person of the Trinity; and in the servant is comprehended Adam, that is to say, all men. And therefore when I say, 'the Son', it means the Godhead, which is equal with the Father, and when I say, 'the servant', it means Christ's humanity, which is truly Adam. By the nearness of the servant is understood the Son, and by the standing on the left side is understood Adam. The lord is the Father, God. The servant is the Son, Christ Jesus. The Holy Spirit is the equal love which is in them both. When Adam fell, God's son fell; because of the true union which was made in heaven, God's son could not be apart from Adam, for by Adam I understand all humanity. Adam fell from life to death, into the hollow of this wretched world, and after that into hell. God's son fell with Adam* into the hollow of the Virgin's womb—she who was the fairest daughter of Adam—and so as to free Adam through that from guilt in heaven and on earth; and through his great might he fetched him out of hell.*

By the wisdom and goodness that was in the servant is understood God's son. By the poor clothing as a labourer standing near the left side is understood Christ's humanity and Adam, with all the misfortune and weakness that follow from that; for in all this our good Lord showed his own son and Adam as but one man. The strength and the goodness that we have is from Jesus Christ, the weakness and the blindness that we have is from Adam; and these two were represented in the servant.

And so our good Lord Jesus has taken upon himself all our guilt; and therefore our Father neither can nor will attribute any more blame to us than to his own son, beloved Christ. So he was the servant before he came upon earth, standing ready before the Father purposefully until the time when he would send him to do that glorious deed by which mankind was brought back into heaven; that is to say, despite the fact that he is God, equal with the Father in respect of the Godhead, yet because of his providential purpose—that he would become man to save man in fulfilment of his Father's will—he therefore stood before his Father like a servant, willingly taking upon

himself all the burden of us. And then he sprang forward very readily* at the Father's will, and at once he fell very low into the Virgin's
womb, having no regard to himself nor to his cruel pains. The white
tunic is the flesh; its unlined single thickness signifies that there was
nothing at all between the Godhead and his humanity; the tight fit is
poverty; its age is because Adam wore it; the staining by sweat is from
Adam's toil; its shortness represents the servant's labouring.

And so I saw the Son standing, expressing what he meant, 'Look,
my dear Father, I am standing before you in Adam's tunic, all ready to
start off and to run. I wish to be upon earth to do what is to your glory
when it is your will to send me. How long am I to remain longing for
this?' The Son knew very truly when it was the Father's will and how
long he was to remain longing for this; that is to say, with respect to
the Godhead, for he is the wisdom of the Father. Therefore this was
shown to represent the understanding of Christ's humanity; for all
mankind that will be saved by the precious incarnation and blessed
Passion of Christ, all are Christ's humanity. For he is the head and
we are his members,* and to these members the day and the time are
unknown* when every passing grief and sorrow will come to an end,
and everlasting joy and bliss will be achieved, a day and time which
all the company of heaven longs to see.* And all those who are below
heaven and shall come there, their way is by longing and yearning,
and this yearning and longing was represented in the servant standing
before the lord, or rather, to put it differently, in the Son's standing
before the Father in Adam's tunic; for the longing and yearning of
all mankind that shall be saved appeared in Jesus; for Jesus is all who
shall be saved, and all who shall be saved are Jesus; and all through
the love of God, with obedience, humility, and patience, and other
virtues that befit us.

Also through this marvellous example I receive instruction, as if
it were the beginning of an ABC,* through which I may gain some
understanding of what our Lord meant; for the mysteries of the
revelation are hidden in it, even though all the revelations are full of
mysteries.

The sitting of the Father signifies his Godhead: that is to say, in
showing rest and peace, for there can be no labour in the Godhead.
And that he showed himself as a lord has a significance with respect
to our humanity. The standing of the servant signifies labour; that he
stands to one side and on the left signifies that he was not fully worthy

to stand right in front of the lord. His springing forward is a reference to the Godhead, and his running refers to Christ's humanity; for the Godhead leapt from the Father into the Virgin's womb, falling into the acceptance of our nature; and in this fall he received grievous injury: the injury that he received was our flesh, in which he soon felt mortal pain. That he stood in awe before the lord, and not right in front, signifies that his clothing was not suitable for him to stand right in front of the lord; nor could nor should that have been his role while he was a labourer; neither could he sit in rest and peace with the lord until he had rightfully earned his peace by his hard labour; and that he stood on the left side signifies how the Father willingly left his own son in his humanity to suffer all man's pains without sparing him. By his tunic being on the point of turning into rags and tatters is understood the blows and the scourges, the thorns and the nails, the pulling and the dragging, tearing his tender flesh;* as I saw in part,* the flesh was torn from the skull, falling in shreds until the time when the bleeding stopped; and then it began to dry again, clinging to the bone. And by writhing about and heaving, groaning and moaning, is to be understood that he could never rise again omnipotently from the time that he fell into the Virgin's womb until his body was slain and dead, he yielding his soul into the Father's hands with all mankind for whom he was sent.*

And at this point he first began to show his power; for he went into hell, and when he was there he raised up out of the deepest depths the great root of those who were rightly joined with him in high heaven.* The body was in the grave until Easter morning, and from that time it lay no more; for then was rightly ended the writhing and the heaving, the groaning and the moaning; and our foul mortal flesh which God's son took upon himself—which was Adam's old tunic,* tight-fitting, threadbare and short—was then made by our Saviour newly beautiful, white and bright* and of endless purity, full and flowing, fairer and richer than was the clothing which I then saw on the Father:* for that clothing was blue, and Christ's clothing is now of a beautiful and befitting mixture which is so marvellous that I cannot describe it, for it is all of true glories.

Now the lord does not sit upon the earth in a wilderness, but he sits in his noblest seat which he made in heaven most to his liking. Now the Son does not stand in awe before the Father like a servant, plainly dressed, half-naked, but he stands immediately before the

Father, richly dressed in joyous bountifulness, with a crown upon his head of inestimable richness; for it was revealed that we are his crown,* and that this crown is the Father's joy, the Son's glory, the Holy Spirit's delight, and endless, marvellous bliss to all who are in heaven. Now the Son does not stand before the Father on the left side like a labourer, but he sits at his Father's right hand* in endless rest and peace. (But this does not mean that the Son sits on the Father's right hand, side by side, as one person sits by another in this life; for, as I see it, there is no such sitting in the Trinity;* but he sits on his Father's right hand, that is to say, in the highest rank of the Father's joys.) Now the spouse, God's Son,* is at peace with his beloved bride, who is the fair Virgin of endless joy. Now the Son, true God and man, sits in his city in rest and peace, which his Father has prepared for him through his eternal purpose; and the Father in the Son, and the Holy Spirit in the Father and in the Son.

52

God rejoices that he is our father, mother, and spouse; and how the chosen have here a mixture of joy and sorrow, but God is with us in three ways; and how we may avoid sin, but never perfectly as in heaven.

AND so I saw that God rejoices that he is our father, God rejoices that he is our mother, and God rejoices that he is our true spouse, and our soul is his beloved wife. And Christ rejoices that he is our brother,* and Jesus rejoices that he is our Saviour. There are five great joys, as I understand, in which he wishes that we rejoice, praising him, thanking him, loving him, endlessly blessing him.

All those who shall be saved, while we are in this life, have in ourselves a marvellous mixture of both happiness and sorrow. We have in us our risen Lord Jesus; we have in us the misery and the harm of Adam's falling.* In dying, we are steadfastly protected by Christ, and by the touch of his grace we are raised into sure trust of salvation. And by Adam's fall our perception is so fragmented in various ways, by sins and by various sufferings, in which we are so overshadowed and so blinded that we can scarcely take any comfort. But in our intention we are waiting for God, and trust faithfully that we shall have mercy and grace; and this is how he works in us. And in his goodness he opens the eye of our understanding, through which we gain insight, sometimes more and sometimes less, according to the ability that God gives us to receive it. And now we are uplifted into the one, and now we are allowed to fall into the other. And so this fluctuation within us is so baffling that we scarcely know what state we ourselves or our fellow Christians are in, because these conflicting feelings are so extraordinary—except for that same holy assent with which we assent to God when we feel him, truly wishing to be with him with all our heart, with all our soul, and with all our might. And then we hate and despise our evil impulses and everything that might be the occasion of sin, spiritual and bodily. And yet nevertheless when this sweetness is hidden we fall back again into blindness, and so into sorrow and tribulation in various ways. But then this is our comfort: that we know through our faith that by the power of Christ, who is our protector, we never assent to it but rail against it, and endure in pain and misery, praying until the time that he shows himself to us again. And so we remain in this mixed state all the days of our life. But he wants us to trust that he is perpetually with us, and in three ways: he is with us in heaven, true man in his own person, drawing us upwards, and that was shown by his spiritual thirst;* and he is with us on earth, guiding us; and that was shown in the third revelation, where I saw God in a point;* and he is with us endlessly dwelling in our soul, ruling and caring for us, and that was shown in the sixteenth revelation,* as I shall recount.

And so in the servant was shown the hurt and blindness of Adam's fall; and in the servant was shown the wisdom and goodness of God's son. And in the lord was shown the compassion and pity for Adam's woe; and in the lord was shown the exalted nobility and the endless glory to which mankind has attained through the power of the Passion and the death of God's beloved son. And therefore he greatly rejoices in his fall, because of the exaltation and fullness of bliss that mankind attains, surpassing what we should have had if he had not fallen; and so to see this surpassing splendour my understanding was led into God at the same time that I saw the servant fall. And so now we have reason for mourning, because our sin is the cause of Christ's sufferings; and we have lasting reason for joy, because endless love made him suffer. And therefore the person who sees and feels the working of love through grace hates nothing but sin; for of all things, as I see it, love and hate are the hardest and most immeasurable contraries. And despite all this, I saw and understood in our Lord's intention that in this life we cannot keep ourselves from sin as completely in perfect purity as we shall in heaven. But we may well, through grace, keep ourselves from the sins which will lead us to endless sufferings, as Holy Church teaches us, and avoid venial sin,* as much as we reasonably can; and if through our blindness and wretchedness we fall at any time, that we promptly rise up again, recognizing the sweet touch of grace, and willingly make amends, according to the teaching of Holy Church, depending on the grievousness of the sin, and go forthwith to God in love; and neither on the one hand fall too low, inclining to despair, nor on the other hand be too heedless, as if we did not care, but openly recognize our weakness, knowing that we cannot remain for the twinkling of an eye unless protected by grace, and reverently clinging to God, trusting only in him.

For God regards things one way and mankind regards things in quite another. For it is for man to accuse himself meekly, and it is for our Lord God's own goodness to excuse man courteously. And these are the two aspects that were shown in the double expression with which the lord regarded the fall of his beloved servant. The one was shown outwardly, very humbly and gently with great compassion and pity, and the other was of inward, endless love. And our Lord wants us to accuse ourselves exactly in this way, willingly and truly seeing and acknowledging our fall and all the harm that comes of that, seeing and knowing that we can never make it good, and at the same time that we willingly and truly see and know his everlasting love which he has for us, and his abundant mercy. And so by grace to see and know both together is the humble self-accusation that our Lord asks of us, and wherever it occurs, he himself brings it about. And this is the lower part of man's life, and it was shown in the lord's outward expression, in which revelation I saw two aspects; one is the pitiable fall of man; the other is the glorious atonement that our Lord has made for man.

The other expression was shown inwardly, and that was more elevated and all of a piece; for the life and the strength that we have in the lower part comes from the higher, and it comes down to us from a natural self-love, through grace. Between the one and the other nothing at all intervenes, for it is all one love, and this one blessed love is now at work doubly within us. For in the lower part there are pains and passions, compassions and pities, mercies, and forgiveness, and such other similar things as are beneficial. But in the higher part there are none of these, but all is one great love and marvellous joy, in which marvellous joy all sufferings are greatly recompensed. And in this our good Lord showed not only our being forgiven, but also the glorious splendour to which he shall bring us, turning all our guilt into endless glory.

53

The kindness of God attributes no blame to his chosen ones, for in them is a godly will that never consents to sin. The pity of God must be so joined to them that a substance is preserved that can never be separated from him.

AND I saw that he wants us to know that he does not view more severely the fall of any created person that shall be saved than he did the fall of Adam, who we know was endlessly loved and safeguarded in the whole time of his need, and is now blissfully recompensed in great and surpassing joys; for our Lord God is so good, so noble, and so courteous that he can never find fault in those by whom he will always be blessed and praised.

And in what I have just said my wish was partly answered, and my great anxiety was somewhat eased by the loving gracious revelation of our good Lord; in which revelation I saw and understood most certainly that in every soul that will be saved is a godly will which never assented to sin, nor ever shall;* which will is so good that it can never intend evil, but always intends good constantly, and does good in the sight of God.

Therefore our Lord wants us to know this as a matter of faith and belief,* and especially and truly that we have all this blessed will kept whole and safe in our Lord Jesus Christ; for all of that kind with which heaven shall be filled must necessarily, through God's righteousness, be so joined and united to him that a substance would be maintained in them which never could nor should be separated from him; and this through his own good will in his endless foreseeing purpose. And despite this rightful conjoining and this endless union, the redemption and the buying back of mankind is still necessary and beneficial in everything, as it is done with the same intent and for the same purpose that Holy Church teaches us in our faith.

For I saw that God never began to love mankind,* for just as mankind shall be in endless bliss, completing the joy of God with regard to his works, just so the same mankind has been known and loved in God's foresight, from without beginning in his righteous intent. And by the endless assent of the whole Trinity in full accord, the Mid-Person* would be the foundation and head of this fair human nature, he from whom we have all come, in whom we are all enclosed, into whom we shall all return; finding in him our full heaven in everlasting joy through the foreseeing purpose of the whole blessed Trinity from without beginning. For before he made us he loved us; and when we were made we loved him; and this is a love made of the substantial goodness natural to the Holy Spirit, mighty by reason of the might of the Father, and wise in mind of the wisdom of the Son; and thus man's soul is made by God, and joined to God at the same point.*

And so I understood that man's soul is made of nothing, that is to say, it is made, but of nothing that is made, in this way: when God was to make man's body he took the slime of the earth,* which is matter mixed and gathered from all bodily things, and from that he made man's body; but for the making of man's soul he would not take anything at all, but made it. And so created nature is rightfully united to the creator, which is essential uncreated nature, that is, God. And so it is that there neither can nor shall be anything at all between God and man's soul. And in this endless love man's soul is kept whole, as the subject matter of the revelations means and shows; and in this endless love we are guided and protected by God and shall never be lost; for he wants us to know that our soul is a life, and this life, through his goodness and his grace, will last in heaven without end, loving him, thanking him, praising him. And just as we shall be without end, so we were treasured and hidden in God,* known and loved from without beginning.

Therefore he wants us to know that the noblest thing he ever made is mankind, and the supreme essence and the most exalted virtue is the blessed soul of Christ. And furthermore he wants us to know that Christ's beloved soul was preciously joined to him in the making; with a knot so subtle and so strong that it is united to God; and in this unity it is made endlessly holy. Furthermore, he wants us to know that all the souls which shall be saved in heaven without end are united and joined in this unity, and made holy in this holiness.*

54

We ought to rejoice that God dwells in our soul and our soul in God, so that between God and our soul there is nothing, but as it were all God; and how faith is foundation of all virtue in our soul, through the Holy Spirit.

AND because of the great, unending love that God has for all mankind, he makes no distinction in love between the blessed soul of Christ and the least soul that will be saved; for it is very easy to believe and to trust that the dwelling of the blessed soul of Christ is most high in the glorious Godhead, and truly, as I understood our Lord to mean, where the blessed soul of Christ is, there is the substance of all the souls that will be saved in Christ.*

We ought to rejoice greatly that God dwells in our soul, and we ought to rejoice much more greatly that our soul dwells in God. Our soul is made to be God's dwelling place, and the dwelling place of the soul is God, who is not made. And it is an exalted understanding to see and to know inwardly that God, who is our maker, dwells in our soul; and it is a more exalted understanding to see and to know that our soul, which is made, dwells in God's substance; and through this substance—God—we are what we are.

And I saw no difference between God and our substance, but as it were, all God, and yet my understanding took it that our substance is in God: that is to say that God is God, and our substance is a creation within God; for the almighty truth of the Trinity is our father, for he made us and keeps us in him; and the deep wisdom of the Trinity is our mother,* in whom we are all enclosed; and the exalted goodness of the Trinity is our Lord, and in him we are enclosed and he in us. We are enclosed in the Father, and we are enclosed in the Son, and we are enclosed in the Holy Spirit; and the Father is enclosed in us, and the Son is enclosed in us, and the Holy Spirit is enclosed in us: almighty, all wisdom, all goodness, one God, one Lord.

And our faith is a virtue that comes from our natural substance into our sensory soul through the Holy Spirit, in which all our virtues come to us—for without that no one can receive virtue—for it is nothing else but a right understanding with true belief and sure trust that in our essential being we are in God and God in us, which we do not see.* And this virtue, along with all the others coming into it that God has ordained to us, works great things in us; for Christ's working mercifully is within us, and we are in accord with him by grace through the gifts and the powers of the Holy Spirit; this working makes it so that we are Christ's children and live Christian lives.

55

Christ is our way, leading and presenting us to the Father; and as soon as the soul is infused into the body, mercy and grace are working. And how the Second Person took upon him our sensory being to deliver us from double death.

AND so Christ is our way,* leading us surely in his laws, and Christ in his body powerfully bears us up into heaven; for I saw that, having within him all of us who shall be saved by him, Christ presents his Father in heaven with us in worship; which present his Father receives most thankfully and courteously gives to his son, Jesus Christ; which gift and deed is joy to the Father, and bliss to the Son, and delight to the Holy Spirit. And out of everything that we are to do, it is the greatest delight to our Lord that we rejoice in this joy over our salvation which is in the blessed Trinity. And this was seen in the ninth revelation,* where more is said about this matter. And in spite of all our feelings, our sorrow or our joy, God wants us to understand and believe that we are more truly in heaven than on earth.

Our faith comes from the natural love of our soul, and from the clear light of our reason, and from the steadfast mindfulness of God which we receive from God at our first creation. And at the moment that our soul is breathed into our body, when we are created as sensory beings, mercy and grace at once begin to work, taking care of us and protecting us with pity and love; and during this process the Holy Spirit forms in our faith the hope that we shall rise up above again to our substance, into the virtue of Christ, increased and accomplished through the Holy Spirit. Thus I understood that the sensory being is grounded in nature, in mercy, and in grace, and this foundation enables us to receive gifts that lead us to eternal life; for I saw most certainly that our substance is in God, and I also saw that God is in our sensory being; for at the very point that our soul is made sensory, at the same point is the city of God, ordained for him from without beginning, into which he enters and shall never vacate, for God is never out of the soul in which he shall dwell blissfully without end.*

And this was seen in the sixteenth revelation, where it says: 'The place that Jesus takes in our soul, he will never vacate.'*

And all the gifts that God can give to those whom he has created, he has given to his son Jesus for us; and he, dwelling in us, has enclosed these gifts in himself until the time when we have grown and matured, our soul with our body and our body with our soul, either of them receiving help from the other, until in the course of nature we reach full stature; and then on the basis of nature through the action of mercy the Holy Spirit, through grace, breathes into us gifts leading to eternal life. And so my understanding was led by God to see in him and to understand, to know, and to recognize, that our soul is a created trinity,* like the uncreated blessed Trinity, known and loved from without beginning; and in the making united to the maker, as is said before.* This insight was very sweet and wonderful to contemplate, peaceful and restful, sure and delectable. And because of the glorious union that was thus made by God between the soul and the body, it has to be that mankind shall be redeemed from a double death;* and this redemption could never have occurred until the time when the Second Person in the Trinity had taken on the lower part of human nature, to which the higher part was united in the first creation.* And these two parts were in Christ, the higher and the lower, which is but one soul. The higher part was at one with God in peace, in full joy and bliss; the lower part, which is sensory being, suffered for the salvation of mankind. And these two parts were seen and felt in the eighth revelation,* in which my body was filled with the recollection and feeling of Christ's Passion and his death. And furthermore, along with this came a subtle feeling and a mysterious inner perception of the higher part, which I was shown at the same time,* when I could not—in response to the suggestion of an intermediary—look up into heaven; and that was because of that powerful contemplative insight into the inner life—the inner life which is that exalted substance, that precious soul, which is endlessly rejoicing in the Godhead.

56

It is easier to know God than our soul, for God is nearer to us than that, and therefore if we want to have knowledge of it, we must seek into God; and he wants us to long to have knowledge of nature, mercy, and grace.

AND so I saw most certainly that it is quicker and easier for us to come to the knowledge of God than to know our own soul; for our soul is so deeply grounded in God, and so endlessly treasured, that we cannot come to the knowledge of our soul until we first have knowledge of God, the creator to whom it is united. But despite this, I saw that naturally, for the fullest understanding, we must long to know our own soul wisely and truly, and through this we are taught to seek it where it is, and that is in God. And so, through grace, by the leading of the Holy Spirit we should know them both in one, whether we are moved to know God or our soul; they are both good and true.

God is nearer to us than our own soul; for he is the foundation on which our soul stands, and he is the means that keeps the substance and the sensory being together, so that they will never separate; for our soul sits in God in true rest, and our soul stands in God in sure strength, and our soul is naturally rooted in God in endless love. And therefore if we want to have knowledge of our soul, and communion and discourse with it, we must seek for it in our Lord God, in whom it is enclosed. And I saw and understood more of this enclosure in the sixteenth revelation, as I shall say.* And as regards our substance, it may rightly be called our soul, and as regards our sensory being, it may rightly be called our soul; and that is because of the union that the soul has in God.

The noble city in which our Lord Jesus sits is our sensory being, in which he is enclosed; and our natural substance is enclosed in Jesus, with the blessed soul of Christ sitting at rest in the Godhead.* And I saw most certainly that it is fitting that we should be in longing and in penance until the time when we are led so deeply into God that we veritably and truly know our own soul. And in truth I saw that our good Lord leads us himself into this exalted profundity, in the same love with which he made us, and in the same love with which he redeemed us through mercy and grace by virtue of his blessed Passion. And despite all this, we can never come to a full knowledge of God until we first know our own soul clearly; for until our soul is in the fullness of its powers we cannot be in complete holiness; and that is when our sensory being, by virtue of Christ's Passion, is raised up to the substance, with all the benefits that our Lord will cause us to derive from our tribulations through mercy and grace.

I had some partial insight into this, and it is based on nature; that is to say, our reason is grounded in God, who is the very essence of being. From this essential nature mercy and grace spring and spread into us, making everything work in fulfilment of our joy. These are the grounds in which we have our being, our growth and our fulfilment; for in nature we have our life and our being, and in mercy and grace we have our growth and our fulfilment. These are three aspects of one goodness, and where one works they all work in the things which involve us now.

God wants us to understand, yearning with all our heart and all our strength to have more and more knowledge of them until the time that we are fulfilled; for to know them fully and to see them clearly is nothing else but endless joy and bliss, which we shall have in heaven, and which God wishes to be begun here in knowledge of his love. For we cannot benefit by our reason alone, unless we truly have insight and love as well; nor can we be saved solely through our natural foundation that we have in God unless we have knowledge of the same foundation, mercy, and grace; for from these three working together we receive all our goodness. Of these, the first are the goods of nature; for in our first creation God gave us as abundant goods and also greater goods such as we could receive only in spirit, but in his endless wisdom his prescient purpose wished that we should have this twofold nature.

57

In our substance we are complete; in our sensory being we are lacking, and God will make this good through mercy and grace. And how the higher part of our nature is joined to God in its creation, and God, Jesus, is joined to the lower part of our nature in taking on our flesh. And how other virtues spring from faith; and Mary is our mother.

AND as regards our substance, God made us so noble and so rich that we always work his will and his glory. When I say 'we', that means those who will be saved;* for I saw truly that we are what he loves and we do what pleases him, lastingly and without ceasing; and from these great riches and this exalted nobility, virtues come to our soul commensurately when it is conjoined with our body, and in this conjoining we are created as sensory beings. And so in our substance we are complete, and in our sensory being we are lacking—and God will remedy and make good this lack through the action of mercy and grace, flowing in to us abundantly from his own natural goodness. And so his natural goodness makes mercy and grace work within us; and the natural goodness that we have from him enables us to receive the working of mercy and grace.

I saw that in God our nature is complete, and in this nature he creates diverse qualities flowing out of him to do his will, which nature maintains, and mercy and grace restore and fulfil. And none of these shall come to nothing; for the higher part of our nature is joined to God in its creation; and God is joined to the lower part of our nature in taking on our flesh. And so in Christ our two natures are united; for the Trinity is comprehended in Christ, in whom the higher part of our nature is grounded and rooted, and the Second Person has taken our lower part, a nature which was ordained for him from the first; for I saw most certainly that all the works which God has done, and ever shall do, were fully known to him and foreseen from without beginning; and he made mankind for love, and for the same love he himself wished to become man.

The next good which we receive is our faith, in which we begin to benefit; and it comes from the great riches of our natural substance into our sensory soul; and it is grounded in us, and we in it, through the natural goodness of God by the operation of mercy and grace. And from this come all the other goods by which we are guided and saved; for from it come the commandments of God, and we ought to have two kinds of understanding of those: one is that we ought to understand and know which are his commandments, so as to love and observe them; the other is that we ought to know what things he forbids, and to hate and reject these; for all that we do is included in these two. Also included in our faith are the seven sacraments,* following each other in order as God has ordained them for us, and all manner of virtues; for by the goodness of God the same virtues that we have received from our substance given to us by nature— those same virtues, by the operation of mercy, are given to us through grace, renewed through the Holy Spirit. These virtues and gifts are treasured up for us in Jesus Christ; for at the same time that God joined himself to our body in the Virgin's womb he took on our sensory soul, and in taking it on, having enclosed us all in himself, he united the sensory soul to our substance. In this union he was perfect man; for Christ, having united in himself everyone who will be saved, is perfect man.

So our Lady is our mother, in whom we are all enclosed and born of her in Christ; for she who is mother of our Saviour is mother of all who will be saved in our Saviour;* and our Saviour is our true mother, in whom we are endlessly born, and out of whom we shall never come to birth.* Abundantly, and fully, and sweetly was this shown; and it is spoken of in the first revelation, where he says that we are all enclosed in him and he is enclosed in us;* and it is spoken of in the sixteenth revelation, where it says he sits in our soul;* for it is his pleasure to reign blissfully in our understanding, and to sit restfully in our soul, and to dwell endlessly in our soul, working us all into himself. In this working he wants us to be his helpers, giving him all our attention, learning his teachings, keeping his laws, desiring that everything that he does should be done, trusting faithfully in him; for I saw truly that our substance is in God.

58

God was never displeased with his chosen spouse; and of the three properties of the Trinity: fatherhood, motherhood, and lordship; and how our substance is in every Person, but our sensory being is in Christ alone.

JUST as God—the blessed Trinity who is everlasting being—is eternal from without beginning, so it was his eternal purpose to create mankind, whose fair nature was first assigned to his own son, the Second Person of the Trinity. And when he so wished, by full agreement of the whole Trinity, he created us all at once;* and in creating us he joined and united us to himself, a union through which we are kept as pure and noble as we were created. By virtue of the same precious union we love our Maker and please him, praise him and thank him and endlessly rejoice in him. And this is the work which is performed continually in every soul that shall be saved, and this is the godly will mentioned before.* And so in our making, God almighty is our loving father by nature; and God all wisdom is our loving mother by nature, together with the love and goodness of the Holy Spirit, which is all one God, one Lord. And in the joining and in the union he is our very true spouse, and we his beloved bride and his fair maiden, a bride with whom he is never displeased; for he says, 'I love you and you love me, and our love shall never be divided in two.'*

I considered the operation of all the blessed Trinity, and in contemplating this I saw and understood these three properties: the property of the fatherhood, the property of the motherhood, and the property of the lordship in one God. In our Father almighty we have our safekeeping and our bliss as regards our natural substance, which is ours by our making from without beginning; and in the Second Person of the Trinity, in understanding and wisdom, we have our safekeeping as regards our sensory being, our redemption and our salvation; for he is our mother, brother, and Saviour.* And in our good Lord the Holy Spirit we have our reward and our recompense for our living and what we undergo, endlessly surpassing all that we desire, in his marvellous courtesy, out of his great and abundant grace.

For our whole life is threefold. In the first part we have our being, and in the second we grow, and in the third we have our fulfilment. The first is nature; the second is mercy; the third is grace. As for the first, I saw and understood that the great power of the Trinity is our Father, and the deep wisdom of the Trinity is our mother, and the great love of the Trinity is our Lord; and we have all this by nature and in the creation of the substantial part of our souls. And further-more, I saw that the same beloved Second Person who is our mother in our substantial being has become our mother in our sensory being; for we are twofold by God's making, that is to say, in substance and sensory being. Our substance is the higher part, which we have in our Father, God almighty; and the Second Person of the Trinity is our mother in nature, in our substantial creation, in whom we are grounded and rooted, and he is our mother in mercy by taking on our sensory being. And so our mother—in whom the parts of us are kept undivided—works within us in various ways; for in our mother, Christ, we profit and grow, and in mercy he reforms and restores us, and, by virtue of his Passion and his death and resurrection, he unites us to our substance. So our mother acts mercifully to all his children who are submissive and obedient to him.

And grace works with mercy, and especially in two ways, as was shown,* and this work belongs to the third Person, the Holy Spirit, who works by rewarding and giving. The rewarding is a generous gift of truth which the Lord gives to those who have laboured, and the giving is a courteous action which he performs generously through grace, fulfilling and surpassing all that is deserved by those he has created. So in our Father, God almighty, we have our being; and in our mother through mercy we have our reforming and restoring, in whom our parts are united and all made perfect man; and by the rewards and gracious gift of the Holy Spirit we are made complete. And our substance is in our Father, God almighty, and our substance is in our mother, God all wisdom, and our substance is in our Lord the Holy Spirit, God all goodness; for our substance is whole in each Person of the Trinity, which is one God. And our sensory being is only in the Second Person, Christ Jesus, in whom are the Father and the Holy Spirit; and in him and by him we are taken out of hell through his might, and out of the wretchedness of earth, and gloriously brought up into heaven and blessedly united to our substance, increased in riches and nobility by all the virtue of Christ, and by the grace and operation of the Holy Spirit.

59

Wickedness is turned into blessedness through mercy and grace in the chosen, for the nature of God is to return good for evil through Jesus, our mother in kind grace; and the soul highest in virtue is the meekest, and on this foundation we have other virtues.

AND this blessedness is ours through mercy and grace—a kind of blessedness we might never have had nor known if that quality of goodness which is in God had not been opposed, for through that we have this blessedness. For wickedness has been allowed to rise up in opposition to goodness, and the goodness of mercy and grace opposed wickedness and turned everything to goodness and to glory for all those who shall be saved; for that is the quality in God which does good against evil.

So Jesus Christ who does good in return for evil is our true mother; we have our being from him where the ground of motherhood begins, with all the precious safekeeping of love which endlessly follows. As truly as God is our father, so truly is God our mother; and he revealed that in everything, and especially in those sweet words where he says:* 'It is I', that is to say: 'It is I: the power and the goodness of fatherhood. It is I: the wisdom and the kindness of motherhood. It is I: the light* and the grace which is all blessed love. It is I: the Trinity. It is I: the unity. I am the supreme goodness of all manner of things. It is I who makes you to love. It is I who makes you to long. It is I: the endless fulfilment of all true desires.'

For the soul is highest, noblest, and worthiest when it is lowest, humblest, and gentlest; and from this essential foundation we have all our virtues and our sensory being by gift of nature and with the help and furtherance of mercy and grace, without which we cannot benefit. Our high Father, God almighty, who is being, knew us and loved us from before there was any time.* Out of this knowledge, in his marvellously deep love through the prescient eternal counsel of all the blessed Trinity, he wanted the Second Person to become our mother, our brother, and our Saviour. From this it follows that as truly as God is our father, so truly is God our mother. Our Father wills, our mother acts, our good Lord the Holy Spirit confirms. And therefore it befits us to love our God in whom we have our being, reverently thanking and praising him for our creation, praying to our mother with all our might for mercy and pity, and to our Lord the Holy Spirit for help and grace; for our whole life is in these three— nature, mercy, and grace; from these we have meekness, gentleness, patience, and pity, and hatred of sin and wickedness; for it is in the nature of virtues to hate sin and wickedness.

And so Jesus is our true mother by nature at our first creation, and he is our true mother in grace by taking on our created nature. All the fair work and all the sweet, loving offices of beloved motherhood are appropriated to the Second Person; for in him we have this godly will, whole and safe without end, both in nature and in grace, out of his own intrinsic goodness.

I understood three ways of regarding motherhood in God: the first is how he is the foundation of our nature's creation; the second is his taking on of our nature (and there the motherhood of grace begins); the third is the motherhood at work, and in this, by the same grace, there is a spreading outwards of length, and breadth, and of height and of depth without end,* and all is one love.

60

How we are redeemed and outspread by the mercy and grace of our sweet, kind, and ever-loving mother, Jesus; and of the properties of motherhood. But Jesus is our true mother, feeding us not with milk but with himself, opening his side to us and claiming all our love.

BUT now it is necessary to say a little more about this spreading outwards as I understood it in our Lord's meaning, how we are redeemed again by the motherhood of mercy and grace into our natural home where we were made by the motherhood of natural love; a natural love which never leaves us. Our mother in nature, our mother in grace—because he wanted* to become our mother wholly and in all things—undertook the foundation of his work very humbly and very gently in the Virgin's womb. And he showed that in the first revelation* where he brought that meek maiden before my mind's eye as the slight figure she was when she conceived; that is to say, our great God, the supreme wisdom of all, made himself ready in this humble place and dressed himself in our poor flesh, himself to perform the service and the office of motherhood in everything. The mother's service is closest, most willing, and most sure: closest because it is most natural, most willing because it is most loving, and most sure because it is most true. No one ever might nor could perform this office fully, nor ever did, but he alone. We know that our mothers bear us and bring us into this world to suffering and to death, and yet our true mother Jesus, he, all love, gives birth to us into joy and to endless life—blessed may he be! So he sustains us within himself in love and was in labour* for the full time, he who wanted to suffer the sharpest pangs and the most grievous sufferings that ever were or ever shall be, and at the last he died. And when he had finished and so given birth to us into bliss, not even all this could satisfy his marvellous love; and he revealed that in these exaltedly surpassing words of love: 'If I could suffer more, I would suffer more.'*

He could not die any more, but he would not cease from working. So then he has to feed us, for a mother's precious love has made him owe us that. The mother can give her child her milk to suck, but our precious mother Jesus, he can feed us with himself*—and does, most courteously and most tenderly with the blessed sacrament that is precious food of true life. And with all the sweet sacraments he sustains us most mercifully and graciously, and so he meant in those blessed words where he said, 'It is I that Holy Church preaches to you and teaches you';* that is to say, 'All the health and life of the sacraments, all the power and grace of my word, all the goodness which is ordained in Holy Church for you, it is I.'

The mother can lay the child tenderly to her breast, but our tender mother Jesus, he can lead us intimately into his blessed breast through his sweet open side and reveal within part of the Godhead and the joys of heaven, with spiritual certainty of endless bliss; and he showed that in the tenth revelation,* giving the same understanding in those sweet words where he says, 'See, how I love you', looking into his side, rejoicing.

This fair, lovely word 'mother' is so sweet and so kind in itself that it cannot truly be said of anyone or to anyone except of him and to him who is the true mother of life and of all things.* To the nature of motherhood belong kind love, wisdom, and knowledge; and it is good, for although the birth of our body may be only humble, lowly, and simple in comparison with the birth of our soul, yet it is he who does it in the created beings by whom it is done.

The kind, loving mother who knows and recognizes the needs of her child protects it very tenderly as the nature and condition of motherhood requires. And as the child grows older she changes her method but not her love. And when it is grown up more, she allows it to be chastised to break down vices so as to make the child gain in virtues and grace. Such actions, with all that is fair and good, our Lord performs through those by whom they are done. So he is our mother in nature by the operation of grace in the lower part of the self, for love of the higher part. And he wants us to know it, for he wants to have all our love made fast to him. And in this I saw that all our debt that we owe, by God's command, to fatherhood and motherhood— because of God's fatherhood and motherhood*—is fulfilled in truly loving God, a blessed love which Christ prompts in us. And this was revealed in everything, and especially in the exalted and bounteous words where he says, 'It is I you love.'*

61

Jesus shows more tenderness in giving birth to us spiritually; though he allows us to fall, so that we come to recognize our sinfulness, he swiftly raises us up, not withholding his love because of our wrongdoing, for he cannot allow his child to perish. For he wants us to have the nature of a child, always hurrying to him in our need.

AND in our spiritual birthing he employs incomparably greater tenderness in caring for us, in as much as our soul is of greater value in his sight. He kindles our understanding, he directs our ways, he eases our conscience, he comforts our soul, he enlightens our heart and gives us, in part, knowledge and love of his blessed Godhead, with recollection through grace of his beloved humanity and his blessed Passion, with courteous wonder at his great, surpassing goodness; and he makes us love all that he loves for love of him, and to be well-pleased with him and all his works. If we fall, he quickly raises us up by calling us lovingly and touching us with grace. And when we are strengthened in this way by his precious actions, then we willingly choose him through his precious grace, and to be his servants and to love him everlastingly without end.

And after this he allows some of us to fall harder and more grievously that we ever did before, as it seems to us. And then we, who are not altogether wise, think that all that we have started upon was of no value. But it is not so; for we need to fall, and we need to see this; for if we did not fall, we should not know how feeble and how wretched we are in ourselves; nor should we know so fully our maker's marvellous love; for we shall see truly in heaven without end that we have sinned grievously in this life and—in spite of this—we shall see that his love for us remains intact, and we were never of any less value in his sight. And through this experience of failure we shall have a great and marvellous knowledge of love in God without end; for strong and marvellous is that love which cannot, nor will not, be broken through our transgressions. And this is one way to understand how we benefit. Another is the humility and meekness which we shall gain through seeing our own fall; for by this we shall be raised high in heaven, and we might never have been so raised up without that humility.* And so we need to see it, and if we do not see it, even though we should fall, it would not do us any good. And usually, we fall first and then we see it, and both through the mercy of God. The mother may allow the child to fall sometimes and be hurt in various ways for its own benefit, but because of her love she can never allow any kind of danger to befall the child. And even though our earthly mother may let her child perish, our heavenly mother Jesus may not allow us who are his children to perish;* for he is almighty, all wisdom, and all love, and so is none but he—blessed may he be!

But often when our falling and our wretchedness are shown to us, we are so much afraid and so greatly ashamed of ourselves that we hardly know where to put ourselves. But then our courteous mother does not want us to flee away, for nothing would be more unwelcome to him. But he wants us then to behave like a child; for when it is upset or frightened it runs quickly to its mother for help as fast as it can; so he wants us to behave like a submissive child, saying, 'My kind mother, my gracious mother, my dearest mother, take pity on me. I have made myself dirty and unlike you, and I neither can nor may put this right except with your very own help and grace.' And if we do not then feel ourselves helped straightaway, let us be sure that he is behaving like a wise mother; for if he sees that it would be more to our advantage for us to mourn and to weep, he allows that with pity and compassion until the right moment, out of love. And then he wants us to take on the characteristics of a child, who always naturally trusts in its mother's love, whether in joy or in sorrow.

And he wants us to hold fast to the faith of Holy Church and find there our dearest mother in the consolation of true understanding, along with all the blessed communion of saints; for a single individual may often feel broken, as it seems to him, but the whole body of Holy Church was never broken nor ever shall be, without end. And therefore it is a safe thing—and good and gracious—to wish humbly and strongly to be sustained by and united to our mother, Holy Church, that is Christ Jesus: for the flood of mercy which is his dearest blood and precious water is plentifully available to make us fair and pure. The blessed wounds of our Saviour are open and rejoice to heal us; the sweet, gracious hands of our mother are ready and enfold us diligently; for in all this he performs the role of a kindly nurse who has nothing else to do but attend to the safety of her child. It is his role to save us, it is his glory to do this, and it is his wish that we know it; for he wants us to love him kindly and trust in him humbly and strongly. And he revealed this in these gracious words: 'I am keeping you very safe.'*

62

The love of God never lets his chosen ones lose time, for all their trouble is turned into endless joy; and how we are beholden to God for his kind nature and for grace; for every kind of nature is in man, and we do not need to seek out different kinds, but instead seek out Holy Church.

FOR at that time he revealed our frailty and our downfalls, our feeling broken and abject, humiliated and isolated: and as much of all our misery as it seemed to me could befall us in this life.

And with this he revealed his blessed power, his blessed wisdom, his blessed love, in which he protects us at such times as tenderly and as sweetly to his glory and as surely to our salvation as he does when we have the greatest consolation and comfort; and with this he raises us in spirit on high in heaven, and turns everything to his glory and to our joy without end; for his precious love never allows us to lose time. And all this springs from the natural goodness of God through the workings of grace.

God in his very being is kindly nature: that is to say, the goodness which is natural is God. He is the ground, he is the substance, he is the same thing as kind nature, and he is true father and true mother of nature. And all the kinds of nature which he has made flow from him to work his will shall be restored and brought back within him again by the salvation of man through the workings of grace; for all the kinds of nature that he has invested in part in various creatures are all wholly present in man, in fullness, in power, in beauty and in goodness, in majesty and nobility, in every kind of dignity of worth and honour. Here we can see that we are all fully bound to God, by nature, and we are all fully bound to God by grace. Here we can see that we do not need to seek far and wide in order to know various kinds of natures but seek them rather in Holy Church, in our mother's breast; that is to say, in our own soul, where our Lord is dwelling.* And there we shall find everything: now, in faith and understanding; and afterwards, truly in himself and clearly in bliss.

But let no man or woman apply this exclusively to themselves; for it is not so, it is universal, for it is our precious mother, Christ, and this fair nature was prepared for him, for the glory and nobility of man's creation, and for the joy and bliss of man's salvation; just as he saw, knew, and recognized from without beginning.

63

Sin is more painful than hell, and is vile and damaging to nature; but grace saves nature and destroys sin. The children of Jesus are not yet all born, and never grow beyond childhood, living in feebleness until they come to heaven, where joys are always beginning anew forever.

HERE we can see that it is truly for us to hate sin by nature, and it is truly for us to hate sin by grace; for nature is all good and fair in itself, and grace was sent forth to save nature and destroy sin and bring fair nature back to the blessed point from which it came, that is God, with greater nobility and glory through the virtuous workings of grace; for it shall be seen before God by all his holy ones in joy without end that nature has been assayed in the fire of tribulation, and no lack or deficiency has been found in it. So nature and grace are of one accord; for grace is God, as nature is God. He is twofold in his way of working and single in love, and neither of them works without the other, nor are they separated. And when through the mercy of God and with his help we find harmony with nature and grace, we shall truly see that sin is incomparably more vile and more painful than hell; for it is contrary to our fair nature; for as truly as sin is unclean, so truly is it unnatural, and so a horrible thing to see for the loved soul that wishes to be all fair and shining in the sight of God, as nature and grace teach.

But let us not be afraid of this, except in so far as fear may help us, but let us meekly lament to our dearest mother, and he will besprinkle us all over with his precious blood* and make our soul very pliant and very gentle, and heal us most beautifully in the course of time, just as is most glory to him and joy to us without end. And he will never cease or desist from this lovely and precious work until all his beloved children are born and delivered. And he revealed that when he showed how spiritual thirst is to be understood,* which is the love-longing which will last until the day of judgement.

So our life is grounded in the prescient wisdom from without beginning of our true mother Jesus, along with the great power of the Father and the great and supreme goodness of the Holy Spirit. And in his taking on of our nature he gave us life; in his blessed dying upon the cross he gave birth to us into eternal life; and from that time, and now, and forever until the day of judgement, he feeds us and fosters us, just as the great and supreme lovingness of motherhood and the natural need of childhood require. Lovely and precious is our heavenly mother in the sight of our soul; precious and lovely are the children of grace in the sight of our heavenly mother, with gentleness and meekness, and all the lovely virtues which belong to children by nature; for naturally the child does not despair of the mother's love; naturally the child does not presume to act by itself; naturally the child loves its mother, and each loves the other; these, and all others that are like them, are the fair virtues with which our heavenly mother is honoured and pleased. And I understood that in this life we never reach any higher state than childhood, in our weakness and deficiency of strength and understanding, until the time when our gracious mother has brought us up into our Father's bliss. And then it will truly be made known to us what he means in those sweet words where he says, 'All shall be well; and you shall see for yourself that all manner of things shall be well.'* And then the bliss of our motherhood in Christ will begin anew in the joys of our God; a new beginning which will last without end, always beginning anew.

So I understood that all his blessed children who have come forth from him by nature shall be brought back within him by grace.

64

The fifteenth revelation as it was shown. The absence of God in this life is a very great affliction to us, besides other sorrows, but we shall suddenly be taken from all suffering, having Jesus for our mother; and our patiently waiting is very pleasing to God; and God wants us to take our suffering lightly, for love, thinking ourselves always at the point of being delivered from this life.

BEFORE this time I had a great longing and desire as a gift from God to be released from this world and from this life;* for I often considered the misery that is here, and the well-being and the bliss that it is to be there. And even if there had been no pain in this life except the absence of our Lord, it seemed to me sometimes more than I could bear; and this made me grieve and yearn intensely, as also did my own miserable state, laziness, and weakness, so that I took no pleasure in living and striving as it fell to me to do. And to all this our courteous Lord replied, to give me comfort and patience, and said these words, 'You shall suddenly be taken from all your pain, from all your sickness, from all your distress, and from all your unhappiness. And you shall come up above, and you shall have me for your reward, and you shall be filled full of love and of bliss. And you shall never have any kind of suffering, any kind of sickness, anything displeasing, any disappointed desires, but always joy and bliss without end. Why then should it bother you to suffer for a while, since it is my will and my glory?'

And in these words—'You shall suddenly be taken'—I saw how

God rewards man for the patience that he shows in awaiting God's will, and for his time, and that man extends his patience over the course of his lifetime; for it is a great advantage that he is in ignorance of when he will pass away; for if a man knew when his time was to be, he would not have patience over the time until then. And it is God's will that, while the soul is in the body, it seems to itself that it is always on the point of being taken; for all this life and this distress that we have here is only a moment, and when we are suddenly taken out of suffering into bliss, then pain will be as nothing.

And at this time* I saw a body lying on the earth, a body which looked dismal and ugly, without shape and form, as if it were a swollen, heaving mass of stinking mire. And suddenly out of this body sprang a very beautiful creature, a little child perfectly shaped and formed, swift and full of life, whiter than a lily, which quickly glided up into heaven.* And the bloatedness of the body signifies the great wretchedness of our mortal flesh, and the smallness of the child signifies the cleanness of purity in the soul. And I thought, 'None of this child's beauty remains with this body, nor does any of this body's foulness remain on this child.'

It is more blessed for man to be taken from suffering than for suffering to be taken from man; for if suffering be taken from us it may come back again. Therefore it is a supreme comfort and a blessed perception for a loving soul that we shall be taken from suffering; for in this promise I saw a marvellous compassion for us which our Lord has on account of our misery, and a courteous promise of pure deliverance; for he wants us to be comforted by this moment of transcendence; and he showed that in these words: 'And you shall come up above; and you shall have me for your reward; and you shall be filled full of joy and bliss.'*

It is God's will that we should concentrate our thoughts on this blessed perception as often as we can and continue with it as long as we can, through his grace; for this is a blessed contemplation to the soul that is led by God, and greatly to his glory for the time that it lasts. If, on account of our weakness, we fall back again into our depression and spiritual blindness and feeling of spiritual and bodily pains, it is God's will that we know that he has not forgotten us. And this is what he means and says for comfort in these words: 'And you shall never have any more suffering, nor any kind of sickness, nor anything displeasing, nor disappointed desires, but always joy and bliss without end. Why should it then grieve you to suffer for a while, seeing that it is my will and my glory?'

It is God's will that we accept his promises and his comfortings as generously and as fully as we can take them. And he also wants us to take our waiting and our distress as lightly as we can take them and count them as nothing; for the more lightly we take them and the less value we set on them out of love, the less pain we shall experience from feeling them, and the more thanks and reward we shall have for them.

65

He who chooses God for love, with reverent humility, is sure to be saved; this reverent humility sees the Lord as marvellously great, and the self as marvellously small; and it is God's will that we fear nothing but him, for the power of our enemy is taken into our friend's hand; and so everything that God does shall be greatly pleasing to us.

AND so I understood that any man or woman who in this life willingly chooses God out of love may be sure of being loved without end, and this endless love works that grace in them. For he wants us to hold to this trustingly: that we may be as certain in our hope of the bliss of heaven while we are here, as we shall be in certitude when we are there. And the more pleasure and joy that we take in this assurance with reverence and humility, the better God is pleased—as it was revealed.

This reverence that I mean is a holy, courteous fear of our Lord, to which humility is conjoined, which means that anyone sees the Lord as marvellously great, and the self as marvellously small; for these virtues are possessed endlessly by those loved by God and may be seen and felt now in some measure through the gracious presence of our Lord, when that presence occurs; a presence which of all things is most longed for, because it brings about marvellous assurance in true faith and sure hope through greatness of love, and in fear that is sweet and delightful.*

It is God's will that I should see myself as much bound to him in love as if all that he has done had been done for me. And so should every soul think inwardly of his lover: that is to say, the love of God creates in us such a unity that when it is truly seen no man can separate himself from another.* And so our soul ought to think that God has done for the soul all that he has done: and he reveals this to make us love him and fear nothing but him; for it is his will that we know that all the power of our enemy is under lock and key in our friend's hand; and therefore the soul that knows this for certain will fear nothing but him whom the soul loves. All other fears the soul reckons along with passions and bodily illness and imaginings.

And therefore, though we are in so much pain, misery, and distress that it seems to us that we can think of nothing at all but the state we are in or what we are feeling, let us, as soon as we can, pass over it lightly and count it as nothing. And why? Because God wants us to know that, if we know him and love him and reverently fear him, we shall have peace and be in complete repose; and all that he does will be great pleasure to us. And our Lord revealed that in these words, 'Why should it then grieve you to suffer for a while, since it is my will and my glory?'*

Now I have told you of fifteen revelations as God was pleased to convey them to my mind, renewed by moments of illumination and inspiration, I hope, of the same spirit that revealed them all. The first of these fifteen revelations began early in the morning, at about four o'clock,* and they lasted, proceeding to reveal themselves over the course of time most beautifully and surely, one after the other, until it was well past the middle of the day.*

66

The sixteenth revelation; and it is conclusion and confirmation of all fifteen; and of her weakness and grieving in distress and speaking lightly of the great comfort of Jesus, saying she had been delirious, which, she being seriously ill, I suppose was only a venial sin. But still, after that the devil had great power to vex her nearly to death.

AND after this the good Lord showed the sixteenth revelation on the following night, as I shall describe later;* and this sixteenth revelation was the conclusion and confirmation to all fifteen. But first I must tell you about my weakness, wretchedness, and blindness. I said at the beginning,* 'And suddenly, at that moment, all my pain was taken from me'; and I had no trouble nor distress from this pain as long as the sequence of fifteen revelations lasted; and at the end everything was at a close, and I saw no more. And soon I felt that I would live and go on suffering; and straightaway my sickness came back: first in my head, with a sound and a din; and suddenly all my body was filled with sickness just as it was before, and I felt as barren and as dry as if I had only ever had little comfort. And like a wretch I mourned and grieved on account of the bodily pain I experienced and the lack of comfort, spiritual and bodily.

Then a member of a religious order* came to me and asked me how I was getting on. And I said I had been raving today, and he laughed loudly and heartily. And I said, 'The cross that was held in front of my face—it seemed to me it was bleeding hard.'* And at these words the person to whom I was speaking was amazed and became very serious. And at once I felt very ashamed and astonished at my carelessness and I thought: 'This man takes seriously the least word I say, yet knows no more of it than that.'

And when I saw that he took it seriously and so very reverently, I grew very much ashamed, and wanted to have been confessed; but at that time I could not tell any priest about it, because I thought, 'How could a priest believe me, when I, by saying I had been delirious, showed myself not to believe our Lord God?' I had truly believed during the time that I was seeing him, and it was then my wish and my intention to do so for ever, without end, but, like a fool, I let it pass from my mind. Ah, look what a wretch I was! This was a great sin and great ingratitude that I—through stupidity, because of feeling a little bodily pain—so foolishly lost for the time being the comfort of all this blessed revelation of our Lord God.

Here you can see what I am in myself; but our courteous Lord would not leave me like this. And I lay still till night, trusting in his mercy, and then I went to sleep. And as soon as I fell asleep, it seemed to me that the devil was at my throat, thrusting forward very close to my face a face like a young man's; it was long and strangely thin; I never saw the like. The colour was red like a tile when it is newly fired, with black spots on it like black freckles, but filthier than the tile. His hair was red as rust, trimmed at the front, with side-locks hanging down at his temples. He grinned at me with a wicked expression, showing white teeth—and so big as to seem all the more menacing to me. His body and hands were misshapen but with his paws he gripped me by the throat* and would have strangled me, but he could not. This horrible apparition occurred while I was asleep, as none of the revelations did.* And during this whole time I trusted I would be saved and protected by the mercy of God. And our courteous Lord gave me grace to wake up, and I was barely alive.

The people who were with me* watched over me and bathed my temples, and my heart began to take comfort. And straightaway a little smoke came in at the door with a great heat and a foul stench.* I said, 'Blessed be the Lord! Is everything here on fire?' And I supposed it to have been an actual fire that would have burned us all to death. I asked those who were with me if they were aware of any stench. They said no, they did not notice anything. I said, 'Blessed be God!' because I well knew it was the devil that had come to assail me. And at once I accepted what our Lord had revealed to me that same day, together with all the faith of Holy Church, for I regarded them both as one, and had recourse to that as to my comfort. And immediately everything vanished away, and I was brought to a state of great rest and peace, without sickness of body or troubled conscience.

67

Of the glorious city of the soul, which is created so nobly that it could not have been made any better, in which the Trinity rejoices everlastingly; and the soul can find rest in nothing but in God, who is seated there, ruling all things.

AND then our Lord opened my spiritual eyes and showed me my soul in the midst of my heart. I saw the soul as large as if it were an endless world, and as if it were a blessed kingdom; and from the properties I saw in it I understood that it is a glorious city.* In the midst of that city sits our Lord Jesus, true God and true man, a handsome person and of great stature, highest bishop, grandest king, most glorious lord; and I saw him dressed resplendently and gloriously. He sits in the midst of the soul in peace and rest.* And the Godhead rules and guards heaven and earth and all that is. The manhood sits at rest with the Godhead; the Godhead rules and guards without any instrument or effort; and the soul is wholly occupied with the blessed Godhead which is supreme power, supreme wisdom, and supreme goodness. Through all eternity Jesus will never vacate the place he takes in our soul, as far as I can see; for in us is the home most familiar to him and his everlasting dwelling.*

And in this he revealed the delight that he has in the making of man's soul; for as well as the Father might make a creature, and as well as the Son could make a creature, so well did the Holy Spirit wish that man's soul be made; and so it was done. And therefore the blessed Trinity rejoices without end in the making of man's soul;* for he saw from without beginning what would delight him without end. Everything that he has made shows his lordship; understanding of this was given at the same time through the example of someone who was to see great splendours and kingdoms belonging to a lord, and when this person had seen all the splendours below, then, marvelling, that person was moved to seek above for the high place where the lord dwelled, knowing by reason that his dwelling is in the place of most worth; and so I understood truly that our soul may never find rest in things that are beneath itself. And when it rises above all created beings into itself, it still cannot remain there contemplating itself, but all its contemplation is blessedly focused on God who is the creator dwelling within; for in man's soul is his true dwelling; and the greatest light in the city, and the most radiant, is the glorious love of our Lord, as it seems to me. And what can make us rejoice more in God than to see in him that he rejoices over us most highly of all his works? For I saw in the same revelation that if the blessed Trinity could have made man's soul any better, any fairer, any nobler than it was made, God would not have been fully satisfied with the making of man's soul. But because he made man's soul as fair, as good, and as precious a creation as he could make it, the blessed Trinity is therefore wholly and endlessly pleased with the making of man's soul. And he wants our hearts to be raised up with strength above the depths of the earth and all vain sorrows and to rejoice in him.

68

Concerning true knowledge that it was Jesus who revealed all this, and it was no delirium; and how we ought to have sure trust in all our tribulation that we shall not be overcome.

THIS was a delectable sight and a restful revelation, that it is so without end. And to contemplate this while we are here is most pleasing to God and of the greatest advantage to us. And the soul that contemplates in this way makes itself like the one that is contemplated* and unites itself in rest and peace through his grace. And this was a special joy and bliss to me that I saw him sitting; for the assurance of his sitting is a revelation of his dwelling without end. And he gave me to know truly that it was he who had revealed everything to me before. And when I had considered this and reflected, then our good Lord revealed words to me very gently, voicelessly, and without opening his lips, just as he had done before, and said very lovingly, 'Be well aware now that what you saw today was no delirium, but accept it and believe it, and hold to it, and comfort yourself with it, and trust in it, and you shall not be overcome.'

These last words were said in order to teach me true certainty that it is our Lord Jesus who revealed everything to me. And just as in the first words that our good Lord revealed, referring to his blessed Passion—'In this way the devil is overcome'*—just so he said the last words with the greatest certainty, referring to us all, 'You shall not be overcome.'

And all this teaching of true comfort applies in general to all my fellow Christians, as is said before, and it is God's will that it is so. And these words, 'You shall not be overcome', were said very distinctly and very powerfully for assurance and comfort against all the tribulations that may come. He did not say, 'You shall not be perturbed, you shall not be troubled, you shall not be distressed', but he said, 'You shall not be overcome.' God wants us to pay attention to these words and always to be trusting strongly and surely in good times and bad; for he loves us and is pleased with us, and so he wishes us to love him, and be pleased with him, and strongly trust in him; and all shall be well.

And soon afterwards everything was at a close, and I saw no more.

69

Concerning the devil's second long temptation to despair; but she trusted strongly in God and in the faith of Holy Church, going over in her mind the Passion of Christ, by which she was delivered.

AFTER this the devil came back with his heat and his stench and preoccupied me; the stench was so foul and so unbearable, and the physical heat was so frightening and troublesome too. I could also hear an audible jabbering, as though it were two people, and both, to my way of thinking, were jabbering away at once, as if they were busily debating something; and as it was all low muttering I understood nothing they said. And I thought all this was to drive me to despair, and it seemed to me as if they were ridiculing the saying of prayers which are rattled off aloud and by rote, lacking the devout attention and thoughtful application which we owe to God in our prayers.* And our Lord God gave me the grace to trust strongly in him, and to comfort my soul by speaking aloud, as I would have done to another person who had been afflicted. I thought this preoccupation could not be compared to any other human anxiety. I fixed my bodily eyes on the same cross which had comforted me before, and set my tongue to speaking of Christ's Passion* and rehearsing the faith of Holy Church, and set my heart on God with all the trust and strength that was in me. And I thought to myself, 'Now you have plenty to do to hold to the faith, for you must not be taken by the enemy. If, from now on, you could always be so intent on keeping yourself from sin, that would be a supremely good way of occupying your time'; for I truly thought that if I were safe from sin I would be completely safe from all the fiends of hell and enemies of my soul.

And so the devil kept me preoccupied all that night and in the morning until it was just after sunrise.* And in a moment they were all gone, all disappeared, with nothing left but stench, and that still lingered for a while. And I scorned them, and so I was delivered from them by virtue of Christ's Passion, for through that the devil is overcome, as our Lord Jesus Christ said before.

70

In all tribulation we ought to be steadfast in the faith, trusting strongly in God; for if our faith had no enemies, it would deserve no reward; and how all these revelations are in the faith.

IN all this blessed revelation our good Lord let it be understood that the vision would pass;* and faith preserves the blessed revelation, through God's good will and his grace; for he left me with neither sign nor token by which I might recall it,* but he left me with his own blessed word in true understanding, telling me very emphatically that I am to believe it. And so I do: blessed may he be! I believe that he who revealed it is our Saviour, and that what he revealed is the faith. And therefore I believe it and rejoice; and I am bound to do so by everything he meant by the words that follow next: 'Hold to it, and comfort yourself with it, and trust in it.' So I am bound to maintain it faithfully. For on the same day that it was revealed, when the vision had passed, like a wretch I denied it, and I said openly that I had been delirious. Then our Lord Jesus in his mercy would not let the vision be lost, but he revealed it all again inwardly in my soul,* with more completeness, with the blessed light of his precious love, saying these words most powerfully and most gently, 'Know it well now, what you saw today was no delirium', as if he had said, 'Because the vision had passed away you lost it and could not keep it; but know it now, that is to say, now that you see it.'

This was said not just for that one occasion, but also to ground my faith on this, as he immediately went on to say the following, 'But accept it, believe it, and hold to it, and comfort yourself with it, and trust in it, and you shall not be overcome.' By these six utterances that follow*—where he says, 'accept it'—he means to fix it faithfully in our hearts; for he wants it to dwell with us in faith until our life's end, and afterwards in fullness of joy, wishing us always to have sure trust in his blessed promises, knowing his goodness; for our faith is opposed in various ways by our own blindness and by our spiritual enemy, within and without, and therefore our dearest lover helps us with spiritual insight and true teaching in various ways, within and without, by which we may know him. And therefore, in whatever way he teaches us, he wants us to perceive him wisely, receive him lovingly, and maintain ourselves full of faith in him; for no goodness above faith may be held to in this life, as I see it; and below faith there is no help for the soul; but it is to the faith that the Lord wants us to hold. For through his goodness and his own works we are to hold to the faith, and, by his permission, we are tested in the faith by spiritual enemies and made strong; for if there were no enmity to our faith it would deserve no reward, as far as I understand all that our Lord intends.

71

Jesus wants our souls to regard him gladly, because he regards us happily and lovingly; and how he shows us three kinds of expression: a suffering, a compassionate, and a blessed countenance.

GLAD and cheerful and sweet is the blessed, loving expression of our Lord towards our souls; for in this life he always keeps us in love-longing, and he wants our soul to regard him gladly, so as to give him his reward. And so I hope that through his grace he has drawn the outward expression closer to the inward, and will do so still more, and make us all at one with him and with each other in the true and lasting joy which is Jesus.

I understand three kinds of expression in our Lord. The first is that of his Passion which he showed while he was here in this life, dying. Although to contemplate this is mournful and sorrowful, it is still glad and joyful, for he is God. The second kind of expression is mercy and pity and compassion; and this he reveals to all who love him, with assurance of safekeeping for those who need his mercy. The third is his blessed countenance as it shall be without end; and this was oftenest revealed and longest continued.

And so in our times of suffering and misery he shows us his face in his Passion and on his cross, helping us to endure by his own blessed strength. And in our times of sinning he shows us his face of mercy and pity, powerfully protecting us and defending us against all our enemies. And these are the two faces he usually shows us in this life, mingled with the third, which is his blessed countenance shown in part as it will be in heaven. And that is a touching by grace and sweet illumination of the spiritual life, through which we are kept in sure faith, hope, and charity, with contrition and devotion, and also with contemplation, and every kind of true pleasure and sweet comfort. The blessed countenance of our Lord God works this in us through grace.

72

Sin in the chosen souls is mortal for a time, but they are not dead in the sight of God; and how we have here a cause for joy and lamentation, and that is on account of our blindness and the burden of the flesh; and of the most comforting face of God; and why these revelations were shown.

BUT now I must tell how I saw mortal sin in those created beings who will not die on account of sin but live in the joy of God without end. I saw that two opposites could never be together in one place. The greatest opposites that exist are the highest bliss and the deepest pain. The highest bliss there is, is to possess God in the radiance of eternal life, seeing him truly, feeling him sweetly, possessing him perfectly in fullness of joy.

And so the blessed face of our Lord was revealed in part, a revelation in which I saw that sin is what is most opposite to this, so much so that as long as we are mixed up with any aspect of sin we shall never see clearly the blessed face of our Lord. And the more horrible and the more grievous that our sins are, the deeper we have fallen below this blessed sight during that time. And therefore it often seems to us as if we were in danger of death, in some part of hell, because of the sorrow and pain that sin is to us.* And so we are dead for a while to the true sight of our blessed life. But in all this I saw truly that we are not dead in the sight of God, nor does he ever leave us; but he will never have his full bliss in us until we have our full bliss in him, truly seeing his fair, blessed face; for we are ordained to this by nature and attain to this through grace. So I saw how sin is mortal for a short time to those blessed creatures who will attain life without end.

And all the more clearly that the soul sees this blessed face through grace of loving, the more it longs to see it in fullness; for even though our Lord God dwells in us and is here with us, and embraces us and enfolds us entirely out of tender love, such that he may never leave us, and is nearer to us than tongue can tell or heart can think, we can still never stop lamenting or weeping, or seeking or longing, until we see his blessed face clearly; for in that precious, blissful sight no sorrow can remain and no joy can be lacking.

And in this I saw cause for celebration and cause for lamentation: cause for celebration, because our Lord, our maker, is so near us and in us, and we in him, through the sure protection of his great goodness; cause for lamentation, because our spiritual eye is so blind and we are so weighed down by the burden of our mortal flesh and the darkness of sin that we cannot see clearly the fair, blessed face of our Lord God. No, and because of this darkness we can scarcely believe and have faith in his great love, our assurance of safekeeping; and so it is that I say we can never stop lamenting or weeping.

This weeping does not only mean the outpouring of tears from our bodily eyes, but it also has a more spiritual understanding; for the natural desire of our soul is so great and so immeasurable that if all the splendours which God ever made in heaven and on earth were given to us for our solace and for our comfort, and we did not see the fair, blessed face of God himself, we still would not cease to lament or weep in spirit—that is to say, in painful longing until we truly see the fair, blessed face of our maker. And if we were in all the pain that heart can think and tongue may tell, if we could at that moment see his fair, blessed face, all this pain would not afflict us. So that blessed sight is the end of every kind of pain to loving souls, and the fulfilment of every kind of joy and bliss. And God revealed that in the great and marvellous words where he said, 'It is I who is highest; it is I whom you love; it is I who am all.'*

It is for us to have three kinds of knowledge: the first is to know our Lord God; the second is to know ourselves, what we are through him in nature and grace; the third is humbly to know ourselves with regard to our sin and weakness. And, as I understand it, the whole revelation was made for these three.

73

These revelations were shown in three ways; and concerning two spiritual sicknesses from which God wishes us to reform ourselves, remembering his Passion, and also recognizing that he is all love; for he wants us to have security and pleasure in love, not being unreasonably depressed about our past sins.

ALL the blessed teaching of our Lord God was revealed in three ways: that is to say, by bodily sight, and by words formed in my understanding, and by spiritual vision. Concerning bodily sight, I have said what I saw as truly as I can; and as for the words, I have reported those words just as our Lord revealed them to me; and as for the spiritual vision, I have said something, but I can never disclose it in full, and therefore I am moved to say more about this spiritual vision, if God will give me grace.

God showed two kinds of sickness that we have: one is impatience or sloth, because our trouble and our suffering are heavy for us to bear; the other is despair or doubting fear,* as I shall explain later. He showed sin in general, in which all sin is included, but he showed only these two in particular. And these two are the ones which most trouble and disturb us, by what our Lord showed me, and the ones from which he wants us to be reformed. I am talking of such men and women who for the love of God hate sin and dispose themselves to do God's will. Then through our spiritual blindness and the burden of our bodies we are most inclined to these sins; and therefore it is God's will that they should be recognized, and then we shall reject them as we do other sins.

And our Lord very humbly revealed what is most helpful for this: the patience that he had in his cruel Passion, and also the joy and the delight that he has in that Passion because of love. And this was shown by way of an example that we should bear our sufferings gladly and wisely, for that is greatly pleasing to him and endless benefit to us. And the reason why we are troubled by them is because of our failure to recognize love. Although the three Persons of the Trinity are all equal in themselves, the soul received most understanding of love; yes, and he wishes that we perceive love in all things and rejoice in it. And we are most blind in recognizing this; for some of us believe that God is almighty and may do everything, and some that he is all wisdom and knows how to do everything; but that he is all love and is willing to do everything—there we stop short. And it is this ignorance that most hinders those who love God, as I see it; for when we begin to hate sin and to mend our ways according to the laws of Holy Church, there still persists a fear which holds us back,* through self-scrutiny of ourselves and our sins committed previously, and some of us because of our sins every day; because we do not keep our promises nor keep to the purity in which our Lord has established us, but often fall into so much baseness that it is shameful to see it.

And it makes us so sorry and so depressed to recognize this that we can hardly find any comfort,* and we sometimes mistake this fear for humility, but it is a reprehensible blindness and weakness. And we are unable to despise it as we do another sin that we recognize, for it derives from our enemy and is contrary to truth; for of all the attributes of the blessed Trinity it is God's will that we find most certainty and delight in love; for love makes power and wisdom very humble towards us; for just as through his courtesy God forgives our sin from the time we repent, just so does he wish us to forget our sin with regard to our unreasonable depression and our doubting fears.

74

There are four kinds of fear, but reverent fear is a loving, true fear which is never without meek love; and yet they are not the same; and how we should pray to God for them.

FOR I understand there to be four kinds of fear.

One is the fear of attack, which comes to a person suddenly through weakness. This fear does good, for it helps to purify a man, as does bodily sickness or any other such suffering which is not sin; for all such sufferings help people if they are patiently accepted.

The second is fear of punishment, through which someone is stirred and woken from the sleep of sin;* for whoever is fast asleep in sin is unable at that time to receive the tender comfort of the Holy Spirit until he has experienced this fear of punishment, of bodily death, and of spiritual enemies. And this fear moves us to seek the comfort and mercy of God; and so this fear serves as an opening to us* and enables us to be contrite, through the blessed inspiration of the Holy Spirit.

The third is doubting fear.* In as much as it draws us on to despair, God wants to have doubting fear turned into love in us through the knowledge of love; that is to say, that the bitterness of doubt is to be turned into the sweetness of kindly love through grace; for it can never please our Lord that his servants doubt his goodness.

The fourth is reverent fear,* for there is no fear in us which fully pleases God except reverent fear; and that is very gentle, for the more we have it, the less we feel it, because of the sweetness of love.

Love and fear are brothers; and they are rooted in us by the goodness of our maker, and through all eternity they will never be taken from us. By nature we are to love, and by grace we are to love; and by nature we are to fear, and by grace we are to fear. It is proper for God's lordship and fatherhood to be feared, as it is proper for his goodness to be loved; and it is proper for us who are his servants and his children to fear him for his lordship and fatherhood, as it is proper for us to love him for his goodness.* And though this reverent fear and love are not separable, they are still not one and the same, but they are two in nature and method, and neither of them may be had without the other. Therefore I am sure that those who love also fear, though they may only feel it a little.

All fears other than reverent fear that confront us, though they may come under the guise of holiness, are not truly so; and this is how they can be told apart. The fear that makes us flee hastily from all that is not good and fall upon our Lord's breast like a child on its mother's bosom, with our whole heart and mind, knowing our own feebleness and our great need, knowing God's everlasting goodness and his blessed love, seeking salvation only in him, and clinging to him with sure trust—the fear that makes us act like this is natural, gracious, good, and true. And all that is opposed to this is either wrong or is mingled with wrong.

This, then, is the remedy: to recognize them both and reject the wrong one. For the natural benefit of fear that we have in this life through the gracious operation of the Holy Spirit will be the same in heaven before God, gentle, courteous and most delightful. And so in love we should be near to God and at home with him, and in our fear we should be gentle and courteous to God, and both equally.

Let us ask our Lord God to fear him reverently and love him humbly and trust in him strongly; for when we fear him reverently, and love him humbly, our trust is never in vain; for the more we trust, and the more strongly, the more we please and honour our Lord in whom we trust. And if we lack this reverent fear and humble love—as God forbid we should—our trust will soon be misdirected for the time being. And therefore we very much need to pray our Lord that through his grace we may have from him his gift of this reverent fear and humble love in our hearts and in our deeds; for without this, no one can please God.

75

We need love, longing, and pity; and concerning three kinds of longing for God which are in us; and how on the Day of Judgement the joy of the blessed will be increased, seeing truly the cause of everything that God has done, trembling in fear and giving thanks for joy, marvelling at the greatness of God and the littleness of all that is made.

I SAW that God can do all that is necessary for us; and these three that I shall describe are necessary: love, longing, and pity. Pity in love protects us in our time of need; and longing in the same love draws us up into heaven;* for the thirst of God is to draw humanity in general into himself, and in that thirst he has drawn up his holy ones who are now in bliss; and in order to gather together his living members, he is always drawing and drinking, and yet he still thirsts and longs.*

I saw three kinds of longing in God, and all to one end; and we have the same in us, and of the same power, and to the same end. The first is that he longs to teach us to know him and love him for evermore, as is proper and advantageous for us. The second is that he longs to have us up in his bliss, as souls are when they are taken out of suffering into heaven. The third is to fill us with bliss; and that will be fulfilled on the last day, to last forever; for I saw, as is known in our faith, that suffering and sorrow will be ended for all who will be saved. And not only shall we receive the same bliss that the souls before us have had in heaven, but we shall also receive a new bliss, which will be abundantly flowing out of God into us and will fulfil us; and this is the good which he has ordained to give us from without beginning; this good is treasured up and hidden in himself;* for until that time no being has either the power or the merit to receive it.

At this time we shall truly see the cause of all that he has done; and for ever more we shall see the cause of all that he has permitted. And the bliss and the fulfilment will be so deep and so profound and so exalted that in their wonder and marvelment all created beings will feel so much reverent fear for God, surpassing what has been seen and felt before, that the pillars of heaven shall tremble and quake.*

But this kind of trembling and fear will cause no suffering; it befits the worth and might of God to be regarded in this way by those he created, fearfully trembling and quaking with humble joy, marvelling at the greatness of God the maker, and at the littleness of all that is made; for to contemplate this makes each created being marvellously meek and subdued. Therefore God wants us to know and recognize this, and it is also fitting for us, both by nature and grace, longing for this sight and this realization; for it leads us in the right way and keeps us in the true life, and unites us to God.

And God is as good as he is great, and it as much befits his goodness to be loved as it befits his greatness to be feared; for this reverent fear is the fair courtesy that is shown before God's face in heaven. And by as much as he shall then be known and loved beyond what he is now, so he will be feared beyond what he is now. Therefore it has to be that all heaven and earth shall tremble and quake when the pillars tremble and quake.

76

A loving soul hates sin for its vileness more than all the pains of hell; and how regarding the sins of others (unless it be with compassion) prevents the

contemplation of God; and the devil, by reminding us of our wretchedness,
wants to hinder us in that too; and concerning our slothfulness.

I AM saying only a little about reverent fear, because I hope it can be
understood from what has already been said. But I am well aware that
our Lord showed me no souls but those that fear him, for I am also
well aware that the soul which truly accepts the teaching of the Holy
Spirit hates sin more for its vileness and hideousness than it hates all
the pains of hell; for the soul which contemplates the kindness of our
Lord Jesus hates no hell but sin, as I see it.* And therefore it is God's
will that we recognize sin, and pray earnestly and labour willingly
and seek humbly for instruction so that we do not fall blindly into it;
and if we fall, that we rise again quickly, for to turn from God for any
length of time through sin is the greatest pain that the soul may have.

The soul that wishes to be in repose should—whenever other people's sins come to mind—flee that like the pains of hell, seeking remedy and help from God against it; for to consider other people's sins
makes, as it were, a thick mist before the eyes of the soul, and during
that time we cannot see the beauty of God unless we regard those sins
with contrition, along with the sinners, with compassion on them,
and with a holy longing for God on their behalf; for without this,
a soul that contemplates sin and sinners is troubled, and disturbed,
and hindered; for I understood this in the revelation of compassion.*

In this blessed revelation of our Lord's I understand two contrary
things: one is the wisest action that anyone can perform in this life; the
other is the most foolish. The wisest action is for people to act in accord
with the wishes and advice of their greatest and supreme friend.* This
blessed friend is Jesus; and it is his will and his advice that we hold
fast to him and adhere to him closely for evermore, in whatever state
we may be; for whether we are unclean or pure, his love for us is the
same. Whether in joy or in sorrow, he never wants us to flee from him;
but because of our own changeability in ourselves, we often fall into
sin. This happens to us through the prompting of our enemy, through
our own folly and blindness, which say, 'You know very well you are
a wretch, a sinner, and also faithless, because you do not keep God's
commands; you often promise our Lord that you will do better, and
immediately afterwards you fall back into the same sin, especially into
sloth and time-wasting', for that is the beginning of sin, as I see it,
and especially for people who have given themselves to serve our Lord

through inward contemplation of his blessed goodness.* And this makes us afraid to appear before our courteous Lord. So it is our enemy who wants to set us back with false fear about our sinfulness, because of the punitive pain with which he threatens us; for it is his purpose in this to make us so miserable and so weary that we should forget the lovely, blessed contemplation of our everlasting friend.

77

Concerning the enmity of the fiend, who loses more by our rising than he gains by our falling, and so is scorned; and how God's chastisement should be borne with his Passion in mind; for that is specially rewarded, more than penance chosen by ourselves; and we must have sorrow, but courteous God is our leader, protector, and bliss.

OUR good Lord revealed the devil's enmity,* and from this I understood that everything that is contrary to love and peace is from the devil and his part. And through our feebleness and our folly we are to fall, and through the mercy and grace of the Holy Spirit we are to rise to greater joy. And if our enemy gains anything from us by our falling—for in that we resemble him—he loses many times more from our rising through love and humility. And this glorious rising is such great sorrow and pain to him, because of the hatred that he has for our souls, that he is continually burning in envy. And all this sorrow that he wishes to cause us will come back upon himself. And this was why our Lord scorned him, and this made me laugh heartily.

This, then, is the remedy: that we should acknowledge our wretchedness and flee to our Lord, for the more prepared we are to do this, the more beneficial it is for us to draw near to him. And let us say this in our thoughts: 'I know very well that I have deserved severe pain, but our Lord is almighty and can punish me mightily, and he is all wisdom and can punish me with reason, and he is all goodness and loves me most tenderly.' And it is necessary for us to keep this in view: for it is a lovely meekness in a sinful soul, accomplished by the mercy and grace of the Holy Spirit, when we willingly and gladly accept the scourging and chastising that our Lord himself wishes to give us. And it will be very gentle and very easy if we will only consider ourselves content with him and with all his works.

For the penance which people impose upon themselves was not

revealed to me; that is to say, it was not revealed specifically; but it was revealed especially and exaltedly, and in a most loving manner, that we should humbly and patiently bear and suffer the penance which God himself gives us, in recalling his blessed Passion; for when we bear in mind his blessed Passion, with pity and love, then we suffer with him as his friends did who saw it, and this was revealed in the thirteenth revelation, near the beginning, where it speaks of pity;* for he says, 'Do not accuse yourself too much, judging that your tribulation and your unhappiness is all your fault; for I do not want you to be unreasonably depressed and sorrowful; for I tell you that, whatever you do, you will experience great unhappiness. And therefore I want you wisely to recognize your penance, which you are in constantly, and humbly to accept it as your penance, and then you will truly see that your whole life is a profitable penance.'*

This place is prison,* and this life is penance, and he wants us to rejoice in the remedy. The remedy is that our Lord is with us, protecting us and leading us into the fullness of joy; for this is an endless joy to us, in our Lord's purpose, that he who will be our bliss when we are there, is our protector while we are here. Our way and our heaven are true love and sure trust; and he made this understood in all the revelations, and especially in the revelation of his Passion, where he made me choose him for my heaven with all my strength.*

Let us fly to our Lord and we shall be comforted. Let us touch him and we shall be made clean.* Let us cleave to him and we shall be safe and secure from all manner of peril. For our courteous Lord wants us to be as friendly with him as heart may think or soul may desire. But let us beware that we do not take this friendliness so casually as to neglect courtesy; for our Lord himself is supreme friendliness, and he is as courteous as he is friendly, for he is truly courteous. And he wants the blessed creatures who will be with him in heaven without end to be like himself in all things. And to be perfectly like our Lord is our true salvation and our utmost bliss. And if we do not know how we shall do all this, let us ask our Lord and he will teach us; for it is his own delight and his glory. Blessed may he be!

78

Our Lord wants us to recognize four kinds of goodness that he shows us; and how we need the light of grace to know our sin and weakness, for in

ourselves we are nothing but wretchedness, and we cannot know the hor-
ribleness of sin as it is. And how our enemy would like us never to recognize
our sin until the last day, and we are therefore much indebted to God who
shows it to us now.

Our Lord in his mercy shows us our sin and our weakness by the
sweet gracious light of himself; for our sin is so vile and so horrible
that in his courtesy he will not show it to us except by the light of his
grace and mercy.

It is his wish that we should have knowledge of four things: the
first is that he is the foundation on which we have all our life and our
being; the second, that he protects us powerfully and mercifully during the time when we are in our sin and among all our enemies who
are so savage to us—and we are in so much the greater danger because
we give them the occasion for it and do not know our own need; the
third, is how courteously he protects us and lets us know that we are
going amiss; the fourth is how steadfastly he waits for us and with
unchanging demeanour, for he wants us to turn to him and be united
to him in love as he is to us.

And so through this grace-given knowledge we may see our sin
profitably, without despair; for we truly need to see it; and the sight
of it will make us ashamed of ourselves and break down our pride
and presumption; for we have to see truly that in ourselves we are
nothing at all but sin and wretchedness. And so by seeing the lesser
part of our sins which our Lord reveals to us, the greater part, which
we do not see, loses its force; for in his courtesy he moderates what
we see, because it is so vile and so horrible that we could not endure
to see it as it is.

And so by humbly recognizing this, through contrition and grace,
we shall be sundered from everything which is not our Lord, and
then our blessed Saviour will perfectly heal us and unite us to himself. This sundering and this healing our Lord intends with reference
to mankind in general; for he who is highest and nearest to God may
see himself as sinful and needy, along with me; and I who am the least
and the lowest of those who will be saved, may be comforted along
with him who is highest. So has our Lord united us in charity when
he showed me that I would sin.

And because of the joy that I felt in contemplating him I did not
pay attention promptly to that revelation; and our courteous Lord

paused then and would not teach me further until he had given me the grace and will to pay attention.

And I was taught by this that though we may be lifted up high into contemplation by the special gift of our Lord, we must still, at the same time, have knowledge and sight of our sin and our weakness; for without this knowledge we cannot have true humility, and without this we cannot be saved. And I also saw that we cannot gain this knowledge by ourselves, nor from any of all our spiritual enemies, for they do not wish us so much good; for if they had their will, we should not see it until our dying day. So then we are greatly indebted to God who will show it to us himself for love's sake, in time and through mercy and grace.

79

We are taught about our sin and not our neighbours', unless it is for their assistance; and God wants us to know that whatever impulse we have contrary to this revelation comes from our enemy. For, knowing God's great love, we should not be more careless about falling; and if we fall, we must rise again quickly or else we are very much lacking in natural gratitude to God.

I ALSO gained greater understanding in this matter: because God showed me that I would sin,* I took this to apply simply to myself in particular, because at that time I was not moved to think otherwise; but through the great and gracious comfort of our Lord which followed later, I saw that he intended it to apply to mankind in general, that is to say, everyone who is sinful and will be until the last day— of whom I am a member, I hope, through the mercy of God, for the blessed comfort which I saw is bountiful enough for us all. And here I was taught that I should consider my own sin and not other people's sins, unless it is for the comfort and help of my fellow Christians.

And also in this same revelation, where I saw that I would sin, I was taught to be fearful on account of my own instability; for I do not know how I shall fall, nor do I know the extent nor the gravity of my sin; for in my anxiety I wanted to know that, but had no answer. Also, at the same time, our courteous Lord revealed most certainly and powerfully the endlessness and the unchangeability of his love; and also, through his great goodness and our inward safekeeping through his grace, that the love between him and our souls shall never be parted in two for all eternity. And so in this fear I have cause for humility which saves me from presumption; and in the blessed revelation of love I have cause for true comfort and for joy which save me from despair.

All this friendly revelation of our courteous Lord is a lovely lesson and a sweet, gracious teaching from himself in comforting of our souls; for he wants us to know, through his sweetness and friendly love, that everything we see or feel which is contrary to this, within or without, is from the enemy and not from God. Thus, if we are moved to be more careless in our way of life or in the custody of our hearts for the very reason that we have knowledge of this abundant love, then we must be very careful; for this impulse, if it arises, is false and we ought to hate it intently, because it bears no resemblance to God's will.

And when we have fallen through frailty or blindness, then our courteous Lord touches us, moves us, and calls us; and then he wants us to see our wretched sinfulness and humbly acknowledge it. But he does not want us to stay like this, nor does he want us to be greatly preoccupied with self-accusation, nor does he want us to be too full of our own misery; but he wants us swiftly to focus our thoughts on him; for he stands all alone* and waits for us, sorrowing and lamenting, until we come, and he hastens to have us with him; for we are his joy and his delight, and he is our salve and our life.

When I say he stands all alone, I am omitting to speak of the blessed company of heaven and speak of his function and way of working here upon earth, in accord with the nature of the revelation.

80

God is worshipped and we are saved by three things; and how our knowledge now is only like an ABC; and sweet Jesus does everything, waiting and grieving with us, but when we are in a state of sin, Christ grieves alone; then it is fitting for us, out of kindness and reverence, to turn swiftly to him again.

MAN depends on three things in this life, and by these three things God is glorified and we are furthered, protected, and saved. The first is the use of man's natural reason; the second is the general teaching of Holy Church; the third is the inner working of grace through the Holy Spirit; and these three are all from one God. God is the source of our natural reason; and God is the teaching of Holy Church; and God is the Holy Spirit. And all are distinct gifts, to which he wants us to have great regard and pay attention; for these are at work in us constantly and altogether, and these are highly important matters, which he wants us to know about here as if it were our ABC;* that is to say, that we have a little knowledge of what we shall know fully in heaven; and that is in order to benefit us.

We know through our faith that God alone took on our nature and none but he; and furthermore that Christ alone performed all the works concerning our salvation, and none but he; and just so he alone is at work now on his final purpose: that is to say, he is dwelling here with us, and rules us and governs us in this life, and brings us to his bliss.* And he will do so as long as any soul is still upon earth who is to come to heaven; and so much so that if there were no such soul on earth but one, he would be with it all alone until he had brought it up to his bliss. I believe and understand what scholars say about the ministrations of angels, but this was not revealed to me; for he himself is nearest and humblest, highest and lowest, and does everything; and not only all that we need, but he also does all that is glorious, for our joy in heaven.

And where I say he waits for us, sorrowing and lamenting, it signifies all the true feelings of contrition and compassion that we have in ourselves, and all the sorrowing and lamenting that we are not united with our Lord. And all such feelings which are beneficial are Christ in us; and though some of us seldom feel this, for Christ it never ends until he has brought us out of all our misery; for love never allows him to be without pity. And when we fall into sin and forget to bear him in mind and to safeguard our own soul, then Christ alone bears all the burden of us, and so he remains, sorrowing and lamenting. Then it is for us, in reverence and kindness, to turn swiftly to our Lord and not to leave him alone. He is here alone with us all; that is to say, he is here only for our sakes. And whenever I am distant towards him through sin, despair, or sloth, then I let my Lord remain alone in as much as it is my doing; and this is how it goes with all of us who are sinners. But although it may be so that we often act like this, his goodness never allows us to be alone, but he is with us continuously, and he excuses us tenderly and always shields us from blame in his eyes.

81

This blessed woman saw God in various ways, but she saw him find no resting place except in the soul of man; and he wants us to rejoice more in his love than sorrow over our frequent falling, remembering our everlasting reward and living gladly in penance; and why God allows sin.

OUR good Lord revealed himself in various ways, both in heaven and on earth, but I saw him take up no place except in man's soul.* He revealed himself on earth in his precious incarnation and in his blessed Passion. And he revealed himself on earth in another way where I say: 'I saw God in a point.'* And he showed himself on earth in another way, as if on pilgrimage:* that is to say, he is here with us, leading us, and will be until he has brought us all up to his bliss in heaven. At different times he showed himself reigning, as is said before,* but principally in man's soul. There he has made his resting place and his glorious city, and from this glorious throne he will never rise nor remove without end. Marvellous and splendid is the place where the Lord dwells.

And so he wants us to respond readily to the touch of his grace, rejoicing more in the completeness of his love than sorrowing in our frequent fallings; for it is the greatest glory to him of anything we can do that we live gladly and cheerfully in our penance for love of him. For he regards us so tenderly that he sees all our life and penance; for our natural longing for him is a lasting penance for us, a suffering which he causes in us and mercifully helps us to bear; for his love makes him long, his wisdom and his truth, together with his righteousness, makes him bear with us while we are here, and he wants to see this in us in the same way; for this is our natural penance and the noblest, as I see it, for this penance never leaves us until the time when we find our fulfilment, when we shall have him for our reward. And so he wants us to set our hearts on our transition: that is to say, from the pain that we feel to the bliss in which we trust.

82

God regards the lamenting of the soul with pity and not with blame, and yet we do nothing but sin, and in this we are kept in joy and in fear; for he wants us to turn to him, clinging readily to his love, seeing that he is our

medicine; and so we must love, in longing and in rejoicing, and anything
contrary to this comes not from God but from the enemy.

BUT here our courteous Lord showed the lamenting and the mourning of the soul, with this meaning: 'I am well aware that you wish to
live for love of me, cheerfully and gladly bearing all the suffering that
may come to you; but in as much as you do not live without sin, you
are therefore depressed and sorrowful, and if you could live without
sin you are willing to suffer for love of me all the misery, and all the
tribulation and distress that could come to you. And it is true. But
do not be upset too much by sin that you commit against your will.'

And here I understood that the Lord regards the servant with pity
and not with blame,* for in this passing life we are not asked to live
entirely free of sin and blame. He loves us without end, and we sin
habitually, and he reveals this to us most gently; and then we sorrow
and mourn appropriately, turning to the contemplation of his mercy,
holding fast to his love and goodness, seeing that he is our medicine,
knowing that we do nothing but sin.

And so by the humility that we gain through seeing our sin, faithfully recognizing his everlasting love, thanking and praising him, we
please him. 'I love you and you love me; and our love shall not be
divided in two,* and it is for your benefit that I suffer.' And all this
was shown in spiritual understanding, these blessed words being said:
'I am keeping you very safe.'*

And through the great desire that I saw in our blessed Lord that
we should live in this way—that is to say, in longing and rejoicing, as
all this lesson of love shows—I understood that all that is against us
comes not from him but from our enemy, and he wants us to know
this through the sweet, gracious light of his kind love.

If there be any such lover of God on earth who is continually kept
from falling, I do not know of it, for it was not revealed to me. But this
was revealed: that in falling and in rising we are always inestimably
protected in one love; for in the sight of God we do not fall, and in
our own view we do not remain standing, and both of these are true,
as I see it, but the sight of our Lord God is the highest truth. So we
are much indebted to God that he wishes to reveal this high truth to
us in this life. And I understood that while we are in this life, it is most
advantageous to us to see both of these at once; for the higher view
keeps us in spiritual solace and true delight in God; the other, that is

the lower view, keeps us in fear and makes us ashamed of ourselves. But our good Lord always wants us to regard ourselves much more in accordance with the higher view, and yet not to relinquish our recognition of the lower one, until the time when we are brought up above, where we shall have our Lord Jesus for our reward, and be filled full of joy and bliss without end.

83

Concerning three properties in God—life, love, and light; and that our reason is in accord with God; it is our highest gift; and how our faith is a light coming from the Father, apportioned to us, and leading us through this night; and at the end of our sorrow, our eyes shall suddenly be opened in the full light and clarity of vision, which is our maker, Father, and Holy Spirit, in Jesus our Saviour.

I RECEIVED in some measure touch, sight, and feeling of three properties of God in which the strength and significance of the revelation consists; and they were seen in every revelation and most particularly in the twelfth, where it says repeatedly 'It is I.'* The properties are these: life, love, and light.* In life there is marvellous familiarity, in love there is noble courtesy, and in light there is endless kindness. These properties were seen in one goodness, a goodness to which my reason wished to be united and to hold fast with all its might. I beheld with reverent fear, greatly marvelling at the sight and feeling of the sweet accord that our reason is in God, understanding that it is the highest gift that we have received, and it is grounded in nature.

Our faith is a light, coming naturally from our endless day, which is our father, God; and in this light our mother, Christ, and our good Lord, the Holy Spirit, lead us in this passing life. This light is apportioned with discretion, standing by us in the night according to our need. The light is the cause of our life, the night is the cause of our pain and of all our woe, in which we deserve reward and thanks from God; for we, through mercy and grace, willingly know and believe our light, walking in it wisely and strongly. And at the end of woe, our eyes will suddenly be opened, and in clearness of light our sight will be complete; a light which is God our maker, and the Holy Spirit in Christ Jesus our Saviour. So I saw and understood that our faith is our light in our night—which light is God, our endless day.

84

Charity is this light which is not so small as not to merit, with toil, the endless, glorious thanks of God; for faith and hope lead us to charity, of which there are three kinds.

THE light is charity, and the apportioning of this light is carried out beneficially for us by the wisdom of God; for the light is neither so full that we can see our blessed day, nor is it shut away from us, but it is such a light as we can live in deservingly, with endeavours deserving the endless glory of God. And this was seen in the sixth revelation, where he said, 'I thank you for your service and your suffering.'* So charity keeps us in faith and in hope, and faith and hope lead us in charity. And at the end, all shall be charity. I understood this light, charity, in three ways: the first is charity uncreated; the second is charity created; the third is charity given. Charity uncreated is God; charity created is our soul in God; charity given is virtue; and that is a way of working, given by grace, in which we love God for himself, and ourselves in God, and all that God loves, for God's sake.

85

God loved his chosen ones from without beginning, and he never allows them to be harmed such that their bliss might be lessened; and how mysteries now hidden in heaven shall be known, so that we shall bless our Lord that everything is so well ordained.

AND I marvelled greatly at this sight; for despite our uninformed way of life and our blindness here, our courteous Lord still endlessly regards us in this conduct of ours, and rejoices. And we can please him best of all by wisely and truly believing this and rejoicing with him and in him: for as truly as we shall be in the bliss of God without end, praising and thanking him, so truly in the foresight of God we have been loved and known in his endless purpose from without beginning. In this love without beginning he created us, and in the same love he protects us and never allows us to be harmed in such a way that our bliss might be lessened. And therefore when the judgement is given, and we are all brought up above, we shall then clearly see in God the mysteries which are now hidden from us. Then none of us will be moved to say in any way, 'Lord, if it had been like so, it would have been very good'; but we shall all say with one voice, 'Lord, blessed may you be, for it is so, and it is well. And now we see truly that all is done as it was ordained before anything was made.'

86

The good Lord showed that this book should be completed differently from how it was first written; and he wants us to pray in this way for his works, thanking him, trusting and rejoicing in him; and how he gave this revelation because he wants it known, and in this knowledge he wants to give us grace to love him; for fifteen years later there came the answer that the cause of all this revelation was love, which may Jesus grant us. Amen.

THIS book was begun by God's gift and his grace, but it is not yet completed,* as I see it. With God working within us, let us all pray to God for charity, thanking, trusting, rejoicing; for it is in this way that our good Lord wishes to be prayed to, according to the understanding that I derived from all that he conveyed, and from the sweet words where he says most cheeringly, 'I am the foundation of your prayers';* for I truly saw and understood in what our Lord conveyed that he revealed it because he wants to have it better known than it is, and through this knowledge he will give us grace to love him and cleave to him. For he regards his heavenly treasure on earth* with such great love that he wants to give us more light and more comfort in heavenly joy in drawing our hearts to him, because of the sorrow and darkness that we are in.

And from the time that this was revealed, I often yearned to know what our Lord's meaning was. And fifteen years and more later* I was answered in my spiritual understanding, and it was said: 'Do you want to know your Lord's meaning in this? Be well aware: love was his meaning. Who showed you this? Love. What did he show you? Love. Why did he show it? For love. Hold fast to this, and you will know and understand more of the same; but you will never understand nor know anything else from this for all eternity.'

So I was taught that love was our Lord's meaning. And I saw most certainly in this and in everything, that before God made us he loved us, and this love has never abated nor ever shall. And in this love he has done all his works; and in this love he has made everything for our benefit; and in this love our life is everlasting. In our making we had our beginning, but the love in which he made us was in him from without beginning, and in this love we have our beginning. And all this shall be seen in God without end, which may Jesus grant us. Amen.

Thus ends* the revelation of love of the blessed Trinity shown by our Saviour, Christ Jesu, for our endless comfort and delight, and also for us to rejoice in him in the transitory journey of this life. Amen, Jesu, amen.

I pray to almighty God that this book come only into the hands of those who wish to be his faithful lovers, and to those who are willing to submit themselves to the faith of Holy Church and obey the sound understanding and teaching of men of virtuous life, mature years, and profound learning; for this revelation is deep theology and great wisdom, and so it should not remain with anyone who is in thrall to sin and to the devil. And beware that you do not select one thing according to your inclination and preference and overlook another; for that is what heretics are like. But take each thing along with everything else, and truly understand that everything is in accord with holy scripture and grounded in the same, and that Jesus, our true love, light, and truth, will reveal this wisdom concerning himself to all pure souls who ask for it humbly and perseveringly. And you to whom this book may come, thank our Saviour, Christ Jesu, intently and with all your heart that he vouchsafed these showings and revelations of his endless love, mercy, and goodness for you and to you, so as to be your and our safe guide and safe-conduct to everlasting bliss—which may Jesus grant us! Amen.

Here end the sublime and wonderful Revelations
of the unutterable love of God in Jesus Christ,
vouchsafed to a dear lover of his and in
her to all his dear friends and
lovers, whose hearts, like
hers, do flame in the
love of our
dearest
Jesu*

APPENDIX 1
LIST OF REVELATIONS IN THE SHORT
AND LONG TEXTS

First Revelation (ST, pp. 6–11; LT, chs. 4–9): Julian sees blood trickling down from under the crown of thorns on a crucifix held before her eyes and comprehends that when Jesus appears, the Trinity is to be understood. Julian also sees the Virgin Mary as she was at the time of the Annunciation.

Second Revelation (ST, p. 11; LT, ch. 10): Julian sees the two sides of the face on the crucifix discolouring.

Third Revelation (ST, pp. 11–12; LT, ch. 11): Julian sees God in a point and understands that he is in all things.

Fourth Revelation (ST, p. 12; LT, ch. 12): Julian sees Christ's body bleeding profusely, as if at his flagellation, and sees that blood streaming through hell, earth, and heaven.

Fifth Revelation (ST, pp. 12–13; LT, ch. 13): Julian understands by means of divine words that through Christ's Passion the devil is defeated.

Sixth Revelation (ST, p. 13; LT, ch. 14): God thanks Julian for her suffering and service, and Julian sees God reigning in his house in heaven.

Seventh Revelation (ST, pp. 13–14; LT, ch. 15): God gives Julian a sequence of alternating experiences of joy and sorrow.

Eighth Revelation (ST, pp. 14–17; LT, chs. 16–21): Christ shows his body dehydrating on the cross as he nears death, and Julian resists an inward prompting that she look up to heaven away from the cross.

Ninth Revelation (ST, pp. 17–18; LT, chs. 22–3): Christ declares his satisfaction at having suffered his Passion for her. If he could suffer more, he would do so, and he shows her three heavens.

Tenth Revelation (ST, pp. 18–19; LT, ch. 24): Christ leads Julian's understanding inside the wound in his side and shows her his heart riven in two.

Eleventh Revelation (ST, p. 19; LT, ch. 25): Christ shows Julian a spiritual vision of his mother Mary, now exalted.

Twelfth Revelation (ST, p. 19; LT, ch. 26): Christ shows himself in glory and utters words surpassing Julian's understanding.

Thirteenth Revelation (ST, pp. 19–26; LT, chs. 27–40): Jesus affirms that sin was befitting and necessary, but all shall be well. God regards the atonement with much greater satisfaction than the Fall of Man was ever harmful.

Fourteenth Revelation (ST, pp. 26–8; LT, chs. 41–3): God reveals that he is the foundation of prayers, inspiring us to pray for what he wishes us to have.

Fifteenth Revelation (ST, pp. 28–30; LT, chs. 64–5): God promises Julian that she will be taken suddenly from suffering and sickness, will come to heaven and have him as her reward.

Sixteenth Revelation (ST, pp. 30–2; LT, chs. 66–8): God shows Julian Jesus seated in her soul and gives reassurance about the authenticity of her revelations.

APPENDIX 2

EXTRACT FROM *THE BOOK OF MARGERY KEMPE*, CH. 18 (MARGERY KEMPE VISITS JULIAN OF NORWICH)[1]

AND then she was commanded by our Lord to go to an anchoress in the same city who was called Dame Julian. And so she did, and told her about the grace, that God had put into her soul, of compunction, contrition, sweetness and devotion, compassion with holy meditation and high contemplation, and very many holy speeches and converse that our Lord spoke to her soul, and also many wonderful revelations, which she described to the anchoress to find out if there were any deception in them, for the anchoress was expert in such things and could give good advice.

The anchoress, hearing the marvellous goodness of our Lord, highly thanked God with all her heart for his visitation, advising this creature to be obedient to the will of our Lord and fulfil with all her might whatever he put into her soul, if it were not against the worship of God and the profit of her fellow Christians. For if it were, then it were not the influence of a good spirit, but rather of an evil spirit. 'The Holy Spirit never urges a thing against charity, and if he did, he would be contrary to his own self, for he is all charity. Also, he moves a soul to all chasteness, for chaste livers are called the temple of the Holy Spirit,[2] and the Holy Spirit makes a soul stable and steadfast in the right faith and the right belief.

'And a double man in soul is always unstable and unsteadfast in all his ways.[3] He that is forever doubting is like the wave of the sea which is moved and borne about with the wind, and that man is not likely to receive the gifts of God.[4]

'Any creature that has these tokens may steadfastly believe that the Holy Spirit dwells in his soul. And much more, when God visits a creature with tears of contrition, devotion or compassion, he may

1 Barry Windeatt (ed.), *The Book of Margery Kempe* (Harlow, 2000; repr. Woodbridge, 2004).

2 1 Corinthians 6: 19.

3 James 1: 8.

4 James 1: 6–7.

and ought to believe that the Holy Spirit is in his soul. St Paul says that the Holy Spirit asks for us with mourning and weeping unspeakable;[5] that is to say, he causes us to ask and pray with mourning and weeping so plentifully that the tears may not be numbered. No evil spirit may give these tokens, for St Jerome says that tears torment the devil more than do the pains of hell.[6] God and the devil are always at odds, and they shall never dwell together in one place, and the devil has no power in a man's soul.

'Holy Writ says that the soul of a righteous man is the seat of God,[7] and so I trust, sister, that you are. I pray God grant you perseverance. Set all your trust in God and do not fear the talk of the world, for the more contempt, shame, and reproof that you have in this world, the greater is your merit in the sight of God.[8] Patience is necessary for you, for in that you keep your soul.'[9]

Great was the holy conversation that the anchoress and this creature had through talking of the love of our Lord Jesus Christ for the many days that they were together.

5 Romans 8: 26.
6 Popularly attributed to St Jerome, but no precise equivalent is to be found in his writings.
7 2 Corinthians 6: 16; Revelation 21: 3; Ezekiel 37: 27–8. See also John 14: 20; 15: 4–5; 17: 23; 6: 57; also 1 John 4: 1, 6, 12–13
8 Luke 6: 22–3.
9 Luke 21: 19.

EXPLANATORY NOTES

THE SHORT TEXT

3 *Here is a vision . . . lovers of Christ*: the scribe of ST, working *c*.1450, has preserved this heading, ostensibly composed during Julian's lifetime by someone who knows her to be still alive in 1413.

relive Christ's Passion in my mind: see Introduction, p. xvii.

bodily sickness: see LT, ch. 2; p. 40, and note.

Nonetheless . . . can attain: this passage, affirming Julian's belief in what is revealed about Christ's sufferings through Church teaching and through works of art like crucifixes, is absent from LT (ch. 2; p. 41).

4 *terrors . . . caused by devils*: it was believed that devils attended deathbeds in hopes of gaining another soul.

Saint Cecilia: a noble Roman virgin and a Christian from infancy, Cecilia preserves her virginity on her wedding night by converting her husband and his brother. When Cecilia refuses to sacrifice to the gods she is placed in a boiling bath for a night and a day but remains perfectly cool, subsequently receiving three great neck-wounds from an executioner who fails to behead her, and then surviving for a further three days. Cecilia was regarded as a model for her practice of sustained contemplation focused on the life of Christ, while her application to good works made her a model of the mixed life of action and contemplation, and she became associated with such female preachers as Mary Magdalene. This reference to how Julian was inspired by hearing about Saint Cecilia disappears from LT. For the life of Cecilia, see William Granger Ryan (ed.), *Jacobus de Voragine, The Golden Legend: Readings on the Saints* (Princeton, 1993), 2.318–23.

thirty and a half years old: translating the Middle English 'thirty winters old and a half'. As Julian dates her revelations to May 1373, this pinpoints the likely date of her birth to late in 1342.

on the third night: although Julian appears to have been ill for a week or so, her report presents this in patterns of threes, possibly recollecting Christ's three days in the tomb from Good Friday to Easter Sunday.

5 *the parson, my curate*: a parson would usually indicate a parish priest and disappears from LT (ch. 3; p. 42), perhaps indicating that in May 1373 Julian was not yet enclosed as an anchoress. A curate might be anyone in religious orders with a responsibility for the cure of souls.

a boy along with him: possibly one of the young clerks who accompanied the priest in the visitation of the sick, carrying the cross or ringing a hand-bell to signal that the eucharist was being carried to the sick person.

5 *Daughter*: this word of address, which reveals the author's gender, is absent from LT (ch. 3; p. 42).

My hands . . . lolled to one side: these details of Julian's posture, perhaps including an allusion to Christ's bowed head on the cross, disappear from LT (ch. 3; p. 43).

6 *'Blessed be thou, Lord!'*: translating the original's Latin, 'Benedicite Dominus'.

7 *'Behold me here, the handmaid of the Lord'*: see Luke 1: 38.

With this . . . its smallness: this revelation of Mary is moved forward in LT, so as to be reported before the revelation of the little thing like a hazelnut (ch. 4; pp. 44–5). For the hazelnut, and the age of Mary at the time of the Annunciation, see LT, chs. 4 and 5 (pp. 44, 45) and notes.

8 *three nothings*: the first nothing is 'everything that is made', as the following lines explain; the other two nothings are probably sin and the devil (see pp. 11, 12).

longs to live contemplatively: this reference to an implied audience of contemplatives is absent from LT (see ch. 5; p. 45).

those who . . . worldly success: replaced by 'we' in LT (ch. 5; p. 45), where Julian assumes an audience no longer concerned with worldly occupation and success.

And all the while . . . bleeding from Christ's head: this is all that Julian reports in ST of one of her most vividly described visions in LT, where she will introduce her pervasive theme of God's marvellous intimacy with us and courtesy towards us (ch. 7; pp. 48–50).

9 *the wretched, worldly, sinful creature*: in LT this becomes 'a wretch' (ch. 8; p. 51), implying that at the time of ST Julian could still think of herself as a 'worldly' person.

And if any man . . . not at peace: this line is not in LT (see ch. 9; p. 52).

10 *And he who loves . . . and suffer for us*: this passage does not survive into LT (see ch. 9; p. 52).

But God forbid . . . loving of God: this passage does not survive into LT (see ch. 9; p. 52). On the theme of Christ as a teacher, see also LT, chs. 34, 40, 70, 73, 78, 79 (pp. 83, 91, 145, 149, 157, 158).

But just because I am a woman . . . teacher of all: this passage does not survive into LT (see ch. 9; p. 52).

I never understood . . . true teaching of Holy Church: this profession of orthodox belief is not retained in LT (ch. 9; p. 52).

11 *you—and so . . . one in love*: not in LT (ch. 9; p. 52).

set less store by the vanity of the world: another line which, by not surviving into LT, suggests that ST was written when Julian was more alert to the perils of worldly temptation, perhaps because still in the world.

And after this . . . no light but him: this brief account of the second revelation is much developed in LT (see ch. 10; pp. 52–5).

And after this I saw God in a point . . . shown me in all this: this report of the third revelation is much developed in LT (see ch. 11; pp. 55–7). On 'I saw God in a point', see note to p. 55.

12 *And after this I saw . . . shares our own nature*: this account of the fourth revelation is much developed in LT (see ch. 12; pp. 57–8).

13 *And afterwards, before God revealed . . . steadfast suffering*: this report of the fifth revelation is somewhat expanded in LT (see ch. 13; pp. 58–9).

the age of everyone will be known in heaven: see note to p. 60.

After this our good Lord said . . . wonderfully thanked: this account of the sixth revelation is doubled in length in LT (see ch. 14; pp. 59–60).

14 *Saint Paul . . . Saint Peter . . . I perish*: cf. Romans 8: 35, 38–9, and Matthew 8: 25, 14: 30; and see the notes to p. 61.

And after this our Lord revealed . . . safeguards us: this report of the seventh revelation is exceptional in undergoing little change between ST and LT (see ch. 15; pp. 60–1).

as far as I could see it: this qualification disappears from LT (see ch. 16; p. 61).

as if he had been dead for a week: in LT Julian moves to explain this startling suggestion (ch. 16; p. 62).

15 *'I thirst'*: see John 19: 28.

I shall say later: see ST, p. 22.

as Saint Paul says . . . in Christ Jesu: see Philippians 2: 5; the Latin text of the Vulgate Bible reads: 'Hoc enim sentite in vobis' (i.e. 'For feel this in you'). The absence from LT of this biblical reference in ST has been attributed to contemporary controversy over access to scripture in the vernacular.

My mother . . . I had for him: this passage—like some earlier details of Julian's experience on 8 May 1373—does not survive into LT (see ch. 17; p. 64). Her distress at having her eyes closed implies that Julian's vision here is still identified with bodily vision.

After this Christ showed me . . . bodily death: this account of the eighth revelation is much expanded in LT (see chs. 16 and 17; pp. 61–4).

16 *And this was the pain*: this passage (ending 'creation failed them') is expanded in LT so as to refer to Pontius Pilate and 'Saint Dionysius of France' (see ch. 18; p. 65, and notes).

sun and moon, withdrew their service: see Matthew 27: 45 and Luke 23: 44–5.

this has always been a comfort to me: sometimes interpreted as indicating a passage of time between the experience of revelation and the composition of ST, although this could be said after a relatively short time filled with intensive meditation.

17 *as I was looking*: translating the Middle English 'me behaldande' which, if modelled on the Latin ablative absolute, may indicate that Julian already knew some Latin at the time when ST was composed.

Then our Lord spoke: this section of ST, ending with the words 'pleasure that he had in our salvation' (p. 18), presents the ninth revelation, which is expanded in LT to form chs. 22 and 23 (pp. 68–71).

18 *He did not say, 'If it were necessary to suffer more'*: see LT, ch. 22 (p. 70) and note.

19 *Very happily . . . joyful and glad*: this brief account of the tenth revelation is developed at double the length and with new understanding in LT (see ch. 24; pp. 71–2).

And with this same expression . . . honour, and joy: this report of the eleventh revelation is much expanded in LT (see ch. 25; pp. 72–3).

And after this . . . as our Lord intended: this account of the twelfth revelation is repeated with some expansion in LT (see ch. 26; p. 74).

And afterwards . . . him before: here begins the thirteenth revelation, already a lengthy sequence in ST which does not end until p. 26, and which is expanded further in LT (chs. 27–40; pp. 74–91).

20 *'Sin is befitting'*: it is only in LT that these words are immediately followed by the reassurance 'But all shall be well, and all shall be well, and all manner of things shall be well' (ch. 27; p. 74).

'But all shall be well . . . shall be well': the repetition 'but all shall be well, and all shall be well'—now famous from LT (see p. 74)—is not found in the ST version of God's words here.

21 *'Our Lord is our portion'*: see Psalms 16: 5, 119: 57, and 142: 5.

23 *with her*: the gender of Julian's friend becomes obscured in LT (ch. 35; p. 83).

24 *no less than the Persons . . . always good*: LT confines itself to affirming that the higher will 'is so good that it can never will evil, but always good' (ch. 37; p. 87).

David . . . Magdalene: well-known sinners, often grouped together by medieval devotional authors. In LT Julian adds the native English saint, John of Beverley, to the list here (see ch. 38; p. 88).

David: King of Israel and Judah (*c*.1000–960 BC), who committed adultery with Bathsheba; see 2 Samuel 11–12.

Peter and Paul: Saint Peter, who denied his connection with Christ three times (Matthew 26: 69–75), and Saint Paul—then named Saul—who was a persecutor of the early Church (Acts 8–9).

Thomas of India: the apostle Thomas, who—absent when the risen Christ appeared to his disciples in John 20: 19–23—doubted his resurrection until Christ appeared again, inviting Thomas to place his hand in Christ's wounded side and remarking, 'Blessed are they that have not seen, and yet have believed' (John 20: 29). Thomas's subsequent career as the apostle to India would be familiar from *The Golden Legend*; see William Granger Ryan (ed.), *Jacobus de Voragine, The Golden Legend: Readings on the Saints* (Princeton, 1993), 1.29–35.

the Magdalene: in apocryphal tradition Mary Magdalene's wedding at Cana to Saint John the Evangelist was interrupted when Christ called John away, and Magdalene subsequently turned to prostitution; she was also identified with the woman taken in adultery (John 8: 3–11), and with the woman sinner who, at the house of Simon, washes Christ's feet with her tears and hair (Luke 7: 37–50). She is named in Luke 8: 1–3 as the woman out of whom Christ cast seven devils. The risen Christ appears first to her in Mark 16: 9, and after Christ's ascension she was believed to have led the life of an evangelist, ended as a hermit, and became the patron of tearful, penitent sinners. See note to p. 41.

any more . . . bliss of heaven: these words are not in LT (ch. 38; p. 88).

26 *a revelation concerning prayer*: this section of ST reports the fourteenth revelation, which is expanded in LT (see chs. 41–3; pp. 91–7).

that they do not want to pray: the remainder of this paragraph (down to 'desire for ourselves') disappears from LT, replaced by a definition of the two attributes in prayer: righteous prayer and sure trust (ch. 41; pp. 91–2).

'Our Father', 'Hail Mary', and the creed: on the recitation of these by anchoresses, see the *Ancrene Wisse*, Part 1 in Bella Millett (trans.), *Ancrene Wisse: Guide for Anchoresses* (Exeter, 2009), 7–19.

27 *there he issues a serious rebuke . . . calm and humble*: this passage is not as such in LT, which includes a section not in ST from 'this was said as an impossibility' until the end of ch. 42 (pp. 92–5).

then it is like God in condition as it is in nature: this is absent from LT, which confines itself to saying that prayer eases the conscience and fits man to receive grace (ch. 43; p. 95).

because everything . . . we never prayed for it: this is absent from LT (ch. 43; p. 95).

28 *for while man's soul . . . as a comfort*: this passage, apparently closer to the experience of revelation, is absent from LT (ch. 43; p. 96).

so powerless . . . gives him sight of himself: this passage in ST lies behind a later passage in LT: 'I understood this . . . conducive to sin' (ch. 47; p. 101).

and then he supposes . . . united to God: this concluding passage to the section in ST has no close parallel in LT (see ch. 43; pp. 96–7). After this, at the equivalent point in LT, comes a major sequence of material without parallel in ST (see LT, chs. 44–63; pp. 97–136).

29 *then it will be nothing*: here follows, in LT's account of the fifteenth

revelation, Julian's vision of the soul leaving a decomposing corpse, together with her subsequent meditation (LT, ch. 64; pp. 137–8).

29 *chosen*: in LT this becomes 'loved without end, and this endless love works that grace in them' (ch. 65; p. 138).

30 *And this was the end . . . that day*: at the equivalent point to this, LT numbers the revelations so far and records the time of their duration (ch. 65; p. 139).

at the foot of my bed . . . bleeding hard: in LT the cross is held 'in front of my face', and Julian's account is phrased more circumspectly as 'it seemed to me it was bleeding hard' (ch. 66; p. 140).

31 *by the throat*: in LT here Julian provides more details of the devil's appearance (ch. 66; p. 140).

But I stayed . . . dwelling most pleasing: this report of the sixteenth revelation is much expanded in LT (ch. 67; pp. 141–2).

32 *gravely*: in LT these divine words are uttered 'lovingly' (ch. 68; p. 143).

'In this way the devil is overcome': see earlier, p. 12.

despair: in LT Julian adds that it seemed as if the devils were mocking the empty recitation of prayer aloud (ch. 69; p. 144).

33 *'Ah, wretched sin!'*: this passage, ending 'we are at peace' (p. 34), is absent from LT. As such, it is one of the longest sections unique to ST and not carried forward into LT.

34 *as I have said before*: see ST, p. 10.

impatience: LT adds 'or sloth' (ch. 73; p. 148).

Then these . . . beset us: rephrased in LT, so that our being beset by sin is rewritten into an inclination to sin born of spiritual blindness and the burden of fleshliness (ch. 73; pp. 148–9).

35 *the fire of purgatory*: replaced in LT by 'spiritual enemies' (ch. 74; p. 150).

to separate ourselves . . . knowledge of love: in LT this becomes not a separation but a transformation: 'fear turned into love in us through the knowledge of love; that is to say, that the bitterness of doubt is to be turned into the sweetness of kindly love through grace' (ch. 74; p. 150).

36 *For this reverent fear . . . perturbs*: this sentence is not in LT (ch. 74; p. 150).

just as we would . . . good angel: this passage, and the following sentences to the end of ST, are not found in LT.

THE LONG TEXT

39 *Revelations . . . not read AD 1373*: a heading presumably provided by a later copyist; see Julian's account of her literacy in ch. 2 (p. 40).

sixteen . . . special revelations: this opening chapter—apparently with readers more than listeners in mind—numbers and summarizes the revelations, but does not refer to chapters, although division into chapters is likely to date from early in the text's transmission.

The first: see chs. 4–9 (pp. 43–52).

Trinity: the Christian dogma that the one God exists in three Persons and one substance: Father, Son, and Holy Spirit. The Trinity is to be a recurrent theme of Julian's text.

incarnation: the Christian doctrine of the incarnation affirms that the eternal son of God took human flesh from his human mother, and that the historical Christ is at once both fully God and fully man, such that there is a union of Godhead and manhood in the person of Christ without the integrity or permanence of either suffering impairment.

The second . . . Passion: see ch. 10 (pp. 52–5).

The third . . . done: see ch. 11 (pp. 55–7). Might, wisdom, and love are the attributes of the Father, Son, and Holy Spirit.

The fourth . . . blood: see ch. 12 (pp. 57–8).

The fifth . . . Christ: see ch. 13 (pp. 58–9).

The sixth . . . heaven: see ch. 14 (pp. 59–60).

The seventh . . . joy: see ch. 15 (pp. 60–1).

The eighth . . . death: see chs. 16–21 (pp. 61–8).

40 *The ninth . . . heaven*: see chs. 22–3 (pp. 68–71).

The tenth . . . rejoices: see ch. 24 (pp. 71–2).

The eleventh . . . mother: see ch. 25 (pp. 72–3).

The twelfth . . . form: see ch. 26 (p. 74).

The thirteenth: see chs. 27–40 (pp. 74–91). The summary here of this revelation does not match precisely with its actual contents.

atonement: mankind's reconciliation or 'at-one-ment' with God through the sacrificial death of Christ.

'Behold and see . . . you shall see it': this does not reproduce one locution by God as reported in the thirteenth revelation.

The fourteenth . . . fulfils them: see chs. 41–3 (pp. 91–7). This summary does not explicitly refer to material in chs. 44–63, which might have been written later.

The fifteenth . . . in heaven: see chs. 64–5 (pp. 136–9).

The sixteenth . . . our enemy: see chs. 66–8 (pp. 139–43). 'Our enemy' is how Julian will often refer to the devil.

simple, uneducated creature: this refers to Julian at the time of her revelations and not necessarily to the degree of literacy that she later attained. In ST (p. 10) Julian describes herself as ignorant, and may be admitting here not to know Latin rather than to be unable to read or write in English.

eighth day of May: since Julian later refers to the popular native English saint, John of Beverley (ch. 38; p. 88), whose feast day was 7 May, it may well be that her revelations occurred on 8 May, but they are dated to 13 May in MS P of Julian's text. The different dates may derive from a copyist's confusion between the two dates as the Roman numerals 'viii' and 'xiii'.

40 *relive his Passion in my mind*: medieval traditions of affective devotion encouraged those meditating on Christ's Passion towards an imaginative projection of themselves into the events and settings of Christ's sufferings, which they are to re-live in their mind's eye. (See Introduction, p. xvii).

bodily sickness: physical illness sent by God may be an opportunity to increase one's spiritual reward through a kind of martyrdom. See Bella Millett (trans.), *Ancrene Wisse: Guide for Anchoresses* (Exeter, 2009), 69.

41 *Mary Magdalene*: named in three Gospels as present at and just after the crucifixion (Matthew 27: 56, 61; Mark 15: 40, 47; John 19: 25). Devotional tradition emphasized Magdalene's weeping at the crucifixion, and also her role at Christ's entombment and in telling the disciples of Christ's resurrection. Also identified (John 11: 2) with Mary, sister of Lazarus and Martha of Bethany, who was defended by Christ as having chosen the 'better part' when she neglected the housework and 'sat at Jesus' feet and heard his word' (Luke 10: 38–42), Mary Magdalene was seen as an archetype of the contemplative life (see ch. 38; p. 88).

terrors . . . caused by devils: it was believed that devils attended deathbeds, in hopes of gaining another soul. Later, Julian will indeed experience visitations by a devil to her sickbed (chs. 66 and 69, pp. 140–1, 143–4).

I only want what you want: see Matthew 26: 39, and Mark 14: 36.

when I was thirty years old: describing herself as thirty and a half years old in May 1373 (ch. 3; p. 42), Julian would have been more or less a contemporary of Chaucer (born *c*.1342). As Christ's ministry began when he was aged thirty, the number thirty was identified with perfection and the perfect age by St Jerome and other patristic writers, who believed Christ waited for the perfect age so as to provide us with a pattern; see Mary Dove, *The Perfect Age of Man's Life* (Cambridge, 1986), 55, 59.

three wounds in my life: the third gift in the form of three wounds derives from Julian's memory of the story of Saint Cecilia and her three great wounds during her martyrdom (see ST, p. 4, and note), which is omitted from LT.

42 *those who were with me*: the presence of these people around Julian's sickbed would suggest that she was not enclosed as an anchoress at the time of her revelations, but it is unclear whether the rules of enclosure would be waived in event of grave illness.

My curate: a curate can be anyone in religious orders; in ST (p. 5) he is also called a parson, which would usually indicate a parish priest. In holding up the crucifix before the gaze of the dying person and in his opening words, the priest follows the directions of the Office of the Visitation of the Sick; see Eamon Duffy, *The Stripping of the Altars* (New Haven, 1992), 314.

43 *mortal man*: Julian disclaims seeking a vision or any kind of revelation, but only that compassionating devotion available to all.

red blood trickling down: many stories circulated about crucifixes and other images that bled. See *The Revelation of the Monk of Eynsham*, ed. Robert Easting (Oxford, 2002), 17, 33–5.

44 *And in the same revelation . . . seems to me*: this passage, not in ST (see p. 6), introduces Julian's recurrent theme of the Trinity's merciful working of our salvation in and through Christ (chs. 23 and 59; pp. 71, 129), in whom the Trinity is comprehended (ch. 57; p. 125). To gaze at the crucified Christ is to perceive the Trinity, and only through Christ may we perceive the Father (ch. 22; p. 69).

'Blessed be thou, Lord!': translating Latin words in the manuscript, 'Benedicite domine'.

friendly: translating the Middle English 'homely'. This passage sees the first of Julian's many links between the homeliness and courtesy perceived in God's intimacy with, and noble graciousness towards, humanity.

when she conceived: Mary is usually said to be fifteen in medieval accounts of the Annunciation. Julian's Mary reflects medieval traditions of the Virgin as precociously wise beyond her years, and of the Annunciation as itself a kind of contemplative moment, in which Mary is an exemplar of the contemplative.

45 *a little thing . . . a hazelnut . . . round as a ball*: on the little thing, see Wisdom 11: 22–6. In referring to the size of a hazelnut Julian may be reflecting the use of the hazelnut as a measurement of size and quantity in surviving medieval English recipes. Just as the little thing, 'as round as a ball', is held in the palm of her own hand, so all creation is sustained by God (see Job 12: 10), and in medieval iconography God is traditionally depicted holding the orb of the world in his hand.

setting at nought . . . unmade: this theme of abnegation will recur; see chs. 18 and 27 (pp. 65, 75).

almighty, all wise, all good: these three attributes of power, wisdom, and goodness of will or love are traditionally appropriated to the Trinity of Father, Son, and Holy Spirit. For Julian's recurrent references to this triad of attributes, see chs. 35, 40, 46, 49, 58 (pp. 83, 91, 100, 104, 126–7).

46 *God wishes to be known*: this may be part of Julian's reason for recording her revelations, although she records no specific divine injunction to do so.

Our Lord God also revealed: from here until 'And all the while he was revealing' in ch. 7 (p. 48) is not in ST (see p. 8).

'God, of your goodness . . . everything': Julian's understanding is expressed through a form of prayer.

intermediaries: Julian proceeds to list these: praying by aspects of Christ's Passion, by Mary and the Holy Cross, and by the saints.

47 *A man walks upright*: Isidore of Seville's immensely influential

seventh-century encyclopaedia explains that 'the human stands erect and looks towards heaven so as to seek God, rather than look at the earth, as do the beasts that nature has made bent over and attentive to their bellies', and cites Ovid, *Metamorphoses*, 1.84–6; see *The* Etymologies *of Isidore of Seville*, trans. Stephen A. Barney et al. (Cambridge, 2006), 231.

47 *food*: this is to translate the manuscript's Middle English 'soule' here as 'souel', which is recorded more frequently meaning something—pottage, sauce, meat—eaten with bread, but may also mean food or nourishment more generally. The passage thus comes to mean not that the soul will leave the body in due course but that God is with us even in such moments of our lowest need as defecation. Various bodily organs are likened to a purse in medieval medical writings; for a comparison to a drawstring purse in an account of the functioning of the anal muscles in a late fourteenth-century anatomical treatise, see Liz Herbert McAvoy, *Authority and the Female Body in the Writings of Julian of Norwich and Margery Kempe* (Cambridge, 2004), 140. The present passage has become something of a touchstone in modern appreciation of Julian's acceptance of humankind's bodiliness, although it is also one of the places where Julian's meaning is most tentatively established. The whole passage from 'A man walks upright' to 'our lowest need' is absent from some manuscripts (S1, S2), perhaps for reasons of fastidiousness. The transition from 'soul' in its usual sense in the previous sentence is certainly abrupt, and the passage may have become somewhat corrupted.

he does not despise what he has made: see Wisdom 11: 24.

clad . . . and enclosed in . . . God: see Job 10: 11.

decay and wear away: see Psalm 102: 26.

48 *ask all that we wish of . . . God*: see John 15: 16.

God's good will is to have us: 1 Timothy 2: 3–4.

filled with grace: see Luke 1: 28.

The great drops of blood: from here until the end of ch. 7 is not in ST (see p. 8).

49 *when it came to the brows, then it vanished*: for Christ's blood as vanishing from view over another edge, see the fourth revelation (ch. 12; p. 57).

like herring scales: herring was a staple of the medieval diet, and the nearby port of Yarmouth was a centre of herring fishery.

clear example: for other exemplary instances of lordship, see chs. 14, 51, and 67 (pp. 59, 106–15, 141–2). Here is introduced what will be Julian's recurrent meditative theme of a lord's true courtesy in being affable and approachable to his subordinates, which represents God's wonderful readiness to be familiar and intimate with us, most of all in taking on human nature in the incarnation.

51 *judged eternally*: reflecting contemporary belief that the eternal judgement of an individual occurs at death. The role of the Last Judgement will be to

confirm publicly these private and particular judgements, thereby demon-
strating their justice within the righteousness of God's will.

52 *I speak of those who will be saved*: by stipulating that she was not shown
other than the saved, Julian sidesteps any universalist claim that all are
saved. The phrase 'who will be saved' is to recur many times.

I believe as Holy Church . . . teaches: the first of Julian's recurrent affirm-
ations that she and her revelations are in accord with Church teachings.

All this . . . spiritual vision: these three modes of revelation (see also
ch. 73; p. 148) may derive ultimately from Saint Augustine's distinctions
between corporeal, spiritual, and intellectual vision. Julian appears exceptional among women visionaries in using such Augustinian terminology,
although there was the example of its application to the revelations of
Saint Bridget of Sweden by Alphonse of Pecha, her redactor and biog-
rapher.

spitting . . . and blows: see Matthew 26: 67. Julian beholds through the face
on the crucifix parts of Christ's Passion which actually preceded the crucifixion itself.

53 *I saw how half his face . . . just as it had come*: ST's conventional devotional
image of Christ's face unchangingly caked with dry blood (see ST, p. 11) is
here rewritten in LT into a dynamic vision of how the two sides of Christ's
face discolour alternately.

he will be your light: see Psalm 27: 1.

bottom of the sea: see Ecclesiasticus 24: 5, and Psalm 139: 9–10. If we could
truly grasp the reality of God's continuous presence with us, we should be
safe, whether beneath the waves or in whatever element.

I was doubtful for a while whether it was a revelation: Julian candidly allows
her prolonged uncertainty over this second revelation to remain part of
her record of how she came to interpret what she was shown.

the holy Vernicle in Rome: the 'Vernicle' was the cloth upon which Christ's
face was miraculously imprinted when Saint Veronica handed it to Christ
to wipe his face on his way to the crucifixion. The Vernicle (Veronica's
'vera icon' or true image) became the great Roman relic of the later Middle Ages, with an indulgence of 12,000 years for non-Italians who trav-
elled to view the image. In response to a miraculous change in the relic in
1216, when the image moved upside down, Pope Innocent III composed
a prayer in honour of the Vernicle, with ten days' indulgence for reciting
it (as the English chronicler Matthew Paris of St Albans recorded). Those
who could not recite the prayer received the same indulgence, provided
they said the Lord's Prayer and Hail Mary five times, and the Creed, while
beholding a Vernicle image. Devotion to the Vernicle much increased
subsequently. Also instituted was an office of the Holy Face, included
in books of hours and illustrated with miniatures sometimes depicting
Christ's face with a dark complexion—brown, grey, or black—and covered by large drops of blood. As Christ's self-portrait, created by himself,

no image could be more truly Christ's likeness than the Vernicle, yet it was not only disconcertingly dark and unbeautiful, but also (as in the story of Innocent III) unfixed and changing to the perception. Given by Christ unmediatedly to a woman, the Vernicle image parallels and authorizes the visions vouchsafed to women visionaries, and it is by association with the miraculous Vernicle that Julian affirms that the crucifix altered miraculously before her eyes. At his 1391 trial the Lollard Walter Brut cites the Vernicle among miracles that Christ enacted for women when concluding that there is no reason why women should not be priests (see Alcuin Blamires (ed.), *Woman Defamed and Woman Defended: An Anthology of Medieval Texts* (Oxford, 1992), 260). Veronica also became identified with the woman afflicted with a discharge of blood who touches Christ's hem and is healed (Matthew 9: 20–2; Mark 5: 25–34), a miracle to which Julian later alludes (ch. 77; p. 155).

53 *fruit of the Virgin's womb*: see Luke 1: 42.

54 *in its image*: see Genesis 1: 26.

as a man without sin could be: see Hebrews 4: 15.

God is hidden: possibly referring to the 'devil's rights' tradition, whereby Christ's divine nature was concealed by his human form so as to deceive the devil into bringing about Christ's death, thus ensuring the redemption of humankind.

never so fair a man as he: see Psalm 45: 2, traditionally interpreted as referring to Christ's beauty.

in the eighth revelation: see chs. 16–17 (pp. 61–4).

faith, hope, and charity: see 1 Corinthians 13: 13.

55 *God in a point*: a point in space rather than an instant in time (which Julian's Middle English 'point' may also signify), although Julian may thus imply both space and time. See also ch. 53 (p. 119) for the point where the soul is knit to God.

without beginning: in his *De Trinitate* (2.5.9) Saint Augustine declared, 'The order of times is certainly without time in the eternal wisdom of God', and it became a medieval commonplace that within God's eternal perspective every moment is eternally present.

56 *everything which is done is well done*: the actions of God cannot but be effective.

at the mid-point of everything: for God 'whose centre is everywhere and whose circumference is nowhere', see Alan of Lille, *Theological Rules* (in *Patrologia Latina*, ed. J. P. Migne (Paris, 1844–65), 210: 627). See also Pseudo-Dionysius, in *The Divine Names*, who writes: 'Now this is unified and one and common to the whole of divinity: that the entire wholeness is participated in by each of those who participate in it; none participates in only a part. It is rather like the case of the circle. The centre point of the circle is shared by the surrounding radii' (2.5). Dionysius continues later:

'All the radii of a circle are brought together in the unity of the centre, which contains all the straight lines brought together within itself. These are linked one to another because of this single point of origin and they are completely unified at this centre' (5.6), in Colm Luibheid (trans.), *Pseudo-Dionysius: The Complete Works* (Mahwah, NJ, 1987).

he does no sin: see Ecclesiasticus 15: 11–13, and also James 1: 13.

sin is no kind of deed: sin is an absence or privation of good, a nullity and nonentity that does not constitute any deed or action. See Boethius, *Consolation of Philosophy*, 4.2, and Saint Augustine, *Confessions*, 3.7, 7.12–16.

just . . . complete: translating Julian's 'right' and 'full', where she is playing on the components of 'rightfulness' (or 'rightfulhede' in Julian's Middle English).

as I shall describe: see ch. 27 (pp. 74–5) and ch. 35 (p. 84).

the best deed is well done: see Ecclesiasticus 39: 33–4.

everything was set in order: see Wisdom 11: 20.

satisfied with all his works: see Genesis 1: 31.

with this meaning: such a mode of exposition through speech attributed to God or Christ recurs in Julian's text, usually introduced by 'as if he had said' or 'with this meaning'. See also chs. 22 (p. 69), 24 (p. 72), 25 (p. 73), 29 (p. 77), 32 (p. 80), 36 (p. 85), and 41 (pp. 92–3).

57 *scourging*: for the flagellation of Christ, see Matthew 27: 26.

tender flesh: created from the female flesh of the Virgin Mary, Christ's flesh was believed to be especially tender, so that his susceptibility to suffering was without parallel.

sharp blows all over . . . body: Julian focuses on the torments not the tormentors, making no mention of those who inflict Christ's wounds, unlike many medieval accounts of the Passion.

if it had been . . . in nature and essence: i.e. if it had been real, natural blood (rather than a vision).

abundant waters on earth: see Psalm 65: 9–10. For Christ's blood as washing away sin, see Revelation 1: 5.

by virtue of his blessed Godhead: see 1 John 5: 6–8.

Behold and see!: see Lamentations 1: 12. The devotional image of Christ's flagellation which forms the corresponding revelation in ST (p. 12) is here transformed in LT into a surreal visionary understanding, in which Christ's actions in delivering souls from hell and ascending into heaven are performed not by his historical person but by his streaming blood.

descended down into hell . . . the court of heaven: referring to Christ's 'Harrowing' or despoiling of hell (from the apocryphal *Gospel of Nicodemus*), when Christ, between his death on Good Friday and resurrection on Easter Sunday, descends into hell and leads forth from limbo into heaven the souls of the just (strictly, only the patriarchs and prophets, but in medieval popular tradition Christ empties hell of all human souls).

57 *ascended up into heaven*: referring to Christ's bodily ascension into heaven, forty days after his resurrection (Mark 16: 19; Luke 24: 51).

58 *bleeding and praying for us to the Father*: see Hebrews 7: 25, 9: 14, and 12: 24.

making up the number that is lacking: the number of saved souls will eventually make up for the number of fallen angels. See Revelation 6: 11.

the devil is overcome: see ch. 69 (p. 144).

incarnation: when the Second Person of the Trinity, Jesus, became human in order to atone through his Passion and death for the original sin of Adam and Eve in Eden, which condemned their descendants to hell.

under lock and key in God's hand: translating Julian's 'locked' (Middle English: 'loken') in God's hand. For the angel bearing the key to the bottomless pit, see Revelation 20: 1–3. In the *Gospel of Nicodemus*, during his Harrowing of Hell, Christ binds Satan with a chain; see J. K. Elliott (ed.), *The Apocryphal New Testament* (Oxford, 1993), 203. See also ch. 65 (p. 139).

But there can be no anger in God . . . against God's will: not in ST (see p. 12). Since God is unchanging, any anger in him would be an eternal wrath incompatible with our being created out of love. See also LT, chs. 46, 48, 49 (pp. 100, 102, 103–4). Julian is choosing, of course, to turn a blind eye to the many biblical passages in which anger is ascribed to God.

I laughed heartily: anchoresses are advised to treat the devil with contempt and laugh him to scorn; see Bella Millett (trans.), *Ancrene Wisse: Guide for Anchoresses* (Exeter, 2009), 94, 103.

But I did not see Christ laughing: the Gospels nowhere record Christ laughing, but Julian's spiritual delight in her revelation enables her to understand that, even if Christ never laughed, we may laugh to comfort ourselves and to rejoice in God.

59 *And when I said, 'He is scorned' . . . forever to hell*: this passage appears only in LT (see ST, p. 13).

your service . . . especially in your youth: conceivably referring to Julian's having been a nun before becoming an anchoress, but some less formal self-dedication may be indicated.

servants and friends: see John 15: 14–15.

splendid feast: see Christ's parable of the king who held a marriage feast for his son in Matthew 22: 1–14, and also Luke 12: 37, where a lord makes his dutiful servants 'sit down to meat, and will come forth and serve them'.

And with this . . . joy and bliss: these lines appear only in LT (see ST, p. 13).

60 *glorious gratitude*: see Matthew 25: 21.

And at this time . . . much increased: this example is only recorded in LT (see ST, p. 13).

the age of everyone will be known in heaven: because it was deemed that Christ had died at the perfect age, it was held that, regardless of its age at death, each soul would be resurrected at that perfect age. See Ephesians 4: 13. In his *De Anima*, Tertullian argues that the soul will preserve whatever age it has reached at the time of death until changed to the perfect age at the Last Judgement; see Mary Dove, *The Perfect Age of Man's Life* (Cambridge, 1986), 57–9, and Caroline Walker Bynum, *The Resurrection of the Body in Western Christianity, 200–1336* (New York, 1995), 122–4.

For I saw . . . life: not in ST (see p. 13). Cf. the parable of the workers in the vineyard in Matthew 20: 1–16.

This only lasted a while: the experience of a fluctuating sense of absence and presence, ease and difficulty, is a topic recurrently addressed in works advising on contemplative life; see Walter Hilton, *The Scale of Perfection*, ed. Thomas Bestul (Kalamazoo, Mich., 2000), 2.41.

61 *Saint Paul: 'Nothing . . . of Christ'*: Julian here invokes but does not quote precisely Romans 8: 35, 38–9.

Saint Peter: 'Lord, save me, I perish': Julian here conflates two appeals to Christ for help on the Sea of Galilee: Peter's 'Lord, save me' (Matthew 14: 30) and the disciples' 'Lord, save us, we perish' (Matthew 8: 25).

sin is not always the cause: traditional teaching would maintain that sin does constitute the cause for withdrawal of grace.

those who are to be saved: all who wish to serve God may hope to number themselves among those predestined to be saved.

deathly pale . . . a darker blue: that Christ's face turns both pale and various shades of blue (livid, blackish, dark grey) is a recurrent theme of medieval Passion lyrics and meditations. This chapter in LT is much supplemented with descriptive detail which does not appear in ST (see ST, pp. 14–15).

62 *a dry, keen wind and terribly cold*: a tradition of cold weather during the Passion derives from the account of Christ's arrest in John 18: 18. A cold wind at the Crucifixion is less commonly mentioned, but cf. a carol of *c*.1500: 'There blows a colde wynd todaye, todaye, | The wynd blows cold todaye; | Cryst sufferyd his passyon for mannys salvacyon, | To kype the cold wynd awaye' (Richard Leighton Greene, *The Early English Carols*, 2nd edn. (Oxford, 1977), 113).

vitality: the 'vital' spirits, emanating from the heart, controlled pulse and breathing. The other two spirits, according to medieval physiology, were the 'natural' spirit in the liver, and the 'animal' spirit in the brain. For an account, see the medieval encyclopaedia in *On the Properties of Things: John Trevisa's Translation of Bartholomaeus Anglicus De Proprietatibus Rerum*, ed. M. C. Seymour et al. (Oxford, 1975), 1.103–8.

And when I said . . . yet continually dying: this clarification is only present in LT (see ST, p. 14).

drying of Christ's flesh . . . his Passion: dehydration of Christ's body during the Crucifixion is a focus of medieval Passion meditations, consequent upon their emphasis on a massive haemorrhaging of Christ's blood, as in Julian's fourth revelation (ch. 12, pp. 57–8).

62 *'I thirst'*: see John 19: 28; fifth of the seven last words or phrases spoken by Christ from the cross.

double thirst: traditionally, Christ's thirst was interpreted as not only a bodily thirst (through dehydration and loss of blood) but also a spiritual thirst for mankind's salvation.

63 *sagged under its own weight*: Julian is picturing the slumped and twisted posture of Christ's body on the cross in much later medieval art.

garland of thorns: the crown of thorns is called a garland in various Middle English writings. A fifteenth-century carol, addressing Christ, wonders 'How shalt thou sufferin the scharp garlond of thorns?'; see Richard Leighton Greene (ed.), *The Early English Carols*, 2nd edn. (Oxford, 1977), 91.

tanned colour: there were sizeable communities of leather-workers in Conesford, the part of Norwich where Julian's anchorhold was situated; see Carole Rawcliffe and Richard Wilson (eds.), *Medieval Norwich* (London, 2004), 309.

as a cloth is hung up to dry: medieval Norwich had an important woollen industry, and the woollen cloth needed to be stretched on frames to dry.

For I understood . . . with shrinking as it dried: this passage is only present in LT (see ST, p. 15).

he only suffered once: see Hebrews 10: 10.

64 *'I little knew what pain . . . I asked for'*: see Matthew 20: 22.

and like a wretch . . . reluctant to pray for it: this regret is not recorded in ST (see ST, p. 15).

'Is any pain in hell like this?': whether Christ's pains during his Passion surpassed the pains of hell was a subject of medieval debate. Julian prefers to see hell as a different rather than a lesser pain.

'Hell is a different pain . . . to see your love suffer': in ST Julian is answered that 'despair is greater because that is spiritual pain, but there is no bodily pain greater than this' (ST, p. 15).

The firmament and the earth failed . . . Christ's death: see Matthew 27: 45, Luke 23: 44–5.

65 *two kinds of people*: those who were and were not converted, represented by Dionysius and Pilate.

Pontius Pilate: according to the *Gospel of Nicodemus* (also known as *The Acts of Pilate*) when Pilate heard of the extraordinary phenomena accompanying Christ's death he 'sent for the Jews and said to them: "Did you see what happened?". But they said: "There was an eclipse of the sun in the usual way"'; see J. K. Elliott (ed.), *The Apocryphal New*

Testament (Oxford, 1993), 177. This is the Gospels' Pilate as a troubled judge, although later medieval tradition developed a villainous Pilate. *The Golden Legend* included an apocryphal biography of Pilate which included several treacherous murders when a young man, his attempts to evade responsibility for Christ's death, his eventual suicide, and the refusal of rivers or earth to accept his body, as dramatized in the Resurrection play in the Cornish mystery plays; see William Granger Ryan (ed.), *Jacobus de Voragine, The Golden Legend: Readings on the Saints* (Princeton, 1993), I.211–14.

Saint Dionysius of France: this figure is a conflation of three separate figures, which Julian may have known from the influential account in *The Golden Legend*: i.e. the Pseudo-Dionysius, author of the *Mystica Theologia* (*c.* AD 500), sometimes called 'the Areopagite' because misidentified in the Middle Ages with the Athenian philosopher converted by Saint Paul on the Areopagus in Athens (Acts 17: 34), and also misidentified by legend with the martyr patron saint of France, Saint Denis, who lived in the third century. According to *The Golden Legend*, Dionysius wrote his mystical works after hearing from Saint Paul of his heavenly visions and was later sent to evangelize in Gaul, where he was martyred. Julian echoes Dionysius's words in *The Golden Legend*, where he is quoted as saying of the noonday darkness and earthquake that accompanied Christ's death: 'Either the order of nature is overturned . . . or the God of nature is suffering and the elements are suffering with him', and the Athenians then 'built an altar to that god and put above it the title "TO THE UNKNOWN GOD" '; see William Granger Ryan (ed.), *Jacobus de Voragine, The Golden Legend: Readings on the Saints* (Princeton, 1993), 2.238. Saint Paul reports seeing this altar in Acts 17: 23.

said . . . in a friendly way: the source of this suggestion is not identified but it follows Julian's horror at the possible presence of the demons believed to attend deathbeds.

you are my heaven: declining the invitation to contemplate God the Father, Julian reaffirms her constancy in devotion to Christ's humanity. See ch. 22 (p. 69), where Julian sees three heavens, all of the manhood of Christ.

67 *he who is highest . . . most utterly despised*: see Philippians 2: 6–8. Christ's abnegation in his Passion serves as an example for that self-abnegation (or 'noughting' in Julian's Middle English) which will be a recurrent theme of Julian's text.

he suffered as much for her sorrows: Christ may not spare his mother her sorrow at his Passion but enters into that sorrow with her.

pains will be turned into . . . joys: see John 16: 20–2.

three ways of contemplating his blessed Passion: for the second and third ways, see chs. 22 (p. 70) and 23 (p. 70).

68 *his blessed countenance changed*: instead of a sight of Christ's death on the

cross to conclude her Passion revelation, Julian witnesses a mysterious change in Christ's countenance, perhaps recalling the Transfiguration in Luke 9: 29. The corresponding change in Julian may recall 2 Corinthians 3: 18.

68 *on his cross with him in our pain and our sufferings*: see Galatians 6: 14 and Romans 8: 17.

if I could suffer more, I would suffer more: see Isaiah 5: 4, echoed in the Good Friday liturgy ('What more should I do for you and have not done?'); see J. Wickham Legg (ed.), *The Sarum Missal* (Oxford, 1916), 113. Julian transforms what is usually understood as a reproach into an expression of Christ's love for humanity.

69 *three heavens*: these three equal heavens are correlated with the three persons of the Trinity in ch. 23 (p. 70), and for Julian the manhood of Christ is coterminous with the Trinity. Cf. Saint Paul's vision as 'one caught up to the third heaven' in 2 Corinthians 12: 2–4.

I saw in Christ what the Father is: see John 14: 6.

he is highly pleased . . . our salvation: see Luke 3: 22.

through his Father's courteous gift: the Father presents to the Son as a gift the humanity that the Son has redeemed. Later, the Son presents humanity to his Father in heaven, a gift which the Father gratefully and courteously returns to the Son (see ch. 55; p. 121).

we are his crown: the suffering consequent on mankind's sins, which is Christ's crown of thorns, becomes a victory crown in the bliss of our salvation. See ch. 51 (p. 115), and also Hebrews 2: 7.

new heavens and a new earth: see Isaiah 65: 17.

70 *He did not say, 'If it were necessary to suffer more'*: because the redemption of humanity was eternally God's purpose, Christ's suffering was not absolutely necessary.

And here I saw: this passage (down to 'he eternally rejoices, as has been said before') is absent from ST, and shows Julian grouping her Passion revelations together.

71 *as has been said before . . . as has been said before*: see chs. 22 (p. 68) and 23 (p. 71).

All the Trinity . . . rejoices eternally: although the Trinity as a whole acts in the Passion and ministers to us its benefits, only Christ's incarnate human aspect suffered.

I ask nothing . . . but that I may please you: a sermon by Archbishop Pecham (1240–92) declares of Christ: 'I tell you that he loved courteously with no expectation of reward'; see Rosemary Woolf, *The English Religious Lyric in the Middle Ages* (Oxford, 1968), 215.

a glad giver: see 2 Corinthians 9: 7.

this word 'ever': see ch. 22 (p. 68).

72 *our Lord looked . . . into his side within*: this revelation may be associated with the iconographical and devotional form known as the *Imago Pietatis*, or Man of Sorrows, where Christ is depicted standing in a tomb-chest after his crucifixion and inclining his head to his right to guide the viewer's attention to the lance wound in his side, from which flow blood and water. See 'History of the *Imago Pietatis*' in Rosemary Woolf, *The English Religious Lyric in the Middle Ages* (Oxford, 1968), 389–91. For the inflicting of the side-wound, see John 19: 34. The blood and water flowing from Christ's side signify the birth of the Church and symbolize the sacraments of baptism and eucharist. The side-wound was conventionally understood as offering a refuge for the sinner and, as a token of Christ's love, the wound is a pervasive devotional theme.

And then he revealed . . . in peace and in love: this revelation is only present in LT (see ST, pp. 18–19).

And with this sweet rejoicing: the remainder of the chapter is much expanded from its earlier form in ST (pp. 18–19), where contemplation of the wounded side is offered in place of contemplation of the Godhead.

For my delight is your holiness: see 1 Thessalonians 4: 3.

on his right side: Mary is traditionally represented as standing on Christ's right side, and hence to the viewer's left, in images of the crucifixion.

73 *not taught . . . bodily presence*: Julian does not aspire to those visions of, and conversations with, the Virgin reported in the much-read and influential revelations of Saint Elizabeth of Hungary and Saint Bridget of Sweden.

as if he had said . . . 'Would you like to see her?': this passage is only present in LT (see ST, p. 19).

he showed her high, and noble, and glorious: possibly at Mary's bodily assumption into heaven and at her coronation in heaven by her son, both popular iconographical subjects in depictions of the life of Mary.

three times: see chs. 4, 7, and 18 (pp. 44–5, 48, and 64).

74 *our soul will never find rest*: cf. Saint Augustine: 'You have made us for yourself, and our hearts are restless until they rest in you' (*Confessions*, 1.1).

It is I: cf. God's words 'I am that I am' (Exodus 3: 14) when appearing to Moses in the burning bush. See also the 'I am' sayings of Jesus in John 6: 35; 8: 24, 28, 58; 9: 5; 10: 7; 11: 25; 13: 19; 14: 6; 15: 1.

The number . . . soul may desire: this sentence is only present in LT (see ST, p. 19).

the longing that I had for him before: that is, the wound of purposeful longing for God, wished for earlier (ST, p. 4, and LT, ch. 2; p. 41).

unreasonably and without discretion: exercise of discretion has a special role in medieval spiritual tradition, and Julian's pairing of discretion with reason reflects a traditional association. See Richard of St Victor's *Benjamin Minor*, as translated, probably by the anonymous medieval English author of *The Cloud of Unknowing*, in *Deonise Hid Divinite*, ed. Phyllis Hodgson (Oxford, 1955), 39–42.

74 *Sin is befitting*: this may have its context in the paradoxical doctrine of the 'felix culpa' (happy fault) or fortunate Fall of Man, by which Adam's sin was happy and necessary in that it was followed by the incarnation (which, however, was held to be not merely occasioned by Adam's fall but was part of God's purposes from all eternity). See also Romans 11: 32 and 2 Corinthians 5: 19. The canticle sung at the Easter Saturday vigil includes the words 'O necessary sin of Adam . . . O happy fault!'; F. H. Dickinson (ed.), *Missale ad usum Sarum* (Oxford, 1861–83), 340.

all shall be well: see Romans 8: 28. Julian's 'shall' has been retained here in perhaps her best-known utterance, but its meaning in Middle English implies necessity ('must') at least as much as futurity ('will'). Julian records no meditation in LT on the significance of the phrase's being repeated.

75 *set at nought*: referring back to Christ's self-abnegation in being incarnated and his humiliations in his Passion; see ch. 20 (p. 67).

But I did not see sin . . . the suffering it causes: see ch. 11 (p. 56).

all who shall be saved: for Julian's references to the saved, see ch. 9 (p. 52).

indicating no kind of blame: on the absence of blame, see also chs. 28, 39, 45, 50, 51, 52, 80, 82 (pp. 76, 89, 98, 105, 107, 116, 159, 161).

mystery hidden in God: for other secrets and mysteries, see chs. 30, 32, 34 (pp. 77, 80, 82–3).

And in these same words . . . our Lord God forever: this passage is only present in LT (see ST, p. 20).

76 *compassion for all my fellow Christians*: most of the remainder of this chapter is only present in LT (see ST, p. 21).

as a cloth is shaken in the wind: the Church is thus identified with Christ's suffering in his Passion, 'hung up in the air as a cloth is hung up to dry' (ch. 17; p. 63). One context for Julian's comment is the doctrinal and political uncertainties of the contemporary Great Schism of 1378–1417.

our Lord rejoices . . . over the tribulations of his servants: the spiritual benefit brought by tribulations was the subject of a substantial medieval literature of counsel and remedy.

I shall . . . break you: see Psalm 2: 9. This appears to be another attributed divine locution.

And then I saw . . . it is Christ in him: this sentence has been retained from ST (see p. 21).

77 *Adam's sin was the greatest harm that was ever done*: while acknowledging the harm of the Fall of Man, Julian's emphasis is on the redemption as more pleasing to God than Adam's fall was harmful.

two parts of this: the 'open' part, concerning our salvation, is addressed in chs. 31 and 34–40 (pp. 78–9 and 82–91), while the secret, hidden part is considered in chs. 32 and 33 (pp. 79–82).

'Our Lord is our portion': see Psalms 16: 5, 119: 57, and 142: 5.

our Lord's private counsels: on God's wisdom as secret and hidden, see 1 Corinthians 2: 7, Romans 11: 33, and Ecclesiasticus 11: 4. Julian's Middle English 'privy councell' here may include some allusion to a sovereign's group of confidential advisers and their business, to which the continuing British institution of the Privy Council is a successor.

78 *Christ's spiritual thirst will come to an end*: Christ's bodily thirst on the cross (John 19: 28) was also interpreted spiritually to signify Christ's continuing longing for mankind's salvation, sometimes understood as a kind of love-longing, and as enduring until the Last Judgement; cf. William Langland, *The Vision of Piers Plowman*, ed. A. V. C. Schmidt (London, 1995), B.18.368–70. See also chs. 40, 52, 63, and 75 (pp. 90, 116, 135, and 151).

some of us who shall be saved . . . until that day: see Matthew 16: 28.

a love-longing: from here, the remainder of the chapter is only present in LT, except the last paragraph, which is present in ST (see p. 22).

79 *'It is I who am highest'*: see ch. 26 (p. 74).

'It is a joy . . . my Passion for you': see ch. 22 (p. 68).

Christ as our head: see Ephesians 4: 15.

his members are joined: see 1 Corinthians 12: 27.

drawing us up to his bliss: see John 12: 32. See ch. 52 (p. 116), and also chs. 43 and 46 (pp. 96 and 100).

80 *same five sayings mentioned previously*: i.e. the five clauses uttered by Christ in ch. 31 (p. 78).

unknown to all creatures under Christ: see Mark 13: 32.

This is the great deed . . . make all things well: possibly indicating some salvific act on God's part, whereby all will be saved at the end of time. This deed is distinct from the mysterious deed treated later, which addresses the salvation of individual Christians (see ch. 36; pp. 85–6).

our faith is founded on God's word: see Romans 10: 17.

God's word will be kept in all things: see Matthew 24: 35.

81 *many will be damned*: i.e. fallen angels, non-Christians, and reprobate Christians. Julian's implicit concern for the possible salvation of the heathen reflects a vivid contemporary interest in the posthumous fate of those virtuous pagans born before Christ's ministry or otherwise unaware of it.

'What is impossible . . . make all things well': see Luke 18: 26–7, Matthew 19: 26, and also Isaiah 55: 11.

in the fifth revelation . . . damned forever: see ch. 13 (pp. 58–9).

82 *no more mentioned . . . than the devil is*: on how the damned go unmentioned before God, see Psalm 69: 28, Revelation 20: 15, and the apocryphal

Apocalypse of Paul, in J. K. Elliott (ed.), *The Apocryphal New Testament* (Oxford, 1993), 637. A conventional view was that the elect rejoice in the torments of the damned, although Julian does not mention this.

82 *various revelations*: for the first, see chs. 4–9 (pp. 43–52); for the second, see ch. 10 (pp. 52–5); for the fourth, see ch. 12 (pp. 57–8); for the eighth, see ch. 18 (pp. 64–5).

as has been said before: see ch. 23 (p. 70).

the Jews who put him to death: the supposed collective responsibility of all Jews for Christ's death prompted a medieval tradition of anti-Semitism that disfigured Christianity, but it is notable that Julian carefully specifies that she did not actually witness herself any Jewish complicity in Christ's murder, even if she accepts the orthodoxy that the Jews stand generally condemned for it. There had been a prominent Jewish community in Norwich until the general expulsion of all Jews from England by Edward I in 1290, although the cult of Saint William of Norwich (d. 1144)—a child supposedly crucified by local Jews—was the earliest instance in England of such a blood-libel story and was part of a wider anti-Semitism recorded in Norwich. See V. D. Lipman, *The Jews of Medieval Norwich* (London, 1967).

wish for nothing . . . but God's will: cf. the petition of the Lord's Prayer, 'Thy will be done'.

two kinds of mystery: for the open and hidden understandings, see ch. 30 (p. 77); for the great mystery, see ch. 32 (p. 80).

83 *in the third revelation*: see ch. 11 (pp. 55–7).

a certain person . . . lead a good life: here Julian exceptionally seeks those gifts of prophecy recorded by such other visionary women as Margery Kempe, but this curiosity about a particular individual hinders her spiritual progress. In LT the fact that Julian's friend is a woman has been concealed, unlike in ST (see p. 23).

For the fullness of joy . . . in everything: from here, the remainder of ch. 35 and all of ch. 36 are only present in LT (see ST, p. 24).

84 *in the first revelation . . . in the third*: see ch. 5 (pp. 45–6) and ch. 11 (p. 55).

ordained from without beginning: see ch. 11 (p. 55).

satisfied with himself . . . his works: i.e. satisfaction is a necessary response to what, by definition, cannot be improved upon.

85 *a deed will be done . . . he himself will do it*: this is distinct from the earlier deed (see ch. 32; p. 80) and will be known in heaven, and can be known here in part (including through miracles), whereas the other deed will only be known at the last day, of judgement. Julian understands herself to represent all who shall be saved.

86 *I am enough for you*: see 2 Corinthians 12: 9.

87 *God brought to mind that I would sin*: from here, LT resumes drawing on ST (see ST, p. 24).

as you will see: see especially chs. 78–9 (pp. 155–8).

I was taught to apply it . . . not to anyone in particular: in ST at this point 'our Lord brought to mind, along with my sins, the sins of all my fellow Christians, all in general and not in particular' (p. 24).

For just as . . . revealed: see Romans 4: 8, echoing Psalm 32: 2.

a godly will which never assented to sin nor ever shall: see 1 John 3: 9. For a later revisiting of this thinking, where Julian expounds the substantial union between the Second Person of the Trinity and the saved, see chs. 53 and 58 (pp. 118–19, 126–8). The present passage looks forward to Julian's treatment of the soul's substance and 'sensuality', or sensory being, in chs. 45–54 (pp. 98–121).

88 *For just as for every sin . . . by surpassing glories*: this passage is only present in LT (see ST, p. 24).

David: see note to p. 24.

of the Old Law: in the Old Testament, living under the old law, as opposed to the 'new law' instituted by Christ.

Mary Magdalene, Peter and Paul, and Thomas of India: see note to p. 24.

Saint John of Beverley: a monk of Whitby, bishop of Hexham (687–706), then of York, John retired (c.714) to the monastery he founded at Beverley. After his death in 721 his tomb became the focus of a major pilgrimage cult and canonization followed in 1037. John's nationwide status as a popular native saint was already long established before Henry V's triumph at Agincourt in 1415 on the feast of the saint's translation (25 October) led to national observance of both 25 October and the feast day of John's death (7 May), which fell on the day before Julian records her revelations as beginning (see ch. 2; p. 40). Most evidence for John's career is preserved by the Venerable Bede, who knew him personally, but Bede does not record any youthful sinfulness, and a legend about this now survives only in a Dutch folktale printed c.1512. In this, the devil tricks the hermit John (son of the Earl of Beverley) into choosing between drunkenness, unchastity, or murder. Choosing drunkenness as the least grave sin, a drunken John then rapes and murders his sister. In repentance, John resolves to go on all fours, drink only water and eat grass like an animal, and keep silent until a day-old infant informs him of God's forgiveness. Seven years later the new Earl of Beverley goes hunting to celebrate the birth of his child and John—now resembling a wild animal—is captured and taken back to court, where the Earl's new-born baby absolves him. Some of John's miracles, as reported by Bede, concern cures from illnesses with symptoms not dissimilar to Julian's in her illness of May 1373. Julian makes no reference to John of Beverley in ST (see ST, p. 24). See Susan E. Wilson, *The Life and After-Life of St John of Beverley: The Evolution of the Cult of an Anglo-Saxon Saint* (Aldershot, 2006).

89 *And this is one form of humility . . . are to be saved*: this section is only present in LT (see ST, p. 25).

89 *healed by these medicines*: Christ is our medicine (ch. 82; p. 161) and our salve (ch. 79; p. 158), and, among other medical references, Christ is the health of the sacraments (ch. 60; p. 130), he heals us (chs. 61 and 63; pp. 133, 135), cures us (ch. 78; p. 156), and is our nurse (ch. 61; p. 133).

For he regards sin as sorrow . . . out of love: not present in ST (see p. 25).

greater joy: after these words, the remainder of ch. 39 is only present in LT (see ST, p. 25).

he is the foundation of our whole life in love: see 1 Corinthians 3: 11.

91 *But now, if any man or woman . . . this comfort*: see Romans 6: 1–2, and also Romans 3: 8. For the corresponding passage in ST, see p. 25.

hate sin only because of love: see Psalm 97: 10.

he taught us to do good in return for evil: see Matthew 5: 38–48.

he is himself this love: see 1 John 4: 8, 16.

acts towards us as he teaches us to do: see Matthew 7: 12.

92 *fifth statement . . . sixth statement*: that is, prayer does not serve to alter God's will or change outcomes, but to align our will with his. For a differently phrased development of the sixth statement, see ST, p. 27.

For everything . . . without beginning: see Matthew 6: 8.

primary recipient of our prayers: as distinct from such other recipients of prayer as Mary, angels, and saints.

a treasury where they will never perish: see Matthew 6: 20, and Luke 12: 33.

93 *pray continually in his sight*: see 1 Thessalonians 5: 17–18.

'You will have me as your reward': see ch. 64 (p. 136).

And thanksgiving is also an aspect of prayer: prayer may be categorized into prayers of petition and intercession for the self and for others, prayers of praise, and prayers of gratitude.

And sometimes when the heart is dry . . . aloud: the 'sometimes' implies that for Julian most prayer is not voiced aloud.

95 *Prayer unites the soul to God*: see 1 Corinthians 6: 17. For the corresponding passage in ST, see p. 27.

Then prayer is a witness . . . to receive grace: this passage in ST reads instead: 'Then prayer makes the soul like God when the soul wills as God wills, and then it is like God in condition as it is in nature' (p. 27).

96 *And so the soul . . . one accord with God*: for ST's version of the next two paragraphs, see ST, pp. 27–8.

he draws us into him by love: see James 4: 8, and John 6: 44.

97 *die in longing for love*: in his treatise *Ego Dormio* the English mystic Richard Rolle (d. 1349) says that those brought into the joy of love 'may not live long afterwards as others do, but as we live in love, so we shall die in

joy and pass to him we have loved' (Windeatt (ed.), *English Mystics of the Middle Ages*, 31).

seeing . . . feeling . . . hearing . . . smelling . . . swallowing him sweetly: the passage is exceptional in Julian in referring to all five senses in one context.

no one can see God . . . in this mortal life: see Exodus 33: 20, and also Genesis 32: 30.

God showed frequently in all the revelations: the end of ch. 43 marks the close of the fourteenth revelation. Before Julian's narrative of her revelations resumes, chs. 44–63 represent a major interpolation of commentary addressing various revelations or all.

in the first revelation: see ch. 4 (p. 44).

98 *I saw him attribute to us no kind of blame*: see chs. 39 and 27 (pp. 89, 75). Cf. Romans 8: 1, 33–4.

so that both judgements might be maintained . . . for me: Julian is concerned to reconcile the judgement of the Church (see ch. 9; p. 52)—and to acknowledge herself a sinner and as such deserving of blame and anger—with her inability to perceive blame or anger in God. Her notion of a higher and a lower judgement allows for orthodox teaching on sin to cede to the higher insight vouchsafed in the revelations, depending on how what the Church teaches is true in God's sight and how Julian is truly to know that.

99 *parable of a lord and a servant . . . very ambiguously*: see ch. 51 (pp. 106–15), although Julian evidently accepts that the answer provided remains an interim and provisional one in this life.

100 *our Lord was never angry . . . he is God*: see ch. 13 (p. 58) and ch. 31 (pp. 78–9).

simple soul: Julian herself. Whatever she has understood from the revelations, God must have wished her to understand.

many mysteries remain hidden: see ch. 34 (p. 82).

my mother, Holy Church: on the Church as mother, see also chs. 60–2 (pp. 129–34).

102 *sweet eye of pity . . . away from us*: this constant merciful gaze looks forward to the lord's beholding of the servant in ch. 51 (p. 107).

103 *Mercy . . . belongs to motherhood in tender love*: this looks forward to chs. 58–62.

God . . . cannot forgive: God does not forgive, because he does not blame us for sin, and in so far as forgiving involves a change of heart, it would be incompatible with God's immutability.

grounded and rooted in love: see Ephesians 3: 17.

friendship: on friendship with God, see Wisdom 7: 14 and James 2: 23.

104 *where our Lord appears, peace reigns*: see John 20: 19, 26.

God is our true peace: John 14: 27.

105 *often dead . . . never dead*: see Wisdom 3: 1–2.

105 *we sin grievously all the time*: see Proverbs 24: 16.

106 *in a mysterious, veiled way*: translating the Middle English 'mystily', indicating something open to figurative or spiritual interpretation.

parable: translating the Middle English 'example', the usual term for any kind of homiletic simile or illustration used in medieval sermons to help explain theological points. See also chs. 7 and 23 (pp. 49, 71).

hollow: this represents the postlapsarian world, but also the Virgin's womb as the site where the Word takes on human flesh and so submits to that fallen world and our human lot. Hence the hollow signifies human experience of sin, and God's love working through the incarnation and Passion. Julian's word 'slade' has often been translated as 'valley', although slade can refer to quite distinct land features in different parts of England. In Norfolk it usually refers to a strip of boggy ground, a slough, although at least in modern English it would be difficult to use this in relation to Mary's womb, as Julian uses 'slade' in Middle English later in the present chapter.

could not . . . look at his loving lord: see Psalm 143: 7.

107 *bruising*: see Isaiah 53: 5.

any help for him: see Lamentations 1: 12, and also Isaiah 63: 5.

with a double aspect: the lord's twofold consideration of the servant represents how God regards Christ's two natures: compassion for his human nature in its sufferings, and joy over the divine nature in its accomplishing of human salvation.

beloved servant: cf. the theme of the 'suffering servant' in Isaiah 42: 1 and 53: 1–12, traditionally interpreted as a figure of Christ.

108 *these three, united as one*: the triad of initial teaching during revelatory experience, subsequent illumination, and the entirety of the revelation as set out in this book may be understood in parallel with two other triads: the traditional attributes of the Persons of the Trinity (might, wisdom, and love), and the triad of human memory, reason, and will, which are the unmade and made Trinities of ch. 44 (p. 97). Analogous to the *perichoresis* (interpenetration) of the three Persons of the Trinity, the mutual indwelling of her visionary experience, subsequent reflection upon it, and God's revelatory activity as a whole, is for Julian a token of the validating oneness of her experience.

three months short of twenty years after the time of the revelation: Julian thus received this inward teaching in February 1393, after the revelations she dates to May 1373.

109 *one man is all men*: see Romans 5: 19.

approve his will: see Isaiah 42: 1 and Mark 1: 11; despite the distraction and impaired perception of sinful falling, man's will remains for God, which God knows even if man now fails to see it.

110 *man's soul to be his own city and his dwelling place*: for the soul as

God's city and dwelling, see also ch. 56 (p. 123), and the sixteenth revelation (ch. 67; p. 141).

mixed with earth: see Genesis 2: 7, and also LT, ch. 53 (p. 119).

hard labour: even though human sinfulness made the human soul unfit for him to inhabit, God sought no substitute habitation but rested upon the bare earth, awaiting the restoration of the human soul.

The blue . . . steadfastness: the colour blue traditionally signifies constancy ('blue is true'); associated with the colour of the Virgin Mary's mantle, blue also carries connotations of intercession and mercy.

shining radiantly around him: see Psalm 104: 2.

'My understanding was led into the lord': a reference back to earlier in ch. 51 (p. 107).

111 *unsuitable clothing*: perhaps recalling the man whom the Lord cast into outer darkness for coming to the feast without a wedding garment (Matthew 22: 11), and traditionally interpreted as wearing unclean and tattered clothes.

The wisdom of the servant . . . honour of the lord: wisdom is the attribute of the Second Person of the Trinity, Christ.

never been sent out before: Adam's torn clothing betokens humanity's toil since the Fall of Man, whereas Christ's incarnation occurs only once in history.

a treasure in the earth which the lord loved: see Matthew 13: 44, and Proverbs 2: 4–5. The treasure may be understood as the souls of mankind.

a food . . . pleasing to the lord: see John 4: 32–4. The treasure apparently becomes conflated with the food and fruits which are to be served to the lord. The reference to serving 'the drink with the food' may carry eucharistic implications in this context.

he was to be a gardener: Mary Magdalene had mistaken the risen Christ for a gardener (John 20: 15), and in medieval homiletic and mystical texts God and Christ were understood to act as gardeners in the garden of the human soul. Cf. also the parables of the vineyard in Isaiah 5: 1–7 and in the Gospels (Matthew 21: 35–44; Mark 12: 1–12; Luke 20: 9–18).

cause sweet streams to flow: possibly the blood and water that flowed from Christ's side; Christ declares that 'rivers of living water', representing the Holy Spirit, shall flow from the believer's heart (John 7: 38–9).

112 *God's son fell with Adam*: see Philippians 2: 6–8, and also ch. 20 (pp. 66–7).

he fetched him out of hell: i.e. at Christ's harrowing of hell; see ch. 12 (p. 57).

113 *he sprang forward very readily*: see Psalm 19: 5, traditionally interpreted as a reference to the incarnation; see also Hebrews 10: 7.

For he is the head . . . his members: see 1 Corinthians 12: 12, 27.

the day and the time are unknown: see Mark 13: 32.

113 *the company of heaven longs to see*: see 1 Peter 1: 12.

the beginning of an ABC: even after twenty years of meditation, Julian likens her state of understanding only to the beginning of elementary learning.

114 *By his tunic . . . tender flesh*: even before the servant hastens to do his lord's will, his torn and tattered tunic prefigures Christ's Passion and thereby the redemption. For Christ's flesh as like a torn cloth, see ch. 17 (p. 63).

as I saw in part: in the eighth revelation; see ch. 17 (pp. 62–4).

yielding his soul . . . he was sent: see Luke 23: 46.

the great root . . . in high heaven: translating the Middle English 'rote'. Depending on whether this is to be understood as 'rout' (company) or 'root'—or indeed, by word-play, as both—it may refer to the company of the saved, rescued by Christ's harrowing of hell (see ch. 12; p. 57), or to the saved 'remnant' or 'root' of Judah (2 Kings 19: 30), taken up in Isaiah 10: 20–2, 37: 31, and Romans 9: 27–9, 11: 16.

Adam's old tunic: cf. 'Our old garment is the flesh, which we have from Adam, our ancestor; we shall receive the new one from God, our rich father, at the resurrection on the Day of Judgement, when our flesh will shine brighter than the sun, if it is torn here with suffering and with pain', Bella Millett (trans.), *Ancrene Wisse: Guide for Anchoresses* (Exeter, 2009), 137.

white and bright: perhaps recalling the radiant whiteness of Christ's apparel at his Transfiguration (Mark 9: 3; Matthew 17: 2).

fairer and richer than . . . I then saw on the Father: see Luke 15: 22, where the father commands that the 'best robe' be placed upon his returning Prodigal Son.

115 *we are his crown*: see ch. 22 (p. 69); the crown signifies redeemed humanity.

at his Father's right hand: see Colossians 3: 1, and Hebrews 1: 3.

no such sitting in the Trinity: Julian echoes a point made by Saint Augustine (*De Trinitate*, 8.2.3) that representations of the Trinity are no more than analogies, but this did not prevent many medieval depictions of the Trinity as two or three of the Persons seated side by side.

the spouse, God's son: Christ as spouse of his beloved is traditionally an image of Christ's mystical union with each believer. In such spousal imagery—which derives from allegorical interpretation of the Song of Songs in the Old Testament—both the Virgin and the Church are also brides of Christ.

he is our mother . . . he is our brother: see Matthew 12: 50 and Mark 3: 35. This looks forward to the theme of Christ our mother in chs. 58–63.

We have in us . . . Adam's falling: see 1 Corinthians 15: 22.

116 *that was shown by his spiritual thirst*: see ch. 31 (pp. 78–9).

I saw God in a point: see ch. 11 (p. 55).

in the sixteenth revelation: see ch. 67 (p. 141).

117 *venial sin*: a mortal sin is a grave transgression committed with the sinner's full consent and knowledge which if not absolved will lead to damnation, whereas a venial sin is a less critical, pardonable offence, which might receive a lesser punishment in purgatory.

118 *a godly will which never assented to sin, nor ever shall*: see ch. 37 (p. 87), but here omitting the earlier distinction between the 'godly' and animal wills. Julian does not imply that the elect never sin, but that their wills are preserved within Christ's perfect will. For Julian, a union between Christ, the Second Person of the Trinity, and the substance of each human soul—foreseen eternally and pre-existing the union between substance and sensory being in the body at birth—implies the salvation of all mankind who thus participate in this union between divine substance and human soul.

a matter of faith and belief: for Julian it is now a divinely sanctioned point of faith that each soul, united at the level of substance with Christ, retains the godly will and orientation to God.

God never began to love mankind: see Ephesians 1: 4–5. See also chs. 58, 59, 63, 85, 86 (pp. 126, 129, 135, 163, 165).

119 *the Mid-Person*: that is, Christ, the Second Person of the Trinity.

at the same point: each soul's highest point is that part of the substance that remains grounded in God's substance (see ch. 11; p. 55).

slime of the earth: see Genesis 2: 7.

treasured and hidden in God: see ch. 32 (p. 80); cf. Colossians 2: 3, 3: 3.

made holy in this holiness: i.e. Christ's soul was united to God in its making, and through this subtle knot all human souls are united to God.

120 *souls that will be saved in Christ*: see John 17: 24.

deep wisdom of the Trinity is our mother: see Wisdom 7: 10–12, where wisdom is mother of qualities and virtues; see also Ecclesiasticus 24: 24–5.

which we do not see: see Hebrews 11: 1.

121 *Christ is our way*: see John 14: 5–6, and Hebrews 10: 20.

in the ninth revelation: see ch. 22 (p. 69).

at the very same point . . . blissfully without end: i.e. God dwells in the soul at that juncture between its substance, which dwells in him, and the 'sensuality', or sensory being.

122 *'The place that Jesus takes . . . vacate'*: see ch. 67 (p. 141).

our soul is a created trinity: in seeing, understanding, knowing, and recognizing, the soul corresponds to the three Persons and the Trinity itself, in a created trinity modelled on the uncreated Holy Trinity.

as is said before: see ch. 53 (pp. 118–19).

double death: of body and soul. Separation of soul from body through natural death will be restored at the resurrection from the dead, while the death that comes to the soul through sin is redressed by the redemption through Christ.

122 *lower part . . . higher part was united in the first creation*: i.e. the sensory physicality and the substance or essence.

in the eighth revelation: see chs. 17–20 (pp. 62–7).

shown at the same time: see ch. 19 (pp. 65–6).

123 *in the sixteenth revelation, as I shall say*: see ch. 67 (p. 141).

The noble city . . . in the Godhead: Jesus will be shown enthroned in the soul in ch. 67, and his enclosure in our sensory being goes along with our substance's enclosure in him, enclosed in turn with Christ's soul in God.

124 *those who will be saved*: see ch. 9 (p. 52).

125 *seven sacraments*: i.e. baptism, confirmation, the eucharist, penance, extreme unction, ordination, matrimony.

126 *So our Lady is our mother . . . all who will be saved in our Saviour*: our enclosure in Christ signifies our being born with him to the Virgin Mary, who thus becomes our mother too.

endlessly born . . . never come to birth: here Julian effects a startling conflation of her themes of Christ's endlessly giving birth to us and of our continuing inclusion within him.

in the first revelation . . . enclosed in us: see ch. 6 (p. 47), although Julian's understanding there is received through spiritual sight rather than words as suggested here.

in the sixteenth revelation . . . in our soul: see ch. 67 (p. 141).

he created us all at once: referring to the creation of the substance of souls in the Second Person of the Trinity, which pre-exists the creation of individual bodies.

the godly will mentioned before: see chs. 37 and 53 (pp. 87, 118).

'I love you . . . never be divided in two': these words are also declared in ch. 82 (p. 161).

127 *our mother, brother, and Saviour*: see ch. 52 (p. 115).

as was shown: see ch. 48 (pp. 102–3).

128 *where he says*: referring back to ch. 26 (p. 74), but the wording is developed here in different terms.

It is I: the light: for Christ as the light, see also chs. 67, 78 and 83 (pp. 142, 156, 162).

129 *before there was any time*: see ch. 53 (pp. 118–19).

of length . . . of depth without end: see Ephesians 3: 17–19.

130 *our mother in grace—because he wanted*: although Julian may explore the theme of Christ as our mother, she never refers to Jesus by other than masculine pronouns.

in the first revelation: see ch. 4 (p. 44).

he . . . was in labour: see Christ's reference to a woman in labour when speaking at the Last Supper of his impending death and the joys that will follow sorrow (John 16: 21).

'If I could suffer more, I would suffer more': see ch. 22 (p. 68).

he can feed us with himself: perhaps alluding to the traditional eucharistic symbolism of the pelican which, as a type of Christ, pierces her breast or side to revive her young with her own blood (as in *Ancrene Wisse*, 3.1). The association of Christ's blood and the eucharist with breast-feeding may be linked to medieval physiological theory that breast milk is processed blood.

'It is I that Holy Church preaches . . . teaches you': see ch. 26 (p. 74).

131 *in the tenth revelation*: see ch. 24 (pp. 71–2), here developed within a devotional tradition that associated Christ's bleeding side-wound with a breast to be suckled.

cannot truly be said . . . of all things: Christ's motherhood of humanity precedes and subsumes all earthly motherhood.

by God's command . . . motherhood: i.e. the fourth of the ten commandments, 'Honour thy father and thy mother' (Exodus 20: 12).

'It is I you love': see ch. 26 (p. 74).

132 *without that humility*: see Matthew 18: 1–4.

his children to perish: see Isaiah 49: 15, and also Psalm 27: 10.

133 *'I am keeping you very safe'*: see ch. 37 (p. 87).

134 *where our Lord is dwelling*: see ch. 67 (p. 141).

135 *besprinkle us . . . with his precious blood*: see 1 Peter 1: 2.

spiritual thirst is to be understood: see ch. 31 (p. 78).

136 *'All shall be well . . . all manner of things shall be well'*: see chs. 27, 32, and also ch. 85 (pp. 74, 79–81, 164).

Before this time . . . from this life: see ch. 2 (p. 41). For this fifteenth revelation in ST, see pp. 28–30.

137 *And at this time*: in this section (down to 'joy and bliss without end') is the only occasion on which Julian describes a bodily sight not already reported in the shorter version. Her reference to the timing is careful to indicate that the vision of the corpse took place at the same time as the rest of the revelation.

a little child . . . glided up into heaven: it was traditional in medieval art to represent the soul leaving the body in the form of a young child.

joy and bliss: slightly rewording the original locution earlier in this chapter (ch. 64; p. 136), which reads 'love' instead of 'joy'.

138 *This reverence that I mean . . . sweet and delightful*: this passage is only present in LT (see ST, p. 29).

139 *It is God's will . . . himself from another*: the corresponding passage in ST reads instead: 'For I am sure that if there had been none but me that should be saved, God would have done all that he has done for me. And so should every soul think, acknowledging that God loves him, forgetting if possible the rest of creation' (p. 29).

'Why should it . . . my glory?': for this locution, see ch. 64 (p. 136).

four o'clock: translating the Middle English 'howre of foure', where Julian is reckoning by clock time. Norwich Cathedral was among the earliest in England to have a mechanical clock (in 1283), and by 1325 there was an elaborate new astronomical clock that struck the hours; see Ian Atherton et al. (eds.), *Norwich Cathedral: Church, City and Diocese 1096–1996* (London, 1996), 441–2.

well past the middle of the day: translating the Middle English 'none', where Julian may mean noon or may be reckoning time not by the clock but by the traditional method of reference to the monastic offices, here that of None (at the ninth hour of the day, around 3.00 p.m.).

as I shall describe later: see ch. 67 (p. 141).

I said at the beginning: see ch. 3 (p. 43).

140 *member of a religious order*: probably a friar or canon; possibly Julian's confessor or spiritual director.

it was bleeding hard: for medieval accounts of images of the crucified Christ and of Mary that had appeared to come alive, see Kathleen Kamerick, *Popular Piety and Art in the Later Middle Ages: Image Worship and Idolatry in England 1350–1500* (London, 2002).

thrusting forward . . . gripped me by the throat: this description of the devil is only present in LT (see ST, p. 31).

141 *while I was asleep, as none of the revelations did*: this is Julian's only non-waking vision, carefully differentiated from her revelations because of traditional distrust of the potential for delusion in dreams.

The people who were with me: the presence of people around her bed may indicate that Julian was not enclosed as an anchoress at the time of this experience.

foul stench: along with the smoke and heat of hell, stench is also associated with devils.

city: the soul as a city recalls the New Jerusalem of Revelation 21: 1–27. Christ's entry into Bethany (Luke 10: 38) was interpreted as signifying his presence in the soul as in a city.

He sits in the . . . soul in peace and rest: Margery Kempe records Julian as declaring to her at their meeting that 'Holy Writ says that the soul of a righteous man is the seat of God', probably referring to 1 Corinthians 3: 16 and 2 Corinthians 6: 16. For the text of their conversation, see Appendix 2 (pp. 168–9).

everlasting dwelling: after these words the remainder of ch. 67 is only present in LT (see ST, p. 31).

142 *the making of man's soul*: the soul has this creatural perfection because human nature was first assigned to Christ, the Second Person, and our souls are joined to Christ (see chs. 53 and 55; pp. 119, 122).

makes itself like the one . . . contemplated: see 2 Corinthians 3: 18.

143 *the first words . . . 'In this way the devil is overcome'*: see ch. 13 (p. 58) for the fifth revelation, containing the first divine locution.

144 *and it seemed to me . . . in our prayers*: this passage is only present in LT (see ST, p. 32). Saying prayers by rote with insufficient heed to their meaning was much warned against in medieval preaching and in works of spiritual counsel.

speaking of Christ's Passion: a recommended recourse against diabolical temptation.

just after sunrise: translating the Middle English 'prime day'. The canonical hour of Prime (6.00 a.m.) would be after sunrise in early May.

the vision would pass: Julian understands that she is not to experience a life-long career of visions, although she has already indicated moments of illumination subsequent to the revelations (ch. 65; p. 139). Chs. 70, 71, and 72 are only present in LT (see ST, p. 34).

neither sign nor token . . . recall it: possibly referring to such tokens as the wedding rings presented by Christ to a historical saint like Catherine of Siena and a legendary one like Catherine of Alexandria, although even by declaring her own non-receipt of any tokens Julian shows herself aware of a possible comparison between herself and such saints who did receive them. What Christ has indeed left with Julian is his blessed word in the divine locutions or utterances within her revelations.

145 *he revealed it all again inwardly in my soul*: this apparently indicates some kind of revisiting of the revelations.

By these six utterances that follow: i.e. 'accept', 'believe', 'hold to it', 'comfort', 'trust', and 'overcome'.

147 *the sorrow and pain that sin is to us*: see the apostrophe against sin in ST (pp. 33–4), which does not survive into LT.

148 *'It is I . . . who am all'*: see ch. 26 (p. 74).

impatience . . . doubting fear: sloth and doubting fear are both branches of the sin of *acedia*˚or spiritual apathy in manuals of the seven deadly sins. Impatience is associated with sloth as a species of spiritual apathy which may lead to despair. For sloth as a special difficulty for those given to contemplation, see ch. 76 (pp. 153–4).

149 *fear which holds us back*: undue preoccupation with one's sins can blind one to God's forgiving love and so sins against that love, and may also lead to excess of scruple or scrupulosity.

149 *and some of us because . . . find any comfort*: only present in LT (see ST, p. 35).

150 *sleep of sin*: on sin as sleep, see 1 Corinthians 15: 34.

an opening to us: see Proverbs 1: 7.

doubting fear: a fearful doubting of whether God's forgiveness can be a reality for oneself.

reverent fear: see 1 John 4: 18.

Love and fear are brothers . . . for his goodness: only present in LT (see ST, p. 35). For the different concluding section which follows in ST, see p. 36.

151 *draws us up into heaven*: see John 6: 44.

thirsts and longs: see ch. 31 (p. 78).

152 *treasured up and hidden in himself*: see Matthew 13: 44, and Isaiah 45: 3.

pillars of heaven shall . . . quake: see Job 9: 6, 26: 11, and Psalm 75: 3.

153 *hates no hell but sin, as I see it*: see ch. 40 (p. 91).

revelation of compassion: see chs. 28 and 31 (pp. 75–6, 79).

supreme friend: John 15: 14–15.

154 *especially . . . blessed goodness*: the perils of indolence form a recurrent theme in writings on contemplative life. This passage implies that the audience of LT remains in part contemplatives, despite the disappearance of the express reference to contemplatives in ST (see pp. 8, 19).

the devil's enmity: see ch. 13 (p. 58).

155 *where it speaks of pity*: see ch. 28 (p. 76).

profitable penance: these words do not figure anywhere as such among Christ's reported locutions in Julian's text but represent some reformulation of ch. 28 as if in Christ's words.

This place is prison: if Julian is referring to her anchorhold as a prison, this would confirm that she was an anchoress when composing the LT. The *Ancrene Wisse* (2.41, 3.4) refers to the anchorhold as God's prison, but it was also traditional to characterize this world as a prison; see Bella Millett (trans.), *Ancrene Wisse: Guide for Anchoresses* (Exeter, 2009), 42, 50–1.

choose him for my heaven with all my strength: see ch. 19 (p. 66).

Let us touch . . . made clean: alluding to the woman in Matthew 9: 20–2 and Mark 5: 25–34, who believed that if she so much as touched Christ's hem she would be healed. This woman was sometimes identified with Saint Veronica (see ch. 10; p. 53, and note).

157 *God showed me that I would sin*: see ch. 37 (p. 87).

158 *he stands all alone*: the loneliness of Christ recalls the isolation of the servant lying alone where he fell, and of the lord seated alone in a wilderness (ch. 51; pp. 107, 109–10).

159 *ABC:* see ch. 51 (p. 113).

to his bliss: see Christ's parable of the one lost sheep out of a hundred (Luke 15: 3–10).

160 *no place except in man's soul*: see ch. 67 (p. 141).

'*I saw God in a point*': see ch. 11 (p. 55).

as if on pilgrimage: the notion of Christ as a pilgrim is not uncommon in medieval devotional literature, but it has not been the subject of one of Julian's reported revelations.

as is said before: see ch. 14 (p. 59).

161 *And here I understood . . . not with blame*: i.e. in ch. 51 (p. 107).

I love you . . . not be divided in two: also declared in ch. 58 (p. 126).

'*I am keeping you very safe*': see chs. 37 and 40 (pp. 87, 91).

162 '*It is I*': see ch. 26 (p. 74).

life, love, and light: see John 1: 4, 8: 12.

163 '*I thank you . . . suffering*': see ch. 14 (p. 59).

164 *not yet completed*: this may refer to the revision of the short text into the long text, or to revisions made within the long text after the insights of 1388 or later. The chapter summary prefacing ch. 86 (most probably not by Julian) evidently understands this as a reference to textual revision between versions of the text.

'*I am the foundation of your prayers*': see ch. 41 (p. 92).

his heavenly treasure on earth: God's heavenly treasure is humanity; see ch. 51 (p. 111).

fifteen years and more later: as Julian dates her original revelations to May 1373 (see ch. 2; p. 40), this spiritual understanding was received sometime in the second half of 1388.

165 *Thus ends*: this concluding injunction in BL MS Sloane 2499 of Julian's *Revelations* was most probably added by a later copyist or editor. The text in the Paris manuscript ends with a rubric in Latin, which may be translated: 'Thanks be to God. Here ends the book of revelations of Julian, anchorite of Norwich, upon whose soul God have mercy.'

165 *Here end the sublime . . . Jesu*: this concluding colophon by a Post-Reformation copyist in this 'diminishing' format is found only in BL MS Sloane 3705 of Julian's *Revelations*.

INDEX OF SCRIPTURAL REFERENCES

GENERAL INDEX

Adam xxix, xxxix–xliii, xlix, 21, 64, 77, 105, 108–18
Aelred of Rievaulx xxxi
Alan of Lille 182
Albert the Great, Saint xxxi
Alphonse of Pecha 181
Ancrene Wisse ix, xii, xxxii, 175, 178, 184, 198, 201, 204
angel(s) 7, 36, 81, 159
anger 28, 58, 90, 98, 100–4
Anselm, Saint xxxi
Apocalypse of Paul 192
Aquinas, Saint Thomas xxxi
Ascension xviii, 57
atonement 21, 40, 46, 67, 77, 117
Augustine, Saint 181, 182, 183, 189, 198

Ball, John xlix
baptism 82
Bernard of Clairvaux, Saint xxxi
bishop 141
blame, blameworthiness: as deserved by sinners 98, 105; excused 159; God beholds with pity not blame 161; God blames us no more than Christ 112; not imputed 75, 76, 89, 98, 100, 105, 107; turned into glory 118
blindness 28, 33–5, 53, 55–6, 80, 82, 105, 107, 116, 139, 148, 153, 158, 163
body: Christ's 3, 11–12, 14–15, 57, 61–4, 67, 70, 114, 121; Church as Christ's 79; human 29, 47, 119, 137; devil's 140; Julian's 5, 6, 140; Saint John of Beverley's 88
Boethius 183
Bonaventure, Saint xxxi
blood, Christ's 6, 8, 11, 12, 19, 43–50, 53, 57, 62–3, 70, 135, 140
Bridget of Sweden, Saint 181, 189
brother, Christ our 10, 49, 72, 115, 127, 129
Brut, Walter 182

Carrow Priory xv
Catherine of Alexandria, Saint 203
Catherine of Siena, Saint 203

Cecilia, Saint 4
charity 9, 11, 51, 52, 73, 76, 78, 81, 91, 100, 113, 129, 154, 156, 163, 164; faith, hope and 50, 60, 86, 138, 146
child, children 121, 130–7, 150
childhood 136
Christ: as Adam 110, 112, 116; as ground, foundation 76, 83, 91, 92, 94, 103, 119, 127, 129, 135; as perfect humanity 119, 125, 129; as protector, keeper, carer 44, 45, 84, 87, 89, 90, 115–16, 127, 133, 146, 155, 156; wishes to be known 56, 80, 85, 93, 100, 101, 123, 149, 156, 158, 164
Christ's crown 17, 69, 71, 79, 115
Christ's friends 59, 65, 82
Christ's lovers 3, 15, 35, 55, 64, 89, 92, 146, 149
Christ's Passion *see* Passion
Church *see* Holy Church
city 31, 121, 123, 141, 160
clothing xli, xliii, 6–7, 31, 45, 47, 109–15, 141
Cloud of Unknowing, The 190
colour 11, 14, 52–4, 61–2, 63, 109–10, 140
comfort 11, 13–14, 16, 22–3, 26–7, 29, 30, 32, 35–6, 51–3, 60–1, 63, 66, 70, 75–6, 91, 101, 106, 116, 134, 136, 140–6, 149, 150, 155, 157
commandments 125, 131, 153
compassion: as wound 4, 41; Christ's 20, 22, 75–7, 137; expression of 146; for Christ 6, 67, 89; for fellow Christians 76; for sinners 153; human 159; revelation of 79, 153
conscience 28, 31, 90, 95, 131, 141
confession 25, 28, 30, 89, 140
contemplation 8, 19, 157
contrition 3, 25, 35, 41, 88–90, 146, 150, 153, 156, 159
courtesy: Christ's 11, 30, 59, 70, 83, 89, 136, 140, 154–6, 161, 163; Christ's courteous love 6; Christ's courteous teaching 19; courteous fear of our Lord 138, 151, 152; God's 23, 35, 49,